Praise for *Our Divided Politi*

"A well-mannered, thoughtful attempt to restore civic grace and productive political conversation."
—*The Boston Globe*

"Ambitiously, [Dionne] situates our current divisions in the full sweep of American history, going back to the founders."
—*The New York Times Book Review*

"[A] mash-up course in philosophy and graduate-level American history."
—*Minneapolis Star Tribune*

"Through all the twists and turns of American history, E. J. Dionne brings his story straight to the point. It delivers a sharp shock of recognition."
—**Thomas Frank, author of *What's the Matter with Kansas?***

"An earnest effort to reach across the political divide . . . Dionne takes his readers on a richly researched tour of history to restore the broken consensus about who we are and what America stands for. His case is strong enough, serious enough and grounded enough to challenge those on the other side of the divide to offer a counterargument as rigorously argued as this one."
—*The Washington Post*

"Dionne's book is outstanding. It is a rich source of historical and contemporary insight. The writing is clear, lively, and accessible. Even though his argument comes from the left, Dionne shows a real respect and appreciation for the conservative tradition . . . This makes the book an excellent example of how to develop a principled political argument free of partisan rancor, one committed to certain ideals while seeking common ground. In other words, just the kind of medicine our body politic needs."
—*Commonweal* magazine

"[Dionne's] extensive knowledge of Washington allows him to ably illustrate our remarkable political history, and he renews our hope that cooler heads can prevail with a renewed balance of individual rights and the needs of the community." **—Kirkus Reviews**

"It would be hard to find a more civil, well-reasoned or hope-filled book about the current polarized state of the country. By all means, read this book." **—America magazine**

"[A] comprehensive, well documented tour through our history." **—Daily Kos**

"[A] much-needed fact-based review of the Constitution, a realistic portrait of its creators, and a balanced history of the ongoing friction in the American psyche between desires for liberty and commonwealth. The book clarifies much misinformation swirling around controversies about the founding fathers, the validity of originalism, and the traditional and historic roles of government and the free market in U.S. society. Tea Partiers and Occupiers alike may be surprised and enlightened by this lucid analysis, all the more convincing for its sympathetic treatment of both sides of the argument." **—Publishers Weekly**

"*Our Divided Political Heart* recalls us to an American past that speaks powerfully, and hopefully, to our present political travails. Every citizen concerned about the state of our politics should read this book." **—Michael J. Sandel, author of *Justice***

"This is E. J. Dionne's best yet, a mature work pulsating with historical discovery, intellectual energy, and moral rigor. One of our most eminent, most up-to-the-minute reporter-columnists turns out to be as wired into the American political past as he is to its present. He takes us on a sweeping, surprising journey that vividly illuminates who we are and how we got here, devastatingly debunks what some among us *think* about who we are and how we got here, and shines a light on the neglected commonalities beneath our seemingly intractable conflicts, revealing some national strengths that, with a bit of wisdom and a bit of luck, just might take us to a better place." **—Hendrik Hertzberg, author of *Politics* and *¡Obámanos!***

"This is a brilliant book about America's current political divide. But more importantly, it's an insightful exploration of our nation's history and our ability to balance individualism with community. That sense of balance has been lost, and this book shows how we can restore a shared appreciation for our historic values."

**—Walter Isaacson, author of *Steve Jobs*
and *Benjamin Franklin***

"E. J. Dionne is the thoughtful conservative's favorite liberal, and the liberal all the rest of us learn from. *Our Divided Political Heart* is at once a grand arc of American thought from the nation's founding, and an up-to-the-minute diagnosis of the weird and sudden turn we've taken in left-right relations. With malice toward none, E. J. nevertheless sounds the alarm about the new threat to the 'long consensus' that's been key to our stability and our national greatness." **—Rachel Maddow**

"E. J. Dionne Jr. sagely reminds us that our country's main political tradition has always been ordered toward flourishing communities as well as free individuals. Conservatives will find much to disagree with in Dionne's interpretation of that tradition, but they will also be educated and stimulated."

**—Ramesh Ponnuru, senior editor of *National Review*,
and author of *The Party of Death***

"E. J. Dionne is the latest in a long line of serious American journalists who are also serious thinkers in their own right. It is therefore not surprising that he has written an extraordinary book at an extraordinary time in our history . . . A book that not only speaks to where we are at this perilous moment, but of where we need to go. In a word, this book is indispensable."

**—Robert N. Bellah, coauthor of *Habits of the Heart*
and author of *Religion in Human Evolution***

"Are Americans rugged individualists? Are we community-loving civic republicans? The answer to both questions, writes E. J. Dionne in his wise new book, is yes . . . Twenty years after his classic of political journalism, *Why*

Americans Hate Politics, Dionne has once again excavated our current political dilemmas and shown how we can rise above them."
—Jacob S. Hacker, author of *Winner-Take-All Politics*

"E. J. Dionne is an intellectual and civic treasure . . . Beautifully written, meticulously researched, and persuasively argued, here is an historically informed how-to manual for recognizing and reversing the worst aspects of our nation's polarized politics . . . Read this book and get ready for the revival." **—John J. DiIulio Jr., author of *Godly Republic***

"In *Our Divided Political Heart*, one of the nation's shrewdest journalists shows he is also a brilliant and empathetic historian . . . Indispensable for anyone who wants to understand how the past both shapes our present conflicts and can help us imagine a better future."
—Michael Kazin, author of *American Dreamers*

"E. J. Dionne is a unique voice in American public life . . . He points the way from our current soul sickness toward a democratic renaissance."
—James T. Kloppenberg, author of *Reading Obama*

Our Divided Political Heart

OUR DIVIDED POLITICAL HEART

THE BATTLE FOR THE AMERICAN IDEA IN AN AGE OF DISCONTENT

E. J. Dionne Jr.

BLOOMSBURY

NEW YORK · LONDON · NEW DELHI · SYDNEY

Published by Bloomsbury USA, New York

All papers used by Bloomsbury USA are natural, recyclable products made
from wood grown in well-managed forests. The manufacturing processes
conform to the environmental regulations of the country of origin.

LIBRARY OF CONGRESS CATALOGING-IN-PUBLICATION DATA HAS BEEN APPLIED FOR.

ISBN: 978-1-60819-201-4 (hardback)

First published by Bloomsbury USA in 2012
This paperback edition published in 2013

Paperback ISBN: 978-1-60819-438-4

1   3   5   7   9   10   8   6   4   2

Typeset by Westchester Book Group
Printed in the U.S.A.

For all of my teachers, including Jim Garman, Norm Hess,
the Rev. Damian Kearney, Bill Schneider, Gary Orren, Nathan
Glazer, Steven Lukes, Michael Hill, Michael Walzer, David
Riesman, Sam Popkin, Martin Shefter, Marty Peretz, Kate
Auspitz, Seymour Martin Lipset, Bob Meister, Doris Kearns Goodwin,
Barbara Herman, Rick Weil, Shelly Binn, and Bill Kovach.

And, again, for Mary, James, Julia, and Margot,
my Beloved Community.

Contents

Who We Are
Liberty, Community, and the American Character

FEAR of decline is one of the oldest American impulses. It speaks, oddly, to our confidence that we occupy a lofty position in history and among nations: we always assume we are in a place from which we *can* decline. It's why there is a vast literature on "American exceptionalism" and why we think of ourselves as "a city on a hill," "the first new nation," "a beacon to the world," and "a light among nations."

When they arise, our declinist sentiments usually have specific sources in economic or foreign policy travails. These apprehensions quickly lead to bouts of soul-searching that go beyond concrete problems to abstract and even spiritual worries about the nation's values and moral purposes. When we feel we are in decline, we sense that we have lost our balance. We argue about what history teaches us—and usually disagree about what history actually says. We conclude that behind every crisis related to economics and the global distribution of power lurks a crisis of the soul.

Because of this, gifted politicians from Franklin Roosevelt and John Kennedy to Ronald Reagan and Barack Obama have been able to transform national anxieties into narratives of hope: "The only thing we have to fear is fear itself." "Get the country moving again." "Let's make America great again." "Change we can believe in."

A yearning to reverse decline played just below the surface in Obama's campaign in 2008. His victory was a response to a national mood conditioned by anxiety. By the end of George W. Bush's second term, Americans worried that in the first decade of the new millennium, their country had squandered its international advantages, degraded its power with a long and unnecessary engagement in Iraq, and wrecked the federal government's finances. Then came the devastation of the worst financial crisis in eighty years. This was happening as not just China but also India and Brazil were widely seen as challenging American preeminence.

Obama's 2008 campaign was well calibrated to respond to the nation's longing for reassurance. Consider the emphasis in his posters featuring the "Hope" and "Change we can believe in" slogans. Whether by design or luck, the words *hope* and *believe* were pointed responses to a spiritual crisis engendered by fears of lost supremacy. They help explain why the Obama campaign so often felt like a religious crusade.

Still, the election of a young, bold, and uplifting president so different in background from all of our earlier leaders—and so different in temperament from his immediate predecessor—was not an elixir. Obama alone could not instantly cure what ailed us or heal all of our wounds. The difficulty in producing a sustainable economic upturn (even if the hopes for a miraculous recovery were always unrealistic) only deepened the nation's sense that something was badly wrong. Obama himself could not fully grasp the opportunity the sense of crisis presented, and he failed, particularly in the first part of his term, to understand how the depth of the nation's political polarization would inevitably foil his pledge to bring the country together across the lines of party and ideology. The same fears of decline that bolstered his 2008 campaign quickly gave force to a rebellion on the right that looked back to the nation's Revolutionary origins in calling itself the Tea Party. Embracing the Tea Party, Republicans swept to victory in the 2010 elections, seizing control of the House and expanding their blocking power in the Senate. Whatever Obama was for, whatever he undertook, whatever he proposed—all of it was seen as undermining traditional American liberties and moving the country toward some ill-defined socialism. Whatever else they did, Republicans would make sure they prevented Obama from accomplishing anything more. Over and over, they vowed to make him a one-term president. The result was an ugliness in Washington typified by the debilitating debt ceiling fight in the summer of 2011. It fed a worldwide sense that the United States could no longer govern itself.

Late in Obama's term, the Occupy Wall Street movement rose up in rebellion against abuses in the financial world that had caused the meltdown. The new wave of protest focused the country's attention on the extent to which the nation's economic gains over the previous three decades had been concentrated among the very wealthiest Americans—the top 1 percent of earners, and especially the top sliver of that 1 percent. Decline was not simply an abstract fear; many Americans sensed its effects in their own lives.

This book is an effort to make sense of our current political unhappiness, to offer an explanation for why divisions in our politics run so deep, and to reflect on why we are arguing so much about our nation's history and what it means.

I believe that Americans are more frustrated with politics and with ourselves than we have to be, more fearful of national decline than our actual position in the world or our difficulties would justify, and less confident than our history suggests we should be. The American past provides us with the resources we need to move beyond a lost decade and the anger that seems to engulf us all. But Americans are right to sense that the country confronts a time of decision. We are right to feel that that the old ways of compromise have become irrelevant to the way we govern ourselves now. We are right to feel that traditional paths to upward mobility have been blocked, that inequalities have grown, and that the old social contract—written in the wake of World War II and based on shared prosperity—has been torn up. Musty bromides about centrism and moderation will do nothing to quell our anxieties and our fears.

At moments of this sort, bookshelves and reading devices quickly fill with political cookbooks and repair kits. They offer recipes for national renewal and carefully wrought step-by-step suggestions for national renovation. Many of these offerings are thoughtful and well conceived. But our current unease arises less from a shortage of specific plans or programs than from a sense that our political system is so obstructed and so polarized that even good ideas commanding broad support have little chance of prevailing. We don't have constructive debate because we cannot agree on the facts or on any common ground defined by shared moral commitments.

We typically blame this on our "polarized politics," our "vicious political culture," our "gotcha" and "partisan" media climate. Our first response is to look for mechanical and technological fixes because these seem within easy reach. Proposals are rolled out to build new websites or media structures, promote electoral reforms that will invigorate the "political center" and draw congressional districting lines in a nonpartisan way, establish new forums for public deliberation, and create new political parties for the fed up and the alienated, or for political moderates.

But procedural, technical, and symbolic reforms are inadequate because our difficulties run deeper. Underlying our political impasse is a lost sense of national balance that in turn reflects a loss of historical memory. *Americans disagree about who we are because we can't agree about who we've been.* We are at odds over the meaning of our own history, over the sources of our national strength, and over what it is, philosophically and spiritually, that makes us "Americans." The consensus that guided our politics through nearly all of the twentieth century is broken. In the absence of a new consensus, we will continue to fight—and to founder.

Building a new consensus will be impossible if the parties to our political struggles continue to insist that a single national trait explains our success as a nation and that a single idea drives and dominates our story. At the heart of this book is a view that American history is defined by an irrepressible and ongoing tension between two core values: our love of individualism and our reverence for community. These values do not simply face off against each other. There is not a party of "individualism" competing at election time against a party of "community." Rather, *both* of these values animate the consciousness and consciences of nearly all Americans. Both are essential to the American story and to America's strength. Both interact, usually fruitfully, sometimes uncomfortably, with that other bedrock American value, equality, whose meaning we debate in every generation.

We ignore this tension within our history and ourselves at our peril. In forgetting who we are, we deny the richness of our national experience and the creative tensions that have always shaped our national character. We begin to lose our gift for managing our contradictions and balancing our competing impulses. We make our nation's narrative less interesting than it is, and ourselves a less interesting people than we are. And because we have forgotten that the tension at the heart of our national experiment is a healthy one, we have pretended that we can resolve our problems by becoming all one thing or all another.

Sometimes all-or-nothing choices must be made. This was certainly the case with slavery, and that "all one thing" phrase alludes to a speech by Abraham Lincoln about human bondage. But when we are confronting not good against evil but one good set against another, we face not a choice but a quest for balance. We are not very skilled at balance anymore. That is why we have lost our gift for reasoning together.

It is with a sense of urgency that I offer an argument here about our politics, our history, and the need to reweave a national consensus. The United States rose to global preeminence because in accepting our commitments to both individualism and community, we were able to see democratic government as a constructive force in our national life and to use it in creative ways. This approach to government, I will argue, is far more consistent with the Founders' intentions and the broad trajectory of our history than are alternatives promoted by the Tea Party and its allies that cast government as inherently oppressive, necessarily wasteful, and nearly always damaging to our nation's growth and prosperity.

We must recover our respect for balance and remember its central role in our history. We are a nation of individualists who care passionately about community. We are also a nation of communitarians who care passionately about individual freedom. We believe in limited government, but also in active and innovative government. Our Founders did not devote so much time and intellectual energy to creating a strong federal government only for it to do nothing.

In the course of this story, I often link our responses to community and individualism with our attitudes toward government and its limits. It's thus important to make clear that I don't believe that "government" is the same thing as "community." But contemporary politics has been shaped by two forces that link our responses to both.

First, our country has witnessed the rise of a radical form of individualism that simultaneously denigrates the role of government and the importance most Americans attach to the quest for community. Critics see both as antithetical to the strivings of free individuals who ought to be as unencumbered as possible by civic duties and social obligations. This extreme individualism sees the "common good" not as a worthy objective but as a manipulative slogan disguising a lust for power by government bureaucrats and the ideological ambitions of left-wing utopians. This view has transformed both American conservatism and the Republican Party.

Second, the American tradition of balancing community and individualism necessarily leads to a balance between government and the private sphere. At the heart of the American idea—common to Jefferson and Hamilton, to Clay and Jackson, to Lincoln and both Roosevelts—is the view that *in a democracy, government is not the realm of "them" but of "us."* In a constitutional and democratic republic, government's power is not used as it would be in a dictatorship or a monarchy—as an instrument that is nearly always oppressive and inevitably invoked on behalf of the few. In our history, government has far more frequently been a liberating force that operated on behalf of the many. This has been true not just since the New Deal but also from the beginning of our national experiment.

The intervention of democratic government has often been necessary to protect individuals from concentrated private power. It is government's failure to live up to this duty that gave rise to the anti–Wall Street protests. Here again, a commitment to balance has been essential: Americans mistrust excesses of power, in both government and the private sphere. Over time, we constructed a system of countervailing power that used government to check private abuses of authority even as we limited government's capacity to dominate the nation's life. We also nurtured vigorous collective forces outside the state in what we commonly call the "third sector" or "civil society." These independent groups are another expression of the American commitment to community. They impressed Tocqueville and continue to strike outsiders as an essential characteristic of our country. At times these forces work with the government and the market. At other times they check the power of one, the other, or both.

There is thus an essential and in some ways paradoxical ambiguity about the relationship between community and government. Government has often been challenged by outside groups rooted in communities and speaking in their name. But because of the democratic character of our system, government also regularly serves as the primary instrument through which the community interest expresses itself. In the American system, private initiative and public enterprise complement each other. This is something that both late nineteenth-century Populists and early twentieth-century Progressives understood well.

The Populists and the Progressives laid the foundation for what I call the Long Consensus. It is a view of public life that created what we came to call, with pride, the American Century. It wrote the social contract for shared prosperity. In the hundred years after Theodore Roosevelt assumed the presidency in 1901, government grew—but so did individual liberty. The state assumed new roles, but individual opportunities expanded. New regulations protected the air and the water, the integrity of food and drugs, the safety of workplaces and consumer products—and American capitalism flourished. Workers organized into unions that advanced the interests of those who depended on their labor, not capital, for their livelihoods. In doing so, labor organizations strengthened a more social form of capitalism based on widespread property ownership and upward mobility. Previously excluded groups were steadily brought into the larger American community to share the economy's bounty and the responsibilities of self-government. The United States continued to welcome newcomers and created the most diverse democracy in the world. G. K. Chesterton observed that the United States sought to make a nation "literally out of any old nation that comes along"—and it succeeded.

In the century of the Long Consensus, the United States became the most powerful nation on earth, its influence enhanced not only (or even primarily) by its advanced weaponry and the martial courage of its men and women in uniform, but also by its economic might, its democratic norms, its cultural creativity, and a moral and intellectual vibrancy that is the product of our constant struggle to preserve liberty while building and rebuilding community. A nation whose intellectual inheritance includes biblical religion and the Enlightenment, the individualism of Ben Franklin and Walt Whitman, the state-building of Hamilton and Clay, the traditionalism of John Adams, the skepticism toward central authority of Jefferson, and the radicalism of Tom Paine is bound to produce a lively life of the mind. Out of this creative conflict arose the balance of the American system and the achievements of the Long Consensus.

American politics is now roiled because the Long Consensus is under the fiercest attack it has faced in its century-long history. The assault comes largely from an individualistic right that has long been part of American politics but began gathering new influence in response to the failures of the Bush administration and the rise of Obama. After Obama's inauguration, it became the most energetic force in the conservative movement and the Republican Party.

But the Long Consensus also fell into difficulty because many Americans outside the ranks of the Tea Party and the right concluded that government was no longer the realm of "us" but was, in fact, under the control of "them." The rise of Occupy Wall Street was powered by a sense that government served the interests of the wealthiest Americans— and those of the banks and the financial institutions—rather than the needs of the remaining "99 percent" of the citizenry. The bailout of the financial system, however necessary it was to preventing a crash, was not accompanied by comparably sweeping measures to ease the burden of the downturn on those facing foreclosure, on underwater mortgage holders, on Americans thrown out of work, or on those with falling incomes. "I bailed out a bank," read one sign carried by an Occupy Wall Street protestor, "and all I got was a new debit card charge." Many Americans who did not join the boisterous protests around the nation nonetheless shared the sense of grievance and injustice the protesters were expressing.

Smaller businesses found themselves starved for credit. Inequalities that grew even in the good times became more glaring in a time of deep trouble. As the journalist and scholar Alexander Stille observed, "The United States has gone from being a comparatively egalitarian society to one of the most unequal democracies in the world." Careful studies by the Congressional Budget Office and the Organisation for Economic Co-operation and Development underscored his point.

Government itself had become the object of scorn on the left, although the reasons for its discontent were very different from those advanced by conservatives. The breakdown and dismantling of government regulation of the financial industry was one of the major causes of the Great Recession, and this was a case of the Long Consensus failing on its own terms. It was a failure in which Democrats, as the principal defenders of the Long Consensus, were complicit. If the strongest initial expressions of political outrage in the Obama years came from those who insisted that government was too powerful, there lay beneath this discontent another form of anger to which the anti–Wall Street protests gave vocal expression. It targeted not government's power, but the failure to use this power as a countervailing force against financial excess and the influence of the wealthy. Worse still, many came to believe that government had used the public's money to strengthen and subsidize the already privileged.

Obama clearly saw his task as restoring support for the core principles behind the American balance and the Long Consensus. Yet he alternated between offering reassurance to Wall Street (in order to get markets moving again) and rhetorical salvos against the economically privileged (to win back those who had concluded he was "soft on Wall Street"). The prominence in the Obama circle of advisors and campaign donors with strong Wall Street ties increased the skepticism among Americans who believed he was too close to those who had caused the nation's problems. Yet his efforts to strengthen Wall Street regulation, to increase taxes on the wealthy, and to critique economic inequality brought forth opposition and even rage from large parts of the financial sector.

Having satisfied neither side, Obama moved steadily toward tougher rhetoric against the world of finance around the moment the Wall Street protests began. He concluded that, as an aide put it in the late fall of 2011, "there is surging sentiment out there among voters that the economy is weighted toward the wealthy." It was a perception that might usefully have come to him earlier, though as the experience of Franklin Roosevelt demonstrated, it often takes a mass movement to push a president further down the path he has tentatively chosen.

Because the loss of trust in government is not simply an ideological matter and extends beyond the political right, I pay particular attention in what follows to the importance of the Populist strain in the American Progressive tradition and the collapse of any controls over the campaign finance system, typified by the Supreme Court's *Citizens United* decision in 2010. It will be difficult to restore public faith in government's capacity to serve as an honest broker as long as large amounts of unregulated cash, often from undisclosed sources, continue to flow into the campaigns of both parties. And liberals will be unable to speak to legitimate popular discontent if they forget the essential role played by American Populism in building support for the Long Consensus. This seemed to dawn gradually on Obama as the battles over his presidency became more ferocious. Before there was Progressivism, a New Deal, or a Great Society, there was Populism. As I will be showing, many liberals have been too eager to embrace historical critiques of Populism that emphasized its more extreme expressions. As a result, they have been insufficiently alive to Populism's deeply democratic character and its roots in America's oldest traditions of republicanism and self-rule. By failing to appreciate Populism's contribution to their own achievements, liberals opened the way for right-wing movements keen on seizing the populist banner. The Tea Party is foremost among them, claiming to speak in the name of populism even as it seeks to sweep aside so many of the reforms for which the original Populists fought.

I I

Our current political struggles make sense only if we understand them in light of the debate over whether we should nurture and refashion the Long Consensus or choose instead to cast it away. This struggle has created a fundamental divide over the most basic questions: Is democratic government primarily constructive or destructive? Does it protect and expand our freedoms, or does it undermine them? Can public action make the private economy work better, or are all attempts to alter the market's course doomed to failure? Do government's efforts to widen opportunities and lessen inequality enhance individual achievement or promote dependency?

Those who disagree on such core questions come to believe that their opponents are bent on pursuing policies that would undermine all they cherish. In such circumstances, compromise becomes not a desirable expedient but "almost treasonous," to use the phrase made briefly famous by Texas governor Rick Perry in remarks about the Federal Reserve. If everything that matters is at stake, then taking enormous risks with the country's well-being, as House Republicans did in the debt ceiling battle, is no longer out of bounds. Rather, pushing the system to its limits—and beyond—becomes a form of patriotism. When your adversary's goals are deemed to be dishonorable, it's better to court chaos, win the fight, and pick up the pieces later.

Because Democrats broadly defend the Long Consensus while Republicans, in their current incarnation, seek to overturn it, the parties are no longer equally distant from the political center. We are in a moment of asymmetric polarization. Since Democrats believe in both government and the private marketplace, they are, by their very nature, always more ready to compromise. On the other side, Republicans (again, given their current preoccupations) believe that compromise will set back their larger project of putting an end to a set of arrangements they no longer believe in.

Obama was slow to acknowledge that his talk of bringing the two parties together was out of sync with the way the parties array themselves now. There was certainly nothing remotely radical about Obama's own proposals. Virtually everyone agreed that the economy needed a strong stimulus at the moment Obama took office—and Obama's own proposals, as many of his aides later conceded, turned out to be smaller than the moment required. His financial reforms, embodied in the Dodd-Frank bill, were serious but relatively mild. And many of Obama's initiatives, even the controversial health insurance reform that Republicans scorned as "Obamacare," were drawn from ideas once favored by moderate and even conservative Republicans, notably former Massachusetts governor Mitt Romney, whose health plan in his state was a model for the 2010 reform.

But these programs, again including Romney's, were the product of a Republican Party that existed before it was taken over by a new sensibility linking radical individualism with a loathing for government that would shock Hamilton, Clay, Lincoln, and even Mr. Conservative himself, Robert A. Taft.

In the fall of 2011, the president woke up to the danger he faces. He began to draw sharper lines against those who believe, as he put it "that the only thing we can do to restore prosperity is just dismantle government, refund everybody's money, and let everyone write their own rules, and tell everyone they're on their own."

He added: "That's not who we are. That's not the story of America."

Who are we? That is now the central issue in American politics.

What follows is inspired in part by the promise of Barack Obama, his successes, and the severe difficulties he has confronted since 2009. But even more, it is inspired by the Tea Party, its reaction to Obama, and its insistence on placing American history at the center of our contemporary political argument.

And so, in a book that is critical of the very core of the Tea Party project, I begin with a few words of thanks. The Tea Party deserves the gratitude of its critics because it pushed the logic of a certain kind of American conservatism to its very limits. It said—plainly, candidly, forcefully, amid much commotion and publicity—what a significant part of the conservative movement believes. It has thus opened a debate about who we are that needs to be settled.

I will speak throughout the book about the ways in which the Tea Party's perspective on our past distorts the American story. Nonetheless, I salute the Tea Party's great interest in our Founding and in the broader American narrative. I hope the movement's passions will encourage those who disagree with its views to reengage the American story ourselves. The Tea Party is not wrong to seek inspiration from our political tradition. It is not mistaken in its fervor for connecting our present with our past.

Yes, we should look toward an authentic past, not an invented one, and we should see our struggles to overcome imperfections and injustices as no less important to our greatness—and our exceptionalism—than our moments of triumph and unity. But there has been a default on the progressive side of politics in embracing an American past that is, at heart, a progressive story about liberty, equality, and community and our efforts to advance all three while struggling to keep them in balance.

A significant part of this book is thus devoted to reclaiming our history from one-sided accounts that cast individualism as the driving American preoccupation and opposition to government as the nation's overriding passion. Such an approach not only does a disservice to the facts, but also offers a stunted view of the meaning of liberty and a flawed understanding of the Constitution. It misreads traditional American attitudes toward government and downplays our struggles over slavery, racism, and nativism.

Too many accounts of the American story—and, these days, far too many talk show rants—emphasize our devotion to individualism to the exclusion of our communitarian impulses. Yet if our history records the many ways in which Americans have struggled to preserve and expand our freedoms, it also shows that our quest for community has taken many forms: conservative and radical, moderate and liberal. It has led some Americans to create small utopian communities, sometimes socialist in inspiration, that promised to model a new world. It has pushed others to yearn for a return to a conservative past. In their 1930s manifesto, the Southern Agrarians preached that traditional ways of living rooted in the soil and in the small town were far superior to the "brutal and hurried lives" of industrialized modernity that led inevitably to "the poverty of the contemporary spirit."

Nor has this hunger for community been confined to the utopian left or the traditionalist right. It has also thrived in the great center of the American discourse, reflected in the community building of Franklin Roosevelt's Tennessee Valley Authority, the Community Action Program of Lyndon Johnson's Great Society, and George W. Bush's faith-based initiatives. Even conservative politicians whose central commitments were to free-market individualism have understood the yearning for human ties that transcend the colder calculations of free exchange; thus Herbert Hoover's invocation of community bonds during the Depression, Ronald Reagan's call to defend "family, work, neighborhood," George H. W. Bush's promotion of "a thousand points of light," and his son's effort to "rally the armies of compassion."

Of course, no one (or practically no one) opposes community outright. In principle, everyone praises vibrant neighborhoods, Little Leagues, YMCAs, active faith institutions, service clubs, veterans groups, and all the other building blocks of civil society. Reagan's "family, work, neighborhood" slogan was effective precisely because virtually everyone has warm feelings about all three. Before he became president, Obama spoke of our fears of "chronic loneliness," drawing on a theme that has inspired hundreds of advice columns and scores of conversations on television's afternoon chat shows.

It's also true that conservatives and progressives offer competing and sometimes clashing visions of how community is created. Their arguments over the role the national government plays in fostering (or weakening) community are especially fierce.

Yet if community is, in principle, uncontroversial—and no doubt many Tea Party members are deeply engaged in PTAs, service clubs, churches, veterans groups, and other builders of local community—asserting community's centrality to the American creed challenges an assumption deeply embedded both in contemporary politics and in a significant (and by no means eccentric) body of historical analysis: that from the very beginning of our republic, the core political values of United States were narrowly defined by individualistic conceptions of liberty. References to "community" or a "common good" or, especially, "collective action" are cast as alien to America's gut commitment to the "rugged individualism" first described by Herbert Hoover. As a result, criticisms of individualism are written off as imports from Europe, as reflecting the unrealistic aspirations of progressive preachers, as speculations of academics far removed from the heart of American life—or, most succinctly these days, as "socialism."

What's forgotten is that challenges to individualism are as American as individualism itself. Robert Bellah and his colleagues were right in their seminal book *Habits of the Heart* to argue that "there is a profound ambivalence about individualism in America among its most articulate defenders." In our literature and popular culture, they argued, "we find the fear that society may overwhelm the individual and destroy any chance of autonomy unless he stands against it, but also recognition that it is only in relation to society that the individual can fulfill himself."

This dualism is a dominant theme of our national narrative, and American politics has always used our democratic system to manage periodic corrections in the ebb and flow between individualism and community. When the country leans too far toward a radical form of individualism, as it did during the Gilded Age after the Civil War, our politics typically produces a communitarian correction. And when the community seems to demand too much, our persistent streak of individualism reasserts itself—as it did in 1933, when the nation ended Prohibition, perhaps the most far-reaching and least successful communitarian experiment in our history.

The unusual American balance between individualism and community helps explain why the United States never gave rise to an enduring socialist or social democratic movement, as did every other industrialized democracy. A relatively strong and popular Socialist Party did win a substantial following during the Progressive Era, and socialist trade unionists and intellectuals influenced the American mainstream for generations after. But over time, left-wing movements came to do most of their work inside the two major parties—within both during the Populist and Progressive years, and primarily within the Democratic Party during and since the New Deal.

Nor have we had an explicitly religious party, akin to European or Latin American Christian Democratic parties. Christian nationalist parties failed in the United States. The Social Gospel movement that inspired so many progressive Christians was influential, but it never sought to form a party of its own. Socially oriented Catholicism was hugely influential in the labor movement and on the New Deal, but it did not inspire the creation of a separate party, as it did in Chile, Italy, Germany, and so many other Latin American and European nations. In recent years, conservative Christians have played an important role among Republicans, but they have not formed a party of their own.

The fact that the United States has neither a feudal past (except, to some degree, in the old slave South) nor a well-developed anti-clerical tradition helps to explain why socialist and Christian parties never gained a foothold: a response to feudalism was critical to the rise of socialism, and a reaction to anti-clericalism often bred religious parties. But it's also true that American politics consistently produced its own brand of tempered communitarianism that filled the space occupied in other countries by socialist and religious parties. The American synthesis was not explicitly Christian, yet Christianity and prophetic Judaism are embedded in our national ethos, and the Old Testament prophets have been a staple of American reformist rhetoric from the beginning. And as the historians James Kloppenberg and Daniel Rodgers have shown, American-style communitarianism often made use of European ideas—from socialists, social democrats, and the British New Liberals—even as European progressives borrowed from our intellectual arsenal. Our politics have never been as indifferent or resistant to ideas from abroad as either critics of an alleged American parochialism or celebrators of our uniqueness would suggest, and Europe, in turn, has long been open to our intellectual innovations.

In these transatlantic dialogues, Americans brought a distinctive set of ideas forged in our own notions of republican government, in Hamiltonian ideas about the role of public authorities in fostering prosperity, in Jeffersonian ideas about democratic responsibility, and in Puritan notions of local autonomy and community. American arguments for individual liberty are always tempered by arguments for personal responsibility, celebrations of community, the idea of fraternity, and the need in self-governing republics for virtuous citizens. The idea that human beings are born to be free is an American instinct. So, too, as Wilson Carey McWilliams argued, is the idea "that fraternity is a need because, at a level no less true because ultimately beyond human imagining, all men are kinsmen and brothers."

This book is thus a plea to restore and refresh the traditional American balance. Doing so is central to reviving our confidence in the future and an approach to politics that brings our country together by speaking to both sides of our political heart.

III

Those who make the assertions that I have already offered about government and the need for a less lopsided distribution of wealth and income are usually seen, in our current climate, as championing a "liberal" or "progressive" view. And my own political commitments are, in fact, liberal, in the American sense of that word. It is a label I have embraced in recent years in part because too many liberals, after looking at the opinion polls, have fled from any association with the honorable history that word embodies. My views can also be fairly described as progressive, center-left, or social democratic. But I most identify with the description of my politics offered by my conservative friends and polemical adversaries at *National Review* magazine. In an exceptionally kind review of my first book, *Why Americans Hate Politics*, *NR* referred to me as a "communitarian liberal."

That was quite accurate, and it helps explain my preoccupations here. It also underscores the extent to which the political shorthand we use typically needs qualifiers. Not every political argument should be seen as a point-counterpoint confrontation between red and blue, left and right, liberal and conservative.

In particular, it is possible to believe passionately that our yearning for community has not received the attention it deserves in our current telling of the American story while still celebrating our enduring devotion to individual freedom. Our nation will never be purely communitarian any more than it will be purely individualistic. Almost everything I have written about politics over the years has seen the essential questions before our country as involving a search for the right equilibrium between these commitments. It is the reason my book *Why Americans Hate Politics* so emphasized how debilitating it is to allow our political life to be defined by false choices. False choices are the enemy of balance.

Conservative readers who know of my commitment to the center-left may be surprised by my affection for the brands of conservatism that emphasize the importance of the social bonds created by tradition, religion, family, and a devotion to place and locality—affections that also help explain my unease with the Tea Party. One conservative writer who has greatly influenced my thinking is Robert A. Nisbet, the sociologist whose classic work *The Quest for Community* found a wide audience across ideological lines.

"The quest for community will not be denied," Nisbet once wrote, "for it springs from some of the powerful needs of human nature—needs for a clear sense of cultural purpose, membership, status, and continuity." What terrified Nisbet were the efforts of the twentieth century's centralizing ideologies, Communism and Nazism, to create artificial forms of community built on "force and terror" in response to the corrosive effects of modernity on traditional social bonds. "Freedom cannot be maintained in a monolithic society," he wrote. "Pluralism and diversity of experience are the essence of true freedom . . . Neither moral values, nor fellowship, nor freedom can easily flourish apart from the existence of diverse communities each capable of enlisting the loyalties of its members." Freedom and a healthy brand of individualism *depend* upon a strong sense of community.

Because of my respect for conservative thought, I try to be careful in distinguishing between brands of contemporary conservatism that have embraced radical individualism and the broader conservative tradition. (I say this knowing that many of my conservative friends will argue that I have not been careful enough.) I readily acknowledge that conservatives going back to Edmund Burke have revered community and what Burke called society's "little platoons." I have always found this sort of conservatism attractive, which explains my affection for Nisbet.

Thus, to be clear, my primary argument is not with the entire conservative tradition, but with the form conservatism is currently taking, typified by the Tea Party. Partisans of this view are trying to break the links between the conservative movement and its more communal and compassionate inclinations. Between communitarian liberals and compassionate conservatives, there is ample room for dialogue and even common action.

But I do go further and argue that even my compassionate conservative friends need to acknowledge more than they do that the American quest for community has taken national as well as local forms, and that action by the federal government has often been constructive and even essential to community building on the local level. Intervention by the national government was required to defend African American communities, particularly but not exclusively in the South, whose rights were violated by state and local governments—violations that were often justified through a defense of the "rights" of local communities to their own peculiar (and oppressive) arrangements. We are, finally, a nation and not simply a collection of states. Our Constitution declares, in Article IV, Section 4, that "the United States shall guarantee to every State in this Union a Republican Form of Government." States' rights do not extend to the "freedom" to create state-based monarchies or despotisms. The Thirteenth, Fourteenth, and Fifteenth Amendments curtailed the rights of states to approve slavery, to deny basic rights to citizens, and to restrict the voting rights of minorities.

Moreover, I argue throughout this account that conservatives face a contradiction in their creed and in their practice. They often find themselves defending state and local rights except where the national economic market is concerned. In this case, they typically choose to deny states the right to regulate national enterprises—and then often turn around and deny the federal government the same ability, sometimes invoking states' rights. It seems to me that conservatives need to acknowledge far more than they do that the existence of a national and international market can require national and local rules and regulations—and that free nations may also be required to pool their sovereignty to impose necessary rules on what has become an increasingly integrated global system.

National and international corporations can be as indifferent to the needs and desires of local communities as any distant government. Communally minded conservatives should accept that if centralized state authority poses challenges to community building, so, too, do centralized, though private, economic enterprises.

IV

American history and its implications are central to this account. This should not be taken to imply that if only we could get our history right and agree on its lessons, all would be well. But I do believe that our inability to share at least some common ground on essential historical matters—how our Constitution was written, how our democracy was created, how we built a thriving and prosperous nation, how we nurtured a society that simultaneously values innovation, tradition, and social justice—places severe limits on our capacity to move forward.

Our argument over history is, after all, a symptom of our polarization as well as a cause. It reflects the rise of personal choice as ever more central to the American value system. If we can choose in all other spheres of life, why not choose our own version of history? That is what is happening now, as Daniel Rodgers observed in his seminal book, *Age of Fracture*. "The terrain of history ha[s] disaggregated," he wrote. "The mystic ribbons of time could not hold it together." Rodgers quotes a colleague who offered a slogan: "Every group its own historian."

While we will always debate how to interpret the American story, we are not free to choose our facts or invent them. Throughout the book, I argue not only that our past holds valuable lessons for the present (a point no less true for being obvious), but also that how we view the development of our democracy powerfully affects how we behave in the present. Especially now, the past is being used as a trump card in our politics. As a general matter, this is a poor way to invoke history. But if history is to have such a large role in our public argument, we ought to play the historical game with a full and unmarked deck.

As it is, we appear to have abandoned the idea of one national history in favor of a series of partial accounts that suit the needs of our respective political tribes. The value we most seem to worship is choice, and so we choose our version of history. The centrality of choice also means that we are building local community in ways that make it ever more difficult to bring ourselves together in a larger community. This was Bill Bishop's insight in his brilliant book *The Big Sort*. Bishop found that we are increasingly inclined to live with people who think and act like us, value the same things, have the same consumer habits, worship in the same way, and live similar personal lives.

Americans are "forming tribes," Bishop wrote, "not only in their neighborhoods but also in churches and volunteer groups. That's not the way people would describe what they were doing, but in every corner of society, people were creating new, more homogeneous relations." Of course, people of like mind have always gravitated toward each other. But Bishop is right to sense that this process is unfolding with a dazzling efficiency, and he is shrewd to observe how this affects the way we tell our national story:

> A friend asked the other evening, "Is it possible now to have a national consensus?" Perhaps not. Maybe the logic of the Big Sort is that there's no longer a national narrative to follow, no longer a communal path to unanimity . . . We have created, and are creating, new institutions distinguished by their isolation and single-mindedness. We have replaced a belief in a nation with a trust in ourselves and our carefully chosen surroundings . . . "Tailor-made" has worked so well for industry and social networking sites, for subdivisions and churches, we expect it from our government, too. But democracy doesn't seem to work that way.

Indeed it doesn't. It is hard to make democracy work when we cannot even agree on what kind of democracy we have created, or how it came about.

My argument might thus be seen as a response both to Rodgers's sense of "fracture" and to Bishop's "Big Sort." In recent decades we have witnessed, as the social thinker Alan Wolfe playfully suggested in a review of Rodgers's book, "the Big Shrink." This is not, he wrote, "a shift from left to right" but "a transformation from big to small." We have given up on large narratives and an expansive sense of community beyond our own enclaves. We have, in theory, challenged old political institutions and mass culture. But by retreating into ourselves, we have in fact empowered those remaining forces that *do* enjoy national and international reach. We can only pretend to escape the national and international, which ought to be the lesson of an economic downturn that began on Wall Street but spread quickly to the rest of the world and reached deeply into our communities of choice.

The broad American narrative is well suited to our circumstances precisely because it is a history of balancing the local and the national, the individual and the communal, the economic and the civic. The American approach understands the vibrancy of the communities that Bishop has discovered, but insists that those communities are embedded in a nation whose story they share, whose laws they depend on, whose prosperity is essential to their own, and whose standing in the world will have a powerful effect on their fate. It is why the desire to prevent American decline is a yearning that unites American communities across nearly all the barriers we have erected against each other.

In the end, we should not be surprised that history seems so important in the politics of our time. Battles over history are always fierce in times of crisis because such moments necessarily involve struggles over self-definition. We had comparable arguments before the Civil War, when partisans on both sides of the slavery question sought to conscript the nation's Founders as allies. That is why what follows is organized around the interaction between our current political impasse and how we read (and sometimes misread) our history.

V

The first chapter explores the rise of the Tea Party and its focus on retelling (and, I argue, rewriting) our nation's story. The Tea Party understood instinctively that Barack Obama could be seen more as a communitarian than as a liberal—although the movement's preferred term for Obama's worldview was "socialist." This made Obama a particular threat to the kind of individualism the movement championed, even if many in the movement would likely have opposed him anyway as too liberal and cosmopolitan a figure. I also note that if the Tea Party was organizationally imaginative, it was not ideologically innovative. On the contrary, many of its ideas depend either on standard varieties of conservative individualism or on old notions popularized by the far right of the 1950s and 1960s. I ask why it is that where mainstream conservatives of a half century ago, notably William F. Buckley Jr., challenged such far-right ideas as cranky, foolish, and extremist, today's conservative leaders have held their tongues or even offered encouragement to notions discredited long ago.

In Chapter 2, I explore the politics of history. Politics has always influenced how we tell our story to ourselves, and this chapter is aimed at putting today's politically tinged arguments in perspective. I pay particular attention to how the rising civil rights movement and historical reassessments of the Reconstruction era after the Civil War influenced each other. The successes of the battle for racial equality encouraged a more accurate view of Reconstruction (a perspective freed from the tinge of racism), even as a more honest accounting of African American achievements in the post–Civil War South encouraged the forces battling segregation.

The next three chapters trace the arguments over individualism and communitarianism through our history and our current politics. Chapter 3 argues that the tension between these tendencies goes back to the Puritan settlements and the early republic. I look at how biblical and republican ideas and individualism in a variety of forms all left their mark on the American character. Chapter 4 describes why progressives in recent years—most prominently Bill Clinton and Barack Obama—concluded that present-day liberalism needed to be tempered by a greater emphasis on community and that rights talk needed to be supplemented by a strong public commitment to civic, social, and personal responsibility. Yet as liberals were becoming more open to community, conservatives were moving the other way. This is the subject of Chapter 5. It asks why today's conservatives have transformed a creed born in skepticism about individualism into a doctrine that now has a radical form of individualism at its very core.

The second half of the book uses four critical moments in our history to shed light on our present controversies. Chapter 6 focuses on the Founding moment and the Constitution. Those who created the American system of government did *not* believe that they had settled every important question permanently. They knew their final product was based on rough-and-ready compromises, a fact that the historian Gordon Wood has underscored in his extraordinary writing on the Founding period. They were alive to the need for innovation precisely because they were innovators themselves. Using what I see as the bookend Supreme Court cases of the first decade of the new millennium, *Bush v. Gore* and *Citizens United*, I argue that Tea Party constitutionalism and conservative originalism more generally are less interested in the Constitution's actual words (or the "real" intentions of the Founders) than they are in rolling back democratic advances that have been made since 1787.

Alexander Hamilton, Henry Clay, and Abraham Lincoln are the heroes of Chapter 7. Contrary to popular notions that government engagement with the American economy began with the Progressive Era and the New Deal, Hamilton, Clay, and Lincoln all acted aggressively on the belief that public enterprise went hand in hand with private initiative. Clay's appropriately named "American System" for developing the country was prophetic in seeing how visionary federal action could bind and build a nation. I draw on the innovative work of the historian Brian Balogh to show that those who now argue for a highly limited government seek their inspiration not from the main line of American development but from the exceptional period of the Gilded Age—roughly 35 years in our 235-year story.

Populism, the subject of the next chapter, inspires a powerful ambivalence that has been productive for historians, fueling a vast industry of revision, counter-revision, and still further revision. Whatever its shortcomings, Populism was profoundly democratic, egalitarian, and communitarian in its aspirations. As I noted earlier, Progressives typically fail when they lose sight of Ralph Waldo Emerson's observation "March without the people and you march into the night."

The original Progressive Era succeeded, I argue in Chapter 9, because it created an alliance between the largely rural Populists and urban, middle-class reformers. The new movement was a revolt against the radical individualism of the Gilded Age and a plea for community at both the national and local levels. It also embodied demands that would be familiar to today's anti–Wall Street activists. Progressives attacked monopoly, the power of "high finance," and an "unregulated and purely individualistic industrialism" (Theodore Roosevelt's words) and warned that the United States was nearing "the time when the combined power of high finance would be greater than the power of the government" (Woodrow Wilson's words).

The Progressives were determined to use democratic government to temper the forces of the marketplace and to write new rules for a rapidly transforming economy. The Progressive surge, reinforced by the New Deal, reasserted the longer American tradition that saw the public and private realms as cooperative, and also as checking each other's power.

This was the basis of the Long Consensus established during the last century, and the final chapter argues that finding its equivalent is urgent if we are to make the next century as successful as the one we have left behind. The irony is that although our new economic circumstances mean that the next consensus cannot simply mimic the Long Consensus, the latter's underlying values of balance, community, and service are at the heart of the next generation's approach to politics. The newest forms of politics pursued by the rising generation that is comfortable with and attuned to technological change are thus likely to be rooted in values deeply embedded in the American tradition.

The anti–Wall Street movement speaks to the new generation's engagement with Jacksonian, Populist, and Progressive demands for a government freed from the power of wealthy elites. At the same time, the Millennial generation's extensive community engagement, its highly developed skills at forming social networks, and its particular forms of idealism—disciplined by a decade of war and years of economic stagnation—suggest a practical resilience that could make it the next great reforming generation in our nation's history. The task of creating a new Long Consensus rests squarely in their hands.

V I

In the declinist talk of recent years, it has become fashionable to suggest that China is leaving us behind because its authoritarian form of government is better suited to making the "enlightened" and "efficient" decisions that a global marketplace requires. This view vastly overrates the efficacy of dictatorships and is startlingly similar to talk in the 1930s that Nazi Germany, Mussolini's Italy, or Stalin's Soviet Union were destined to make democracy obsolete. Skeptics of democracy in general and of America's approach to it in particular were proven badly mistaken in the past. They underestimated American democracy's capacity for self-correction and the vitality of a free, democratic, and egalitarian society.

But the resurgence of the United States is by no means assured. In the Roosevelt years, the country proved the prophets of dictatorship wrong by renovating our democracy. We created a durable political majority for effective government, bolstered the nation's sense of community, and built new partnerships between the public and private spheres. By using new methods that were thoroughly consistent with the American past, the nation moved simultaneously toward a greater degree of social justice and a more dynamic economy. We are now summoned to this task again.

Richard McGregor, the Washington bureau chief for the *Financial Times*, recently pointed to the lesson of experience for our time. "America's problem is not that it does not work like China," he wrote. "It is that it no longer works like America."

This book examines our history to explore what "working like America" means. We are a nation that has protected liberty while also fostering the sense of fellowship and common commitment that a free society requires. It is in restoring this balance that we will rediscover the idea of progress, and the confidence that we can achieve it.

Part One

Why Are We Yelling
at Each Other?

CHAPTER I

Two Cups of Tea
The Tea Party in History and on History

I T began with the rant that shook the country. When CNBC's Rick Santelli exploded on the air in fury at government bailouts *not* of big bankers but of financially stressed homeowners, he changed the nation's political calculus and sought to redefine the objects of its rage over an economic catastrophe.

"The government is promoting bad behavior!" Santelli declared on February 19, 2009, complaining about President Obama's mortgage rescue plan, one day shy of a month after his inauguration. "This is America! How many of you people want to pay for your neighbor's mortgage that has an extra bathroom and can't pay their bills?" He then transformed those suffering from the financial meltdown from sympathetic victims to inferior beings. The Obama plan, Santelli said, would "subsidize the losers' mortgages."

Appropriately, Santelli issued his condemnation of extra-bathroom subsidies from the floor of the Chicago Board of Trade, one of the holy places of American high finance. The well-to-do traders cheered on their comrade-in-rage-against-government as if they were at a political rally—which of course they suddenly were. Santelli made clear he was engaged not in financial analysis but in ideological rabble-rousing when he described the wreckage of the Cuban economy after "they moved from the individual to the collective." Could it be that Barack Obama was pursuing Fidel Castro's economic policies?

Suddenly a nation with ample reason to be furious at the financiers who engineered wealth for themselves and catastrophe for so many others was being told to be mad instead at government, and at the profligate parts of the middle class—those "losers." Santelli's subliminal message: *Don't be angry about the extra Gulfstreams or vacation homes of the very, very wealthy. Get mad over your neighbor's imprudent addition.* It would take two and a half years for anger at Wall Street to find its expression.

And then Santelli gave political bite to his tirade. "We're thinking of having a Chicago Tea Party in July!" he shouted. "All you capitalists who want to show up at Lake Michigan, I'm going to start organizing!" Thus was one of the sacred terms in American history reborn in 2009 as a capitalist call to arms. Quickly the conservative and libertarian neighborhoods of the Internet, including the canonical Drudge Report, turned Santelli's rant viral. A new movement was born. All over the country, conservative citizens pledged their loyalty to the new rebellion.

But was all this really so new? As groups claiming the Tea Party mantle proliferated—many existing organizations simply rebaptized themselves in the waters of a media phenomenon—their words suggested not that they were the next new thing but rather that very old tendencies on the American right and far right were being wrapped up in shiny new packaging. "Some people say I'm extreme," Kelly Khuri, founder of the Clark County Tea Party Patriots in Indiana, told the *New York Times*, "but they said the John Birch Society was extreme, too." Well, yes.

In fact, as Kate Zernike noted in *Boiling Mad: Inside Tea Party America*, the first reported Tea Party actually took place three days before Santelli's rant, organized in Seattle by twenty-nine-year-old Keli Carender. According to Zernike, "little more than a hundred people" showed up at the protest, "mostly older people, along with a few in their twenties" who had supported Ron Paul's libertarian campaign in the 2008 Republican primaries. What was striking about that crowd is what was striking about Carender: neither she nor the protesters she brought out were in any way exotic political creatures. On the contrary, Carender was a regular sort of conservative who, in another time and circumstance, might have become a conventional Republican precinct captain. She had come to her views, Zernike noted, by reading *National Review*, the thoroughly orthodox conservative magazine, and the works of the libertarian economist Thomas Sowell.

At its heart, the Tea Party consisted of nothing more (or less) than conservative Republicans who had opposed Barack Obama in 2008 and were angry that he was pursuing the policies he'd run on. Many were also upset over the failures of the Bush presidency and their sense that Bush had been a "big spender," which was certainly true when it came to Iraq.

Astute marketing, not philosophical innovation, is what set the Tea Party apart. It was conservative Republicanism with a sharper tilt rightward. It enjoyed the additional advantages of its own television network in Fox News, a nationwide troupe of talk radio hosts, a considerable bankroll—its most famous angels being the wealthy Koch brothers—and the energies of Sarah Palin, whom every segment of the media could not get enough of in the years 2009 and 2010, before she began to fade.

A *New York Times*/CBS News survey in April 2010 was especially helpful in debunking the idea that the Tea Party was a bold new populist movement. The *Times* reported that Tea Party supporters accounted for about a fifth of the country and tended to be "Republican, white, male, married and older than 45." It was hard to find a better description of the GOP base. They were also more affluent and better educated than Americans as a whole. If this was populism, it was the populism of the privileged, or at least the comfortable.

The Tea Party was in many ways a throwback movement—to the 1930s and also to the 1950s and early 1960s. Like the right wing in those earlier years, it saw most of the domestic policies the federal government had undertaken since the Progressive Era and the New Deal as unconstitutional. Like its forebears, the Tea Party typically perceived the most dangerous threats to freedom as coming not from abroad but from the designs of well-educated elitists out of touch with "American values."

The language of these Obama-era anti-statists, like the language of the 1950s right, regularly invoked the Founders by way of describing the threats to liberty presented by socialists disguised as liberals. A group called Tea Party Patriots (many Tea Party groups donned the colors of patriotism) described itself as "a community committed to standing together, shoulder to shoulder, to protect our country and the Constitution upon which we were founded!" Tea Party Nation called itself "a user-driven group of like-minded people who desire our God-given individual freedoms written out by the Founding Fathers."

This was old right-wing stuff. Americans for Constitutional Action, a mainstream conservative group founded in 1958 (which was also the John Birch Society's founding year), had declared itself against "compulsory participation in social security, mandatory wage rates, compulsory member-ship in labor organizations, fixed rent controls, restrictions on choice of ten-ants and purchasers of one's property" [a protest against civil rights laws then beginning to win public support] and in support of "progressive repeal of the socialistic laws now on our books."

Attacks on a highly educated class have become a staple of conserva-tive criticisms of Obama and his circle, and these, too, have a long right-wing pedigree. Typical of this style of anti-elitism were comments on a Web site called conservativeteapartycaliforniastyle.com that included a pictorial assault on what it called "Obamunism," with the sickle and hammer inte-grated into Obama's 2008 campaign logo. "You attempt to be Professorial, Mr. President, and no one is impressed," wrote a blogger called Paul. "Americans are now resentful of anyone who has an Ivy League Education because this demonstrates how far detached the Ivy Leaguers are from the American People. Demonizing the Tea Party will be your downfall. The more you insult them, the stronger they will become."

Robert Welch, the founder of the John Birch Society, had a similar message in 1966, although he expressed it more jauntily. "I can find you a lot more Harvard accents in Communist circles in America today," he declared, "than you can find me overalls." A 1967 Birch Society publication asserted: "From Woodrow Wilson—himself a professor—to Lyndon Johnson, we have had nothing but Presidents surrounded by professors and scholars." The writer warned against a "conspiracy conceived, organized and activated by professionals and intellectuals, many of them brilliant but cunning and clever, who decided to put their minds in the service of total evil."

The similarities between parts of the Tea Party and the old far right pointed to a darker side of the movement—a minority, perhaps, but a vocal one—that veered toward both extremism and racism. The Obama ascendancy clearly radicalized parts of the conservative movement, giving life to conspiracy theories long buried and explicit forms of racial politics that had largely gone underground since the successes of the civil rights movement.

Defenders of the Tea Party cried foul whenever anyone suggested that, in light of the president's background, race might have something to do with the movement's ferocity. And it's true that a conservative, libertarian, and right-wing ideology was more central to the movement than race. A white female progressive president might also have incited a backlash. Nonetheless, the *Times*/CBS News Poll made clear that the racial attitudes of Tea Party supporters were significantly different from those of the rest of the country.

The survey asked a classic question designed to measure racial attitudes without requiring respondents to give explicitly racist responses: "In recent years, do you think too much has been made of the problems facing black people, too little has been made, or is it about right?" Twenty-eight percent of all Americans—and just 19 percent of those who were not Tea Party loyalists—answered "too much." But among Tea Party supporters, the figure was 52 percent, *almost three times the proportion of the rest of the country*. A quarter of Tea Partiers said the Obama administration's policies favored blacks over whites, compared with only 11 percent in the country as a whole. A survey in the summer of 2011 by the Public Religion Research Institute found a very similar relationship between membership in the Tea Party and attitudes toward race.

It was hard to miss the racial overtones in a speech that former representative Tom Tancredo delivered to a cheering Tea Party crowd in February 2010. Tancredo declared that in 2008 "something really odd happened, mostly because I think that we do not have a civics literacy test before people can vote in this country. People who could not even spell the word 'vote,' or say it in English, put a committed socialist ideologue in the White House, name is Barack Hussein Obama."

For African Americans, who remembered "literacy tests" as phony devices once used in the South to keep blacks from voting, Tancredo's words had a familiar and insidious ring. But the Tea Party conventioneers welcomed them.

There were other memory losses where America's history with race was concerned. As the country began commemorating the 150th anniversary of the Civil War, defenders of the South's "Lost Cause" sought to play down the role of slavery as the conflict's primary cause and instead linked the Confederate revolt against Washington to Tea Party–style concerns about "big government." One Georgia blogger captured the identification with the Confederacy on parts of the right: "Some say simplistically that the Civil War was fought over slavery. Unfortunately, there is no 'simple' reason. The causes of the war were a complex series of events . . . Many of the problems Georgians saw more than one hundred fifty years ago are being reiterated today. The 'oppressive' federal government. High taxes (tariffs before the war). A growing government unwilling to listen to law abiding citizens. Sound familiar? They were complaints levied from 1816 on in Georgia."

The Civil War entered the national political debate when Virginia's Republican governor, Bob McDonnell, named April 2010 "Confederate History Month" in a proclamation that didn't mention slavery. (McDonnell later revised the document to denounce slavery as "evil and inhumane.") Mississippi's then governor, Haley Barbour, spoke up for McDonnell by declaring that the controversy surrounding the proclamation's rather substantial omission "doesn't amount to diddly." When Barbour took himself out of the GOP presidential race, his wading into the Civil War argument was often cited as one reason why a popular conservative with strong ties to party officials around the country decided to forgo his opportunity.

The episode underscored not only the extent to which the battle over history had entered contemporary politics, but also how much history was being distorted in the process. Drew Gilpin Faust, Harvard's president and a celebrated chronicler of the war, cited fellow historian C. Vann Woodward's wry observation that history itself "becomes the continuation of war by other means." In a powerful lecture inspired by the war's anniversary, Faust made note that some continued to see the aftermath of the great struggle as a defeat for American principles. "The powers of the centralized nation-state achieved by the war are now questioned and challenged," she observed, "seen as the betrayal rather than the fulfillment of the Founders' vision."

Moreover, "significant segments of the American population, particularly in the South, continue to reject slavery as a fundamental cause of the war, even in the face of irrefutable evidence that what southerners called the 'peculiar institution' played a critical role in secession debates, declarations, and decisions across the South." Even the National Park Service's chief historian, Robert Sutton, was drawn into politics—simply by doing his job. As Faust observed, when Sutton "insisted that the nation's historic sites emphasize that 'slavery is the principal cause' of the war," he "encountered widespread resistance and controversy."

One after another, historians took to op-ed pages and lecture halls to explain that slavery had indeed been the central issue behind the conflict, and that no amount of revisionism could alter this. "A century and a half after the civil war, many white Americans, especially in the South, seem to take the idea that slavery caused the war as a personal accusation," the great Civil War historian Eric Foner wrote in the *Guardian*. "The point, however, is not to condemn individuals or an entire region of the country, but to face candidly the central role of slavery in our national history." After all, it had been Confederate vice president Alexander Stephens who declared that the "cornerstone" of the Confederacy "rests upon the great truth that the negro is not equal to the white man; that Slavery, subordination to the superior race, is his natural and normal condition," and that "this, our new Government, is the first, in the history of the world, based upon this great physical, philosophical and moral truth." That racism and slavery, not states' rights, lay at the heart of the southern rebellion was an inconvenient truth for some of the conservative rebels of 2011.

Again and again, contemporary politics became the staging ground for arguments about the past, some of them quite surprising. Relitigating history became a central characteristic of the Obama era, as the perceptive progressive writer Elbert Ventura noted in the spring of 2011. "Beyond the circumscribed world of academic journals and conferences, history is being taught—on TV and talk radio, in blogs and grassroots seminars, in high school textbooks and on Barnes & Noble bookshelves," he wrote in *Democracy* magazine. "In all those forums, conservatives have been conspicuous by their activity—and progressives by their absence."

The new right-wing historical revisionism needed to be taken seriously as a political matter, if not as an approach to history itself. Revisionist historians on the left had long come under attack from conservatives for using the past primarily for the political purposes of the present. Such conservative criticism is very much alive. Writing in 2011, James W. Ceaser, a neoconservative scholar, offered a lovely and apt metaphor for the value of history: "Like the experience of foreign travel," he wrote, "it can refresh the mind and provide a sense of distance from the familiar." Then Ceaser added: "How sad it is, therefore, that so much academic history today does just the opposite, projecting current issues back onto the past, invariably for the purpose of promoting a contemporary ideological viewpoint. Instead of freeing us from the present, 'history' of this kind ends by imprisoning the past."

Yet at the moment Ceaser was writing, his criticism of reading the present into the past for polemical purposes had far more relevance to the historical excursions of the right wing than to the work of academic historians. Indeed, many of the professional historians had to spend a great deal of time during the early Obama years rescuing the actual American story from the distortions and inventions of conservative talk show hosts and publicists for whom no issue was too small to escape fictionalization.

II

Thanksgiving may well be the most unifying of American holidays, even if Thanksgiving dinners have often been staging grounds for fierce if (usually) friendly arguments about politics among extended family and friends. Yet a passion for debunking that was once a habit of the left led many on the far right to assert that our common interpretations of Thanksgiving were tainted. The distortions, they insisted, arose from the socialist assumptions of academic mythmakers. It was a big lie, the right-wing revisionists insisted, to use Thanksgiving to celebrate how the Pilgrims pulled together and, with the help of God, prospered through communal assistance and a little help from their Indian neighbors.

As with almost all of the new historical "accounts," this one had deep roots in earlier polemics. Rush Limbaugh began promoting the "corrected" vision of Thanksgiving in his 1993 book, *See, I Told You So.* Year after year, he used his talk show to teach that the settlers suffered because, at the outset, their land and their homes "belonged to the community." As Limbaugh exclaimed on a 2007 show, "They were collectivists!" The hero of Limbaugh's commentary was the colony's governor, William Bradford, who was wise enough to understand the dangers of common ownership and took what Limbaugh called "bold action" by assigning "a plot of land to each family to work and manage, thus turning loose the power of the market-place." Limbaugh drew what for his audience was the obvious moral: "Long before Karl Marx was even born, the Pilgrims had discovered and experimented with what could only be described as socialism. And what happened? It didn't work!"

Limbaugh's persistence in promoting this view of the *real* Thanksgiving won it an ever wider following, to the point where in 2010 it drew the attention of the *New York Times* and Zernike, the paper's able chronicler of the new New Right. She pointed out that the actual story of the Pilgrims was a bit more complicated than Limbaugh and his philosophical forebears would like it to be. For this, she was rebuked by Limbaugh as arguing that, "hey, socialism wasn't that bad for the Pilgrims." (That this is not what Zernike actually said did not deter Limbaugh.)

Limbaugh has been wrong about many things, but he was right to understand the extent to which our understanding of the past shapes our present. His reinterpretation of Thanksgiving almost perfectly illustrated the loss of balance that is at the heart of our current discontent. Putting aside that all the facts about the first Thanksgiving cannot be known—and that there has been much mythmaking around the holiday beyond the confines of Limbaugh's radio show—the more complicated version of the story is certainly truer both to who we are and to who we have been. Capitalism is part of our narrative, but so are solidarity and the idea that no one ever really "goes it alone." Our rights are embedded in a web of social bonds and mutual obligations. We have a responsibility not just to take care of ourselves and our families but also to look out for one another. And we hope that if we run into trouble, someone, maybe even the entire community, will look out for us.

Such homely sentiments, edited down a bit, could be stitched on a holiday sampler. They are the values not of an angry and radical individualism but of a tempered individualism that is truer to the Pilgrims' faith and our national experience. Those early Massachusetts farmers were, on the whole, industrious and hardworking, but they also believed passionately in a common good and the promise of mutual assistance.

One might simply dismiss Limbaugh's Thanksgiving obsession as good conservative radio theater but for the source of his storytelling. Zernike traced Limbaugh's Thanksgiving revisionism to the work of W. Cleon Skousen, whose writings were popularized by right-wing talk show host Glenn Beck in his one-day course called "The Making of America."

And who was Skousen? In a fine piece of what might be called investigative-scholarly reporting published shortly before the 2010 elections, the historian Sean Wilentz took to the pages of the *New Yorker* to explain where Limbaugh, Beck, and parts of the Tea Party movement were getting their ideas. Wilentz traced Beck's approach to American history to Skousen in particular and to the John Birch Society more generally. "The political universe is, of course, very different today from what it was during the Cold War," Wilentz wrote. "Yet the Birchers' politics and their view of American history—which focussed more on totalitarian threats at home than on those posed by the Soviet Union and Communist China— has proved remarkably persistent. The pressing historical question is how extremist ideas held at bay for decades inside the Republican Party have exploded anew—and why, this time, Party leaders have done virtually nothing to challenge those ideas, and a great deal to abet them."

As is often the case with extremists, Skousen's career had its colorful moments. A "transplanted Canadian who served as a Mormon missionary in his teens," Wilentz wrote, "Skousen was considered so radical in the early nineteen-sixties that even J. Edgar Hoover's F.B.I. watched him closely." Skousen was employed by the FBI from 1935 until 1951, "much of that time as a special agent working chiefly in administration. These desk jobs, he claimed implausibly, gave him access to confidential domestic intelligence about Communism." Skousen also claimed he had served as Hoover's administrative assistant, though "Hoover informed inquirers that there was no such position." Skousen was Salt Lake City's police chief from 1956 to 1960, and as Wilentz wrote: "His time in office was contentious, and after he raided a friendly card game attended by the city's right-wing mayor, J. Bracken Lee, he was promptly fired. Lee called Skousen 'a master of half truths' and said that he ran the police department 'like a Gestapo'; Skousen's supporters placed burning crosses on the Mayor's lawn."

Skousen then turned to writing the volumes that made him famous in far-right circles in the 1950s and 1960s—and posthumously, thanks to Glenn Beck, with parts of the Tea Party in the Obama years. There was *The Naked Communist*, which Wilentz described as "a lengthy primer published in 1958." In this provocatively titled book, "he enlivened a survey of the worldwide leftist threat with outlandish claims, writing that F.D.R.'s adviser Harry Hopkins had treasonously delivered to the Soviets a large supply of uranium." It was followed by *The Naked Capitalist*, which "decried the Ivy League Establishment, who, through the Federal Reserve, the Council on Foreign Relations, and the Rockefeller Foundation," formed what Skousen saw as "the world's secret power structure."

The book that grabbed Beck's attention was *The 5,000 Year Leap*, which Wilentz describes as "a treatise that assembles selective quotations and groundless assertions to claim that the U.S. Constitution is rooted not in the Enlightenment but in the Bible, and that the framers believed in minimal central government." The historian in Wilentz felt compelled to note that both propositions "would have astounded James Madison, often described as the guiding spirit behind the Constitution, who rejected state-established religions and, like Alexander Hamilton, proposed a central government so strong that it could veto state laws."

The 5,000 Year Leap also challenged the separation of church and state, asserting that "the Founders were not indulging in any idle gesture when they adopted the motto 'In God We Trust.'" In reality, as Wilentz notes, "the motto that came out of the Constitutional Convention was 'E Pluribus Unum': out of many, one. 'In God We Trust' came much later; its use on coins was first permitted in 1864, and only in 1955, at the height of the Cold War, did Congress mandate that it appear on all currency. The following year, President Eisenhower—who [the Birch Society's Robert] Welch charged was a Communist agent—approved 'In God We Trust' as the national motto."

Beck took this old, strange, and fanciful book and turned it into a kind of historical bible, calling it "essential to understanding why our Founders built this Republic the way they did." When Beck "put the book in the first spot on his required-reading list—and wrote an enthusiastic new introduction for its reissue," Wilentz notes, "it shot to the top of the Amazon bestseller list. In the first half of 2009, it sold more than two hundred and fifty thousand copies" as "branches of the Tea Party Patriots, the United American Tea Party, and other groups across the country have since organized study groups around it."

Wilentz's article undertook the essential work of historians. He showed how so many of the assertions about the American past that were being taken for granted in certain political quarters were flatly wrong. He also brought home what so much of the mainstream commentary ignored: that ideas popular among the Tea Party rank and file could only be characterized as extremist and involved breathtaking fabrications and distortions of the American story. These ideas, associated with the Birch Society and other far-right groups a half century earlier, had been discredited before, and not just by liberals.

And that was Wilentz's other essential point: how reluctant established conservatives in our time have been to take on crackpot theories. (Beck, it should be recalled, eventually ran into controversy for reasons other than his embrace of these theories.) By contrast, an earlier conservative generation had shown no such reticence. In the heyday of the Birch Society, it had been William F. Buckley Jr., the premier voice of contemporary American conservatism, who denounced its foolishness as dangerous to the conservative cause.

In 1962, Buckley had published a 5,000-word "excoriation" of Welch and the Birch Society, as Buckley called his commentary in a loving retelling of the episode shortly before his 2008 death. "The underlying problem," he wrote in the sixties, "is whether conservatives can continue to acquiesce quietly in a rendition of the causes of the decline of the Republic and the entire Western world which is false, and, besides that, crucially different in practical emphasis from their own." In a 1965 column, Buckley chronicled the Birch Society's views on issues ranging from Medicaid to John Kennedy's assassination, concluding that they amounted to "paranoid and unpatriotic drivel."

By contrast, much of the right in the years after Obama's election either was silent about the extremism and distortion or actually played off the ideas put forward by Beck and, by extension, the old Birch heroes. Amity Shlaes, writing from a perch at the Council on Foreign Relations— yes, the institution once seen by the Birchers as a guiding force behind the international conspiracy—defended Beck against the "university guild" of historians and treated Skousen as just another book writer. Praising Beck for breaking the usual television rules, Shlaes wrote: "He insists viewers read books by dead men—W. Cleon Skousen's work on the Constitution, the '5000 Year Leap.' It is all a long way from 'Oprah,' 'The Newshour' or even much of public television." Well, yes. *Oprah* or the *NewsHour* might have provided a little background on who Skousen was and what he believed. Shlaes, once a writer for the *Wall Street Journal*'s editorial page, was honest enough to note her views might have been influenced by Beck's plugging of her own anti-Roosevelt history of the New Deal, *The Forgotten Man: A New History of the Great Depression.* But she embraced Beck in full:

> Every author is glad to sell books. But the victory is far more Mr. Beck's than any individual writer's or publisher's. His genius has been in his recognition that viewers do not want merely the odd, one-off book, duly pegged to news. They want a coherent vision, a competing canon that the regulated airwaves and academy have denied them. So he, Glenn Beck, is building that canon, book by book from the forgotten shelf. Since the man is a riveting entertainer, the professors are correct to be concerned. He's not just reacting or shaping individual thoughts. He is bringing competition into the Ed Biz.

By this definition, of course, Skousen, Welch, and anyone else who managed to offer a "coherent vision," no matter how distorted, qualified as part of "the Ed Biz." And one "competing canon" was just as good as another. It was, as we have seen, an odd stance for conservatives to adopt, since so many in their ranks (and with some justification, too) had railed against abuses committed in the name of multiculturalism, postmodernism, and "political correctness." The truth of a historical account suddenly didn't matter as much as its political utility—exactly what conservatives had complained about in the days when the left sought to find "a useable past." And Beck—with his "coherent vision," his "competing canon," and, most important of all, the reach his television and radio broadcasts enjoyed at the time—was politically useful to a right desperate to turn back the Obama tide. Some fifty years after they were rejected by responsible conservatives, Welch's old Birch Society notions had powerful media outlets standing behind them. Much of the conservative movement was happy to go along, at least for a while.

To see how deeply in debt the contemporary far right is to the far right of two and three generations ago, consider the thoroughly contemporary sound of the observations offered by Richard Hofstadter in his justly famous essay "The Paranoid Style of American Politics," first delivered as a lecture in November 1963. Note his emphasis on the "coherence" of the paranoid view:

> The typical procedure of the higher paranoid scholarship is to start with . . . defensible assumptions and with a careful accumulation of facts, or at least of what appear to be facts, and to marshal these facts toward an overwhelming "proof" of the particular conspiracy that is to be established. It is nothing if not coherent—in fact, the paranoid mentality is far more coherent than the real world, since it leaves no room for failures, mistakes, or ambiguities. It is, if not wholly rational, at least intensely rationalistic . . . What distinguishes the paranoid style is not, then, the absence of verifiable facts (though it is occasionally true that in his extravagant passion for facts the paranoid occasionally manufactures them), but rather the curious leap in imagination that is always made at some critical point in the recital of events.

Hofstadter concluded: "We are all sufferers from history, but the paranoid is a double sufferer, since he is afflicted not only by the real world, with the rest of us, but by his fantasies as well."

If Beck and the Tea Party had simply been marginal players on the right end of the political spectrum, their exertions might have been of some scholarly and journalistic interest, but hardly the stuff of a politically transformative movement. Their power came from the willingness of the conservative mainstream to embrace them—and also from fear among more moderately conservative politicians of the movement's power in the Republican primary electorate. The Tea Party's 2010 success in ousting the respected conservative senator Robert Bennett in Utah and its defeat of the popular moderate representative Mike Castle in a Delaware Senate primary gave it standing to intimidate Republicans who might otherwise have considered resistance. The fact that Castle lost to Christine O'Donnell, a figure destined to face electoral defeat as well as easy mockery, only underscored the extent to which exotic ideology had trumped any sense of realism on the right. Even Karl Rove was enraged that the stronger Republican candidate had been brought down by the right wing.

The Tea Party's strength owed to a broader crisis on the right created by the failures of the Bush presidency as well as the rise of an Obama movement that, on election night 2008, seemed destined to sweep the country toward a new, long-term engagement with progressivism.

If it was obvious that the Tea Party signaled a new level and kind of conservative activism characterized by an extreme reading of the Constitution, it was less obvious that its revolt was also aimed at Bush. But the president loathed by so many liberals was the far right's target, too. The historian Gary Gerstle provided an important clue to the sources of the Tea Party's disaffection in an essay that described Bush's "religiously inflected multiculturalism," an approach Gerstle characterized as the "multiculturalism of the godly."

Gerstle argued that Bush and Rove had set out to develop a brand of Republicanism that they believed "offered groups of minority voters reason to rethink their traditional hostility to the GOP." Gerstle noted that on "questions of immigration and diversity, Bush was worlds apart from Patrick Buchanan and the social-conservative wing of the Republican Party that wanted to restore America to its imagined Anglo Saxon and Anglo

Celtic glory." After all, Bush "was comfortable with diversity, bilingualism, and cultural pluralism, as long as members of America's ethnic and racial subcultures shared his patriotism, religious faith, and political conservatism." It is particularly notable, Gerstle added, that "during a time in which the United States was at war and Europe was exploding with tension and violence over Islam, Bush played a positive role in keeping interethnic and interracial relations in the United States relatively calm." Gerstle concluded that Republican politicians are likely someday to return to Bush's "multiculturalist project . . . as a way of building winning electoral coalitions."

But in the medium term, Bush's approach created a quiet backlash on the right that came back, ironically, to haunt Barack Obama.

In a *Financial Times* column written shortly after Gerstle's essay was published, the conservative writer Christopher Caldwell built on Gerstle's analysis to explain the Tea Party. This is how Caldwell characterized Bush's multicultural accomplishments, offering the perspective of a critic moderately sympathetic to the Tea Party's complaints.

> His "faith-based initiatives" were not a harbinger of creeping theocracy, but they did funnel a lot of federal money to urban welfare and substance-abuse programmes. He expanded Bill Clinton's ill-advised plans to increase minority home ownership. His No Child Left Behind Act, meant to improve educational outcomes for minorities, did so at the price of centralising authority in Washington. Mr Bush hoped for a free trade and migration zone for the Americas, deepening the North American Free Trade Agreement so that it would become more like the European Union. Conservatives' angry rejection of his 2007 immigration reform—which resembles Mr Obama's ideas—was the clearest sign that he was losing the ear of his party.

Caldwell argued that "many of the Tea Party's gripes about President Barack Obama can also be laid at the door of Mr Bush," and he concluded provocatively that if Obama "has come to grief through his failure to realize the electorate is poor soil for cultivating social democracy," then Bush failed to realize that "Christian Democracy was just as alien a plant."

Gerstle was on to something important about the Bush presidency, and one did not have to agree with Caldwell's views to accept the shrewd distinctions he drew between the Tea Party's ideology and the politics of compassionate conservatism. While white Christian conservatives and Tea Party supporters were in broad agreement on many issues, there was a harder edge to the Tea Party's views on immigration, multiculturalism, and Islam. There was also a radical character to the Tea Party's individualism that was missing on the religious right, whose Christian commitments demanded at least some fealty to a more communitarian disposition.

A poll conducted by the Public Religion Research Institute after the 2010 elections underscored the overlap between the Tea Party and the religious right but also highlighted subtle though important differences. For example, while 57 percent of white evangelicals believed that the values of Islam are at odds with American values, 66 percent of Tea Party members took this view. Sixty-five percent of white evangelicals said that Obama's religious views were different from their own; 76 percent of Tea Party members said this. While 50 percent of white evangelicals and 46 percent of Christian conservatives said "it is not a big problem if some people have more of a chance in life than others," 64 percent of Tea Party supporters felt this way. Tea Party supporters were also less likely to back an increase in the minimum wage than either white evangelicals or Christian conservatives.

To the extent that the Tea Party was attempting a "correction" to Bushism, it sought to move conservatism away from its more open and tolerant features. As we'll explore in more detail later, it was also a revolt against the idea that compassion is a legitimate object of public policy, and against Bush's modest, religiously based communitarian tilt.

But if the movement was partially a reaction against Bush, the energy behind it came from its fierce response to Barack Obama.

IV

The rise of the anti–Wall Street movement in the fall of 2011 inevitably invited comparisons with the Tea Party, and some of them were appropriate. In the broadest sense, both movements were the product of the anger unleashed by the country's economic troubles and the anxiety created by fears of American decline. Both spoke in angry tones. In quite different ways, both condemned the bailouts of bankers and financiers. Each also reflected the cocooning of American sensibilities that Bill Bishop described. Even protest movements were subject to cultural sorting: the Tea Party expressed its rage by reaching back to older right-wing views, Occupy Wall Streeters to some of the protest traditions on the left.

But therein lay the profound difference between the two groups. The Tea Party insisted that the concentrated power Americans needed to fear lay in government. The anti–Wall Streeters argued that most fearsome power was exercised by the masters of the financial world. The Tea Party disliked the bailouts primarily because they involved government meddling with the economy. The Occupy Wall Street movement did not reject activist government as such. Indeed, many in its ranks criticized government for insufficient rigor in regulating the bankers and the large investors. They objected to the *beneficiaries* of the government's largesse: the financiers who, they believed, already had too much influence on how government was run.

Polling on support for the two movements showed just how different they were. A *Washington Post*/Pew Research Center Poll in late October 2011 found that while 64 percent of the supporters of the Occupy Wall Street movement were either Democrats or independents leaning toward the Democrats, 71 percent of the Tea Party's supporters were Republicans or Republican-leaners. Among the Tea Partiers, 56 percent called themselves conservative; only 21 percent of the Occupy Wall Street supporters did. Interestingly, given efforts to discredit the anti–Wall Street movement as extreme, a plurality of its supporters (45 percent) described themselves as moderate; only 31 percent called themselves liberal. Occupy Wall Street supporters were only slightly younger than Tea Party supporters, but the Tea Party sympathizers were somewhat more likely to be southerners. The idea that there was a large overlap between these two movements was simply wrong: among Occupy's supporters, 64 percent said they opposed the Tea Party, while 25 percent supported it. Among the Tea Party's supporters, 52 percent said they opposed Occupy Wall Street, while 31 percent supported it. When these findings were combined, it turned out that 14 percent of all Americans opposed both movements and *only 10 percent said they supported both the Tea Party and Occupy Wall Street.* Such limited overlap hardly provides the basis for cooperation between these very different protest initiatives.

The survey also traced what other polls were showing: a steady decline in sympathy for the Tea Party outside conservative circles, a reflection, perhaps, of the growing unpopularity of the new House Republican leadership. In the *Post*/Pew survey, only 32 percent said they supported the Tea Party, while 44 percent opposed it. Occupy Wall Street fared somewhat better: 39 percent supported the movement, according to the *Post*/Pew research, while 35 percent opposed it.

Why did it take so much longer for a left-of-center protest movement to gather strength comparable to the Tea Party's? Some of the answers were obvious. The right felt closed out of government after 2008 and in desperate need of new forms of organization and activism. The left thought it had won the 2008 election. With Democrats in control of the White House and both houses of Congress, stepped-up organizing didn't seem quite so urgent. The administration was complicit in this, allowing Obama's vast organization to atrophy and viewing the left's primary role as supporting whatever the president believed needed to be done. Dissent to his left was discouraged as counterproductive.

In certain respects, the Obama response was understandable. Facing ferocious resistance from the right, Obama needed all the friends he could get. He feared that left-wing criticism would further weaken him as it joined in the public mind with right-wing assaults. But in the end, what seemed sensible as a tactical matter proved to be a strategic mistake. The absence of a strong, organized left made it easier for conservatives to label Obama a left-winger. It gave the Tea Party a temporary monopoly on the symbols of populism. And it deprived Obama of the sort of productive interaction with outside groups that Franklin Roosevelt enjoyed with the labor movement and Lyndon B. Johnson had with the civil rights movement. Those movements pushed FDR and LBJ in more progressive directions while also lending them support against their conservative adversaries.

Curiously, the absence of a left was also bad for the cause of moderation itself. With the Tea Party steadily pushing the political dialogue toward the right, the dominant political narrative became unbalanced—and, from the point of view of Obama and those to his left, unfair as well. Because the voices laying blame for the nation's troubles in the failures of the financial system were muted, responsibility for the continuing economic stagnation fell to Obama and "big government." In the short run, individualism had a powerful hold on the public debate. Those more sympathetic to the cause of community, including Obama himself, were placed on the defensive.

V

Understanding the tension between individualism and a more communitarian view helps explain the ferociousness of the Tea Party's anti-Obama backlash in a way that a focus solely on left and right, liberalism and conservatism, does not. Obama's critics understood instinctively that his ascent to power was a communitarian correction to a long individualistic era that could be traced back to both the 1980s and the 1960s. Calling him a "socialist" was a convenient if inaccurate way of protesting this shift. Of course, this wasn't the only reason the right opposed Obama. But it was an important and insufficiently appreciated cause of the Tea Party's rise.

It's true, of course, that Obama's election was made possible by the specific failures of the Bush administration in both foreign policy and economic policy. It was a reaction to the war in Iraq and the economic collapse. But Obama's larger message—that we had been off track for a long time and that it was "time to turn the page"—was rooted in a more sweeping critique of a country that had become too selfish and too self-involved. Obama sensed that Americans felt increasingly disconnected from each other and sought stronger social bonds. He pledged to change Bush's policies, yes, but his larger promise was to mix a stronger social glue, to link Americans to each other, to roll back extreme individualism. Consider this early Obama speech, given in 2006 before he formally launched his presidential campaign:

> Each day, it seems, thousands of Americans are going about their daily rounds—dropping off the kids at school, driving to the office, flying to a business meeting, shopping at the mall, trying to stay on

their diets—and they're coming to the realization that something is missing. They are deciding that their work, their possessions, their diversions, their sheer busyness, is not enough. They want a sense of purpose, a narrative arc to their lives. They're looking to relieve a chronic loneliness, a feeling supported by a recent study that shows Americans have fewer close friends and confidants than ever before. And so they need an assurance that somebody out there cares about them, is listening to them—that they are not just destined to travel down that long highway towards nothingness.

Obama's politics, including his open sympathy for religion's role in American life, have been mystifying to those who viewed him only as a conventional liberal. In fact, he is at least as much a communitarian as he is a progressive. What could be more appropriate for a former community organizer?

He made this absolutely clear in his inaugural address, proposing to reverse two kinds of extreme individualism that had permeated the American political soul for perhaps four decades. He set his face against the expressive individualism of the 1960s that defined "do your own thing" and "if it feels good, do it" as the highest forms of freedom. Against this view, Obama spoke of responsibilities, of acting on behalf of others, even highlighting that classic bourgeois obligation reflected in "a parent's willingness to nurture a child."

But he also rejected the economic individualism of the 1980s, which he diagnosed as a principal cause of the nation's economic implosion. Discounting "the pleasures of riches and fame," he spoke of Americans not as consumers but as citizens. His references to freedom were glowing, but he emphasized our "duties" to preserve it as much as he extolled the rights it conveys.

A good case can be made that Obama would have placed himself in a stronger position to battle for his program had he given a more practical and focused inaugural address that highlighted the depth of the economic difficulties the country faced. Such a speech would have explained the causes of the downturn, emphasizing the flawed policies of the recent past.

And in describing the long struggle the country faced in emerging from the financial wreckage, he could have prepared the country for what would prove to be a more difficult recovery than many Americans expected at the time. He might usefully have linked candor about the medium-term difficulties with his signature emphasis on hope for the long run. It can be seen as a lost opportunity.

Yet the speech he did give plainly laid out Obama's moral challenge to the country. His criticism was directed against flaws in the forms of individualism embraced by each of the country's ideological camps. He took on a large rhetorical challenge, since rights are so much easier to talk about than duties, and freedom's gifts are always more prized than its obligations. He was also fighting against the prevailing narrative of our history as one long march toward individualism.

Glenn Beck, Dick Armey, and partisans of the Tea Party understood this as well as anyone. A deep belief that individualism is the one American value that counts lies at the heart of the Tea Party. Like similar groups at other moments in our history, the Tea Partiers claim a direct lineage to Jeffersonian notions that only small government is compatible with liberty, individual initiative, and individual responsibility. Freedom Works, former representative Dick Armey's organization that latched onto the Tea Party, described its goals compactly: "lower taxes, less government and more economic freedom for all Americans." The rhetoric of the Tea Party and its allies typically speaks of heroic individuals under siege, the central theme of Ayn Rand's novels. And sales of her books soared after Obama's election.

Glenn Beck's extreme and at times rabid conservatism eventually led to his departure from Fox News (though not before he had helped Republicans win the 2010 elections). But in the first year or so of the Obama administration, he built a large audience as one of the primary voices of the rising Tea Party opposition. It's important to remember how influential Beck's voice was during Obama's first two years in office.

And Beck nicely summarized the Tea Party's view of American history during a radio conversation in the spring of 2009 with a young woman who described herself as a student at a Baptist college. She had called in to

complain about a professor's sharp criticisms of capitalism. Beck spoke in
direct reply to the caller's instructor:

> Mr. Professor: Do you believe this country was founded on divine
> providence? Do you believe that George Washington, Thomas
> Jefferson, Ben Franklin, Madison, Adams, do you believe those men
> were enlightened men? I do. Well, their crazy idea was to allow men
> to be free and free in their own business to allow them to be able to
> engage in capitalism. I didn't think a bad tree could bear good fruit.
> I didn't know a good tree could bear bad fruit or bad trees bear
> good fruit. I didn't think that was possible. I've read that some place
> in some big thick book. You'd know better than I do because you're a
> professor, and the elite professors always have the right answer.

Beck is by no means eccentric in seeing the nation's founders as committed to a view that men should be "free in their own business to allow
them to be able to engage in capitalism." And the conservative habit of
criticizing supposedly know-it-all college professors had a particular resonance against a former law school professor named Barack Obama, and
also against Beck's other great historical nemesis, the former Princeton
professor Woodrow Wilson.

But if Beck, Limbaugh, and Skousen are guilty of distorting American
history for their own purposes, they did not invent the idea of revisiting and
reinterpreting the past. On the contrary, Americans' understandings of ourselves have changed over the course of our national life. Parts of our story
have been contested as fiercely as any contemporary political issue. New
political eras have opened our eyes to parts of our past that we had
ignored—and, on occasion, have also closed our eyes to aspects of our story
we once understood clearly. There has always been a politics of history.

CHAPTER II

The Politics of History
Why the Past Can Never Escape the Present

IF so many public controversies during Barack Obama's first term seemed part of an extended American history course, many politicians consistently got failing grades. Speaking in New Hampshire at an event sponsored by the Republican Liberty Caucus in the late winter of 2011, Representative Michele Bachmann tried to establish a link with the local folks by declaring: "You're the state where the shot was heard 'round the world at Lexington and Concord." The problem for Bachmann: the Concord where the battle happened was the one in Massachusetts.

A few months later, Sarah Palin got into the news by offering a rather peculiar gloss on a story familiar to every American schoolchild. Speaking in Boston, she declared that Paul Revere had "warned the British that they weren't going to be taking away our arms, by ringing those bells and making sure as he was riding his horse through town to send those warning shots and bells that we were going to be secure and we were going to be free." Palin was determined to turn America's best-known silversmith into a Second Amendment hero, and historians spent several days debating exactly what was true and what wasn't in her unusual account of Revere's famous ride.

The routine botching of the American story by politicians is not unique to this era, nor has it been confined to politicians on the right. But the gaffes may be more a habit of the right at the moment simply because the Tea Party so insists upon rooting itself in the American past. The movement's very name goes back to the signal event in Boston Harbor on December 16, 1773. Whether they intend it or not, their name suggests that the current elected government in Washington is as illegitimate as a distant, unelected monarchy was two and a half centuries ago. And it hints that methods outside the normal political channels are justified in confronting such oppression.

But the Tea Party is far from alone among American political movements in trying to establish a consistency with the past. It is an important truth about history *within* our history: when large matters are at stake, Americans have a habit of searching for precedent and identifying useful heroes. We all claim to be sons and daughters of our Revolution. We all desperately want to be *American* and devoutly wish to avoid being labeled otherwise. It's hard to imagine another country having a committee within its legislative branch bearing a name akin to that of our House Un-American Activities Committee, which did its work rooting out un-Americans from 1938 to 1975. Even the American Communist Party, HUAC's main target, was moved during the crisis of the 1930s to proclaim Communism as nothing more (or less) than "twentieth century Americanism."

Our historical heroes themselves looked back for heroes of their own. A significant portion of Abraham Lincoln's 1860 address at Cooper Union in New York City, the speech that helped to make him president, was an argument over where the Founders of our republic—"our fathers," Lincoln called them—*really* stood on the question of slavery. His learned speech concluded that he was on their side in opposing the spread of slavery, and they on his.

In his war against the Bank of the United States a generation earlier, Andrew Jackson (whom Lincoln had opposed) thought of himself as "the guardian of a threatened Republican tradition" defending the nation's Founding principles against what Jackson saw as the "tyranny and despotism" of the big financiers.

And in his 1932 Commonwealth Club speech, the campaign address that most closely prefigured the New Deal, Franklin Roosevelt carefully defended his proposals for a stronger national government by harking back to the American Revolution and Thomas Jefferson's intentions. "A government must so order its functions as not to interfere with the individual,"

FDR declared. "But even Jefferson realized that the exercise of the property rights might so interfere with the rights of the individual that the government, without whose assistance the property rights could not exist, must intervene, not to destroy individualism but to protect it."

Of course, the homage that politicians pay to the past is often a form of opportunistic piety. If the devil can quote scripture for his purposes, politicians can ransack our national tradition to justify virtually any course they are commending to the country. Lincoln's opponents, after all, invoked the Founders in *support* of slavery. Jackson's critics accused him of subverting the Constitution's conception of the presidency and turning himself into a king. Opponents of the New Deal organized the Liberty League under a Jeffersonian banner of their own. Many old Liberty League arguments have been brought back to life by the Tea Party against Obama. References to the Founders and the Constitution, so routine in today's conservative rhetoric, also studded the polemics against the New Deal.

No American orator was more steeped in the American story than Martin Luther King Jr. His "I Have a Dream" speech was an extended and impassioned essay on the American promise, rooted in our Founding. From the speech's second sentence—"Five score years ago, a great American, in whose symbolic shadow we stand today, signed the Emancipation Proclamation"—King made clear that the civil rights movement's demands reflected American history's own vows. "When the architects of our republic wrote the magnificent words of the Constitution and the Declaration of Independence," King declared, "they were signing a promissory note to which every American was to fall heir. This note was a promise that all men, yes, black men as well as white men, would be guaranteed the 'unalienable Rights' of 'Life, Liberty and the pursuit of Happiness.'" One of the most dramatic moments in the speech came next. "It is obvious today that America has defaulted on this promissory note, insofar as her citizens of color are concerned," King said. "Instead of honoring this sacred obligation, America has given the Negro people a bad check, a check which has come back marked 'insufficient funds.'" And all this within the first four paragraphs of the speech.

Our debate over our history is only rarely over whether our past should be seen as noble or ignoble, defined primarily by our love for freedom and justice or by the oppressions of race or class or gender. These debates do occur, especially in disputes over how American history should be taught in the schools and how much schoolchildren and teenagers should learn about our nation's mistakes. My own view, for what it's worth, is that giving students an accurate account of the country's shortcomings as well as its triumphs will not endanger anyone's patriotism. On the contrary, doing so is just as likely to show how acknowledging and correcting mistakes is an American long suit.

But most of our politically relevant debates reflect a widely shared respect and affection for the American story across philosophical lines. American history has been contested terrain from the beginning of the republic precisely because even critics of a particular American present have tended to view the past as a resource. Egalitarians, from abolitionists and trade unionists to civil rights leaders and feminists, have drawn on the Declaration of Independence's promises of *universal* liberty in a land where all are created equal. Libertarians have used the pledges in the Bill of Rights to highlight the American promise of *negative* liberty, a guarantee against the power of an overweening state. Traditionalist conservatives have stressed that ours, from the beginning, was an experiment in *ordered* liberty, resisting radicals who were seen as threatening the stability on which freedom depends. Contemporary liberals have seen the Constitution as containing an inherent drive toward greater democracy, toward *active* liberty, Supreme Court justice Stephen Breyer's phrase to describe our commitment to "the principle of participatory self-government."

But politics has also shaped historical writing. In their interpretations, in the stories they tell, and in the evidence they select, America's historians are powerfully influenced by the political culture in which they work. This is not, it should be emphasized, simply a habit of the Tea Party.

To say that the politics of the moment influences history is neither to justify the intentional distortion of our story for partisan purposes, nor to assert that one account is as "good" or "valid" as another, regardless of its factual basis. It is simply to acknowledge that the heart of the historian's task lies "in explanation and in selection," as the scholar Morton White noted in his classic book *Foundations of Historical Knowledge*. In describing events, the historian "depends upon generalizations," White noted, and "because he records certain events rather than others, he may depend upon value judgments that guide his selection." How a historian explains, selects, and generalizes is affected by many factors, and politics is one of them. White noted Samuel Eliot Morison's classic observation: that at the turn of the last century, it was difficult to find a general history of the United States that did not "present the Federalist-Whig-Republican point of view, or express a very dim view of all Democratic leaders except Grover Cleveland." But by the 1950s, it was hard to find a good history of the country "that did not follow the Jefferson-Jackson-Franklin D. Roosevelt line." Some intervening elections, which ended a long Republican era and inaugurated an extended period of Democratic rule, had a large impact inside the quiet studies where historians wrote their books.

"Memory is the thread of personal identity, history of public identity," Richard Hofstadter observed in *The Progressive Historians*, and "the business of history always involves a subtle transaction with civic identity." In turn, civic identity is defined by a set of political and philosophical assumptions. "Historians," wrote Eric Foner, whose exceptional work on Reconstruction I turn to later, "view the constant search for new perspectives as the lifeblood of historical understanding." He recounts a conversation he had with a reporter for *Newsweek* during the debate a few years ago over standards for the teaching of American history. "'Professor,' she asked, 'when did historians stop relating facts and start all this revising of interpretations of the past?' Around the time of Thucydides, I told her." Foner is fond of James Baldwin's observation that history "does not refer mainly, or even principally, to the past. On the contrary, the great force of history comes from the fact that we carry it within us, are unconsciously controlled by it in many ways, and history is literally *present* in all we do."

The work of George Bancroft, "the first great American historian of America," as Hofstadter called him, was inflected with his Jacksonian partisanship. Bancroft saw all history, as one of his admirers put it, as representing "the progress of the democratic principle." For Bancroft, Hofstadter said, "history taught a lesson, the inevitable movement of human affairs toward the goal of liberty under providential guidance." It was Bancroft who contributed one of the great refrains of American populism, decades before populism was born. "The popular voice is all powerful with us," Bancroft wrote; "this, we acknowledge, is the voice of God."

In 1945, roughly a century after Bancroft, Arthur Schlesinger Jr. published his landmark account *The Age of Jackson*, which viewed Old Hickory as a prototype for Franklin Roosevelt. He saw Jackson, like FDR, as giving voice to the discontents of the working class. "History can contribute nothing in the way of panaceas," the young Schlesinger wrote in his foreword. "But it can assist vitally in that sense of what is democratic, of what is in line with our republican traditions, which alone can save us." It was a heroic view of the role played by the study of history. Yet as Sean Wilentz has noted, Schlesinger, an honest self-critic, was later willing to concede the merit of the observation that he had voted for Roosevelt on every page of his book about Jackson.

In one sense, the notion that historians are influenced by their views is a truism. All historians make choices as to which subjects they deem important and which themes they see as worthy of their energies. It is thus not surprising that one of the best recent histories of conservatism, *The Conservative Intellectual Movement in America*, was written by George H. Nash, himself a conservative. Some of the most compelling recent historical work on American trade unions has come from Nelson Lichtenstein, Steve Fraser, and Gary Gerstle, all of them sympathizers with the contemporary labor movement. Nor is it surprising that individual historians with a strong commitment to the causes of gender and racial equality—scholars such as Meredith Tax, Elaine Tyler May, and Manning Marable—have produced a series of innovative studies of the role played by women and African Americans in our national story.

Differences in the outlooks of individual historians working in the same field have produced some of our most revealing intellectual discussions. In recent years, Sean Wilentz and Daniel Walker Howe have written dueling, monumental, and hugely valuable accounts of American democracy in the period before the Civil War. Both accounts are true and accurate. Neither historian manufactures evidence. Both tell moving stories.

Yet Wilentz and Howe differ sharply in their assessments of the Jacksonian Democrats and the Whigs. Wilentz, like Schlesinger before him, offers a largely positive assessment of the role of the Jacksonians. He sees their warts but highlights their role in making the United States more democratic. Howe has rehabilitated the Whigs in historical memory. A few years ago, their argument commanded the attention of the *New Yorker*. It is the sort of notice that disagreements among historians receive only rarely, yet the magazine was right to see that their work and their differences mattered far beyond the realm of the academy.

Morton White, whose book on historical knowledge was published in 1965, long before the rise of deconstruction, observed flatly that "some of our apparently logical statements turn out to be moral and relative in character." White acknowledged this even as he strongly defended the role of fact and logic in the writing of history. Foner, citing the work of Herbert Gutman, argued that history "is not simply a collection of facts, not a politically sanctioned listing of indisputable 'truths,' but an ongoing means of collective self-understanding about the nature of our society." As the *New Yorker* recognized in calling attention to the Wilentz-Howe debate, their argument mattered not just for what it said about our past, but also for the light it shed on how we view the present.

But the politics of history cannot be explained simply by the personal predilections of individual historians. Our historical understanding is also enriched by the interplay between current political and civic struggles and our efforts to arrive at new and better understandings of what came before.

Nowhere has this been more evident recently than in the response of a group of younger historians to the emergence of a new conservative movement that arose in the 1960s and took power with Ronald Reagan's election in 1980. The habit of historians and social scientists in the period after World War II was to dismiss conservatism. This attitude came naturally to writers convinced that a liberal consensus characterized American reality, a view captured famously by the literary critic Lionel Trilling, who observed in 1954 that "in the United States at this time, liberalism is not only the dominant but even the sole intellectual tradition." Such conservative impulses that did exist, he wrote, manifested themselves not "in ideas but only in action or irritable mental gestures which seek to resemble ideas." Hofstadter broadly shared this view and was inclined to use clinical psychology to explain the radical right. The ideas these movements put forward seemed secondary. In explaining this new right, Hofstadter, Daniel Bell, and Seymour Martin Lipset all stressed that an older, non-Anglo-Saxon Protestant middle class felt displaced by newly mobile children of immigrants and were using politics as an outlet for their "status anxieties." (These theories have come around again to explain opposition to Obama.)

But with Ronald Reagan's victory in 1980, a creative group of historians (many of them younger and left-leaning in their own politics) began suspecting that the right could not be reduced to a collection of "irritable mental gestures." A raft of new histories—among them Rick Perlstein's *Before the Storm: Barry Goldwater and the Unmaking of the American Consensus*, Lisa McGirr's *Suburban Warriors: The Origins of the New American Right*, and Mary Brennan's *Turning Right in the Sixties: The Conservative Capture of the GOP*—chose to take American conservatism seriously. More recently, Patrick Allitt's *The Conservatives* traced a conservative tradition through the entirety of American history. The new historians of conservatism cast a skeptical eye on assertions that the subjects of their studies were only anxious, backward-looking, and paranoid. McGirr, who focused on conservatism's heartland in California's Orange County, conceded that "a segment of the Right appealed to traditional ideas, [and] embraced a fundamentalist religious worldview and apocalyptic strands of thought." But conservative ideas also "took hold among a highly educated and thoroughly modern group of men and women." Their mobilization, she argued, was "not a rural 'remnant' of the displaced and maladapted but a gathering around principles that were found to be relevant in the most modern of communities." These new historians are correct to take conservatism seriously. But it's worth asking if this trove of good historical work would have been undertaken had Ronald Reagan lost the 1980 election.

No discussion of revisionism is complete without a bow to the work of revisionists on the left end of the historical profession during the 1960s and 1970s. Their objective was summarized by the evocative title of a collection of their essays published in 1968, *Towards a New Past*. The editor of the volume, Barton Bernstein, pioneered the view of the New Deal as largely a conservative achievement. Similarly, Gabriel Kolko argued in *The Triumph of Conservatism* that the Progressive Era reforms, far from being particularly progressive or radical, were pushed by "important business leaders" who realized "that only the national government could rationalize the economy." The effect of the period's reforms was to "preserve the basic social and economic relations essential to a capitalist society." William Appleman Williams and Gar Alperovitz offered important books debunking aspects of American foreign policy, in Alperovitz's case challenging the stated reasons behind the decision to drop the atomic bomb on Japan. Herbert Gutman pioneered new approaches to the history of both slavery and the American working class, while Howard Zinn spent a long lifetime captivating students with his bottom-up approach to the writing of the American story. As the historian Jill Lepore noted in the *New Yorker*, Zinn "introduced a whole lot of people who hadn't thought about it before to the idea that history has a point of view."

The revisionists provoked a new generation of historians to focus far more than their elders had on the role of race, class, and gender in our story. Because of their work, Jacksonian democracy's achievements and its vision of equality among white men came to be measured against its grave moral failures on slavery and its brutal policies against Native Americans. Visionary radicals—Tom Paine, William Lloyd Garrison, Frederick Douglass, Eugene Debs, W. E. B. Du Bois—were read back into the American narrative.

Critics of the New Left historians certainly had a point when they argued that their accounts of the past were heavily influenced by their political preoccupations in the present. "New Left academics," wrote the historian John Patrick Diggins, "would write about the American past with a romantic determination to find there what they could never find in the American present outside their own enclaves: moral community, feminine consciousness, and a radical working class." But there was also a refreshing candor among the left's revisionists about their political objectives. "I am less interested in eighteenth-century radicalism than in twentieth-century radicalism," Staughton Lynd, one of the pioneers of dissenting history, wrote in his *Intellectual Origins of American Radicalism*. "The characteristic concepts of the existential radicalism of today have a long and honorable history. Acquaintance with that history may help in sharpening intellectual tools for the work of tomorrow."

But it was not only the scholars on the left in the 1960s who embarked on the quest for a new past. Their work simply made explicit a revisionist temper that, to one degree or another, motivates *all* historians, often inspired by their engagement with the problems of their day. "All of my books have been, in a certain sense, topical in their inspiration," said Hofstadter, a revisionist in his own time, later revised by others. "That is to say, I have always begun with a concern with some present reality."

It is easy enough to understand that all historians start from *somewhere*—they write at a given time in a given place, and have moral, political, religious, and ethical commitments. They are inevitably affected by the currents of their era, even if they struggle heroically to free their accounts from bias and distortion. And what they write, in turn, affects how others view not only the past but also the present and the future.

But in certain areas, the politics of history is especially raw and contentious. Nowhere is this more obvious than in how historians have dealt with our nation's long struggle with race, and no aspect of our story has undergone a more thoroughgoing revision and counter-revision than our view of what happened during Reconstruction in the South after the Civil War. I turn briefly to that history because it may be the very best example of why I believe the word "struggle" is appropriate to how we have continually grappled with our past. It is also important to our own time, when some on the right are eager to downplay the role of race in our national story, and the role of slavery in our Civil War.

III

The bold effort by the radical Republicans to transform the South's aristocratic, planter-dominated society into a more egalitarian and democratic order was, from the outset, a brave, visionary, and imaginative project. It was also destined to run into vicious opposition from those whose power was challenged.

Reconstruction took place at a moment of widespread corruption in

American politics, so it's not surprising that this corruption affected the Reconstruction governments. And the political interests of the new Republican Party were as tied up in the power struggles around Reconstruction as were those of the Democrats, then allied with the old white southern elites. But at the heart of the argument over Reconstruction, from the beginning and ever since, was the moral and political question of whether southern blacks would be offered rights genuinely equal to those of whites. Would African Americans be empowered to shape the decisions that determined their fate as individuals and as a community? Or would they be denied the basic rights of citizenship and treated as an inferior group?

"The answer to the all-important question of what kinds of lives black people might live in the South," wrote Nicholas Lemann in *Redemption*, "depended on the freed slaves' organizing abilities and on the reliability of their voting rights. From these, governmental power—and then schools and jobs and justice—would flow." For an extended period during Reconstruction, black people enjoyed these rights. But over time, as Lemann observed, the forces of white supremacy triumphed through "an organized, if unofficial, military effort to take away by terrorist violence the black political rights that were now part of the Constitution." It's strange to our ears now, but the whites who overthrew the Reconstruction governments, imposed a color line, and stripped African Americans of their rights were known, proudly, as "Redeemers."

The scholars who wrote the history of Reconstruction from the turn of the last century into the 1920s saw the foes of Reconstruction just that way in accounts offered when the nation's inclinations had turned conservative (one could also fairly say racist) on matters of civil rights. Works by James Ford Rhodes, William Dunning, John W. Burgess, and their students painted Reconstruction as a disastrous interlude. They described the Reconstruction governments as dominated by corrupt "carpetbaggers" and "scalawags" and accused them of imposing misrule on the South, partly by granting power to "ignorant" freed slaves. Southern whites who used violence and fraud at the polls to overthrow the Reconstruction governments were defended, not condemned. Burgess called Reconstruction "the most soul-sickening spectacle that Americans had ever been called upon to behold." Rhodes called the work of the Radical Republicans "repressive" and "uncivilized" and cast them as politicians who "pandered to the ignorant negroes, the knavish white natives and the vulturous adventurers who flocked from the North." Bear in mind that Dunning, Burgess, and other scholars who worked in that tradition were broadly respected figures who did extensive new research on the era about which they wrote. The center for much of this revisionist work was Columbia University, well known then and since for providing the nation with many of its most distinguished historians. Their accounts became the conventional wisdom of American history—and they were still affecting the presentation of the period in the American history textbooks I first encountered in elementary school in the 1950s and early 1960s. These approaches to Reconstruction, in turn, reinforced racial attitudes that undergirded southern segregation.

As Kenneth M. Stampp argued in *The Era of Reconstruction*, his 1965 volume that played an enormous rôle in overturning the Dunning interpretation, social trends in the North after the Civil War prepared the way for this negative view of the Radical Republicans. A reaction against the wave of southern European immigration popularized the invocation among the native-born of "cruel racial stereotypes" against the newcomers. These turned out to match rather closely the racial stereotypes that were common in the South. "In due time," Stampp observed, "those who repeated these stereotypes awoke to the realization that what they were saying was not really very original—that, as a matter of fact, these generalizations were *precisely* the ones southern white men had been making about Negroes for years." As a result, Stampp noted archly, "the old middle classes of the North looked with new understanding upon the problems of the beleaguered white men of the South."

The "vogue of social Darwinism," the view that the fittest survived and that government help for the underprivileged, including blacks, only disturbed a "natural" process, "encouraged the belief that a solution to the race problem could only evolve slowly as the Negroes gradually improved themselves." This squared with the era's popular sentiments that Anglo-Saxons "were superior to other peoples, especially when it came to politics." Stampp noted the publication in 1916 of *The Passing of the Great Race*, which asserted—again, in words jarring in our time—that the Civil War had destroyed "great numbers of the best breeding stock on both sides." If the war had not occurred, the author asserted, descendants of those men "would have populated the Western States instead of the racial nondescripts who are now flocking there." In a climate that could produce a phrase such as "racial nondescripts," it is not surprising that a historian such as Rhodes would conclude: "No large policy in our country has ever been so conspicuous a failure as that of forcing universal negro suffrage upon the South." A powerful dissent from this view was lodged by the civil rights leader and scholar W. E. B. Du Bois in his 1935 work *Black Reconstruction in America*, but it would take years for the historical profession to catch up with Du Bois.

It was against a history rooted in racism that the post–World War II revisionists did their work. At the dawn of the civil rights era, a group of talented historians—among them Stampp, James McPherson, John Hope Franklin, Eric McKitrick, and Howard K. Beale—set out to rehabilitate the exertions of the Radical Republicans. They reminded Americans of the achievements of the Reconstruction governments in building schools, developing the southern economy, successfully enfranchising African Americans, and enacting the Fourteenth and Fifteenth Amendments to the Constitution. As Stampp argued, these great egalitarian amendments "could have been adopted only under the conditions of radical reconstruction" and they "make the blunders of that era, tragic though they were, dwindle into insignificance." And against the view that white politicians had foisted the vote on African Americans for partisan Republican purposes, the revisionists demonstrated that African Americans had been the authors of their own fate and major architects of the successes of the era. As Stampp wrote, "Suffrage was not something thrust upon an indifferent mass of Negroes. Their leaders had demanded it from the start."

Building on the work of the original revisionists and going beyond it, Eric Foner offered his monumental 1988 history, *Reconstruction*. It is likely to stand as the authoritative account of the era for many years—even if Foner would be the first to assert that all historical accounts, including his own, should be open to revision. Foner's ambition was to "combine the Dunning School's aspiration to a broad interpretive framework with the findings and concerns of recent scholarship." *Reconstruction* was notable in many respects, particularly in the emphasis it placed on the role of African

Americans as leading actors in the South's post–Civil War political drama. "Rather than passive victims of the actions of others or simply a 'problem' confronting white society," Foner wrote, "blacks were active agents in the making of Reconstruction."

Foner also emphasized how southern society was "remodeled" in the Reconstruction period and "how the status of white planters, merchants, and yeomen, and their relations with one another, changed over time." He stressed that while racism was "pervasive," a significant number of southern whites were "willing to link their political fortunes with those of blacks" and that northern Republicans, for a time, came "to associate the fate of former slaves with their party's raison d'être."

To read Foner is to realize that the 1960s civil rights movement did not emerge from nowhere. It reflected the memory of an earlier time when racial justice was an inspiring ideal, informing social reforms that were at once practical and far-reaching. As Foner notes, what emerged from the Civil War and Reconstruction was "a national state possessing vastly expanded authority and a new set of purposes, including an unprecedented commitment to the ideal of a national citizenship whose equal rights belonged to all Americans regardless of race." This was the national state Martin Luther King Jr. coaxed into action and Lyndon B. Johnson mobilized when he embarked upon the Second Reconstruction in the 1960s.

The transformation of the history of Reconstruction was in itself an important part of our nation's political history. It helped open the way for the demands of African Americans who sought nothing more than the rights they had once, if briefly, enjoyed. The civil rights movement, in turn, inspired historians to revisit the old accounts of Reconstruction that had been distorted by racism. This interaction between politics and history created both a more accurate history *and* a political climate more hospitable to racial justice.

Foner has been as close as anyone to the center of this interpretative struggle, and his coda about his own role is delightfully revealing:

> There is a certain irony in the fact that a Columbia historian produced this new history of Reconstruction, exemplified by the fact that my research expenses were partly covered by the department's

Dunning Fund and much of my reading took place in Burgess Library. For it was at Columbia at the turn of the century that William A. Dunning and John W. Burgess had established the traditional school of Reconstruction politics, teaching that blacks were "children" incapable of appreciating the freedom that had been thrust upon them, and that the North did a "monstrous" thing in granting them suffrage. There is no better illustration than Reconstruction of how historical interpretation both reflects and helps to shape current policies. The views of the Dunning School helped freeze the white South for generations in unalterable opposition to any change in race relations, and justified decades of Northern indifference to Southern nullification of the Fourteenth and Fifteenth Amendments. The civil rights revolution, in turn, produced an outpouring of revisionist literature, far more favorable to the aspirations of former slaves.

Foner shared with Dunning and Burgess a Columbia connection, a deep engagement with the same period in American history, and a passion to interpret it. Substantively, he disagreed with his Morningside Heights forebears on almost everything that mattered.

I V

The battle over Reconstruction history has another lesson for this moment. The 1870s revolt against Reconstruction, accompanied as it was by an increasingly reactionary view of African Americans, provides an object lesson in how the energies of reform eras dissipate. The idealism of one period can congeal into a sour view of those who undertake the difficult and visionary work of change. Note how Reconstruction's advocates, who were motivated by a desire to achieve equality across the color line and revolutionize social and economic relations in the South, were reduced by later historians to power-hungry and corrupt politicians merely using African Americans for their own selfish purposes. African Americans who saw themselves as the subjects of history during Reconstruction were reduced to being mere objects for political schemers. A project of community transformation was recast as a series of plots for individual self-aggrandizement.

Such rewrites of the past are very much with us again. The activists of the Progressive Era and the New Deal saw themselves as social reformers battling against an unjust and outmoded economic system on behalf of working- and middle-class Americans. But the struggles of those eras are being repainted as selfish efforts on the part of liberal politicians, government bureaucrats, labor bosses, and anti-business intellectuals who sought to gain control over the economic system. The reforms of the Great Society are being denigrated in a similar way. The successes of the period—among them Medicare, Medicaid, civil rights, and voting rights—are ignored in an effort to pronounce the entire effort a failure. The best way to discredit today's social reformers is to tear down those who came before them, to ignore their successes and belittle their achievements.

An even more daring approach involves rewriting our national self-understanding from the very beginning. This is at once bold and subtle. Our understandings of Reconstruction, after all, went through a sharp, open process of revision. Our views of the larger trajectory of our story have been changed by taking propositions we broadly agree on—our love of liberty, our devotion to individual achievement, and our belief in limits on government—and using them to push aside all competing, supplementary, or complementary visions of the American character and national philosophy.

Our current polarization arises in part because liberals and Democrats—notably our last two Democratic presidents—have become more open to a communitarian view of our national story at the very moment when conservatives have been casting aside their own strong communitarian traditions and denying the robust role played by the federal government in the nation's growth and development from the earliest days of our republic. This conflict is fed by the very complexity of our national character.

CHAPTER III

Lessons from the Humble Penny
The Striver, the Seeker, the Puritan, and the Patriot

W E Americans are a confusing people, perhaps especially to ourselves. The self-portraits we offer the world are contradictory. Our movies include such gloriously communitarian films as *It's a Wonderful Life*, *Witness*, and *The Last Hurrah*—and the powerfully individualistic characters of *Dirty Harry*, *High Noon*, *Scarface*, and *Rebel Without a Cause*. The novels of John Steinbeck, John Sayles, and Toni Morrison call for community and speak of the limits of individualism. Our popular fiction also celebrates loners: Jack Kerouac as Sal Paradise took us *On the Road* while Sam Spade, Travis McGee, Lew Archer, and Kinsey Millhone disdain interference from anyone in their private efforts to create pockets of order in a chaotic world. And then there is Spenser, the late Robert B. Parker's splendidly self-contained and iconoclastic hero. Is he a pure individualist, as he so often presents himself? Or was his entire fictional life a celebration of the Boston communities in which he remained so unapologetically embedded?

Our confusion arises not from misperceptions about ourselves, but from an awareness of our twin longings. As I have been suggesting, one of our country's peculiar achievements has been to nurture communitarian individualists—and individualistic communitarians. At our worst, this can make us seem schizophrenic. At our best, we approach a sensible equilibrium. And at a moment of so much fruitless and angry political polarization, the homely idea of restoring the balance between our two sides may be the most radical option on offer. For a people no less than for individuals, asserting one aspect of our character at the cost of obliterating another is an act of self-destruction.

Understanding the duality of the American character has been a national pastime (and a passion of foreign observers) since at least the time of Tocqueville. *Democracy in America* brims with examples of how Americans in the Jacksonian era tempered their individualistic spirit with a regard for the community. "When an American needs the assistance of his fellows, it is very rare for that to be refused," Tocqueville wrote. "When some unexpected disaster strikes a family, a thousand strangers willingly open their purses." Beyond his gift for aphorism and for striking observations that seem timelessly relevant to the American experience—one of my favorites: "The great privilege of the Americans does not simply consist in their being more enlightened than other nations, but in their being able to repair the faults they may commit"—Tocqueville understood American tensions and contradictions as clearly as any other student of our nation's life. He was one of the first to use the very word "individualism," and he knew how much a hunger for private property drove us. "In no other country in the world is the love of property keener or more alert than in the United States," he declared, "and nowhere else does the majority display less inclination toward doctrines which in any way threaten the way property is owned."

Tocqueville worried that American individualism, untempered, might lead to the isolation of Americans from each other and thereby undermine the very freedom they celebrated. Yet Americans had other tendencies to which Tocqueville was highly attentive. "I have already shown, in several parts of this work, by what means the inhabitants of the United States almost always manage to combine their own advantage with that of their fellow citizens," Tocqueville wrote in *Democracy in America*. "In the United States hardly anybody talks of the beauty of virtue, but they maintain that virtue is useful and prove it every day. The American moralists do not profess that men ought to sacrifice themselves for their fellow creatures because it is noble to make such sacrifices, but they boldly aver that such sacrifices are as necessary to him who imposes them upon himself as to him for whose sake they are made."

Bill Clinton liked to illustrate America's twin commitments by calling attention to our most unassuming piece of currency. "Take a penny from your pocket," Clinton said. "On one side, next to Lincoln's portrait is a single word: 'Liberty.' On the other side is our national motto. It says 'E Pluribus Unum'—'Out of Many, One.' It does not say 'Every man for himself.'

"That humble penny," he would continue, "is an explicit declaration—one you can carry around in your pocket—that America is about both individual liberty and community obligation. These two commitments—to protect personal freedom and to seek common ground—are the coin of our realm, the measure of our worth."

We may carry in our pockets the lesson the penny teaches, but we often resist it. Overwhelmingly, our public language about who we are and what we believe emphasizes liberty, individual rights, freedom of conscience, and personal autonomy. All are of infinite value, but the communitarian slogan on the other side of the penny is invoked only rarely, and not just because it's in Latin. Except when it's used in the most bland and anodyne sense, the word "community" regularly provokes controversy in a way the word "liberty" does not.

Applying "community standards" to the availability of pornography immediately implies censorship. The "community action" program was the most controversial aspect of Lyndon Johnson's War on Poverty, seen as utopian, impractical, open to corruption, and disruptive of the usual ways in which local governments did business. "Community schools" are typically praised, yet the term has also been seen as a vehicle for defending segregation and exclusion by people in one community at the expense of those in another. While "community policing" now enjoys widespread support, it aroused suspicion on both the left and the right. There were civil libertarians who feared that giving police officers too much discretion would undermine individual rights, and there were conservatives who worried that the program would reduce the forces of order to social workers, diminishing their attention to law enforcement. In health insurance, the use of "community rating" to create large pools of customers by way of lowering overall rates is criticized by those who say the practice unfairly raises costs for the younger and the healthier, and especially for those who are more responsible than others in their exercise and eating habits. And it's hard to forget the controversy during the 2008 campaign over Barack

Obama's first professional role as a "community organizer," including Sarah Palin's memorable comment at the Republican National Convention: "I guess a small-town mayor is sort of like a 'community organizer,' except that you have actual responsibilities."

That "community" inspires admiration in the abstract but suspicion in many of its concrete uses speaks to the power of individualistic assumptions about our country and its history. The central idea of "the political philosophy by which we live," the philosopher Michael Sandel has written, "is that government should be neutral toward the moral and religious views its citizens espouse . . . it should provide a framework of rights that respects persons as free and independent selves, capable of choosing their own values and ends . . . So familiar is this vision of freedom that it seems a permanent feature of the American political and constitutional tradition."

The vision is familiar in part because the idea that individualism is central to the American creed was dominant in the academy for decades, expressed most forcefully by Louis Hartz in his hugely influential 1955 book, *The Liberal Tradition in America*. Hartz argued that individualistic liberalism is the United States' *only* authentic political tradition. In explaining the failure of strong socialist and conservative movements to find a footing in American politics, Hartz pointed to a "moral unanimity" in America behind a "fixed, dogmatic liberalism," which he defined as "the reality of atomistic social freedom." In Hartz's view, John Locke was our master philosopher. As the historian James T. Kloppenberg has argued, Hartz used Locke "as a shorthand for the self-interested, profit-maximizing behaviors of liberal capitalism, against which he counterposed, on the one hand, the revolutionary egalitarian fervor of Jacobins and Marxian socialists and, on the other, the traditional hierarchical values of church elites and aristocrats under various European ancien régimes."

Hartz's work was certainly "elegant and dazzling," as Kloppenberg conceded. But Kloppenberg is right to argue that Hartz should be understood not as offering "timeless truths about America" but as himself the product of history. Hartz was writing, after all, in a very particular period after World War II when the Cold War consensus reigned in politics. Hartz was, in essence, reading the consensus of his moment back into the

American story. Daniel Bell's *The End of Ideology*, a brilliant book that defined the era, referred in its subtitle to "the exhaustion of political ideas in the fifties." The "middle way" that British prime minister Harold Macmillan announced and that Dwight Eisenhower followed in the United States militated against both socialist and right-wing politics. Hartz turned the exhaustion of political ideas in the fifties into a shortage of political ideas in American history altogether. This led him to wonder whether American history was even worth the time, a remarkable assertion from one of our great historical commentators. As Kloppenberg pointed out, Hartz acknowledged that his approach "seems suddenly to shrink our domestic struggles to insignificance, robbing them of their glamour, challenging even the worth of their historical study." It was very hard to square this view with our long struggles over slavery, government's role in the economy during the Progressive Era and the New Deal, and the dueling domestic legacies of Lyndon Johnson and Ronald Reagan.

Yet as Sandel made clear in his seminal book *Democracy's Discontent*, this liberal version of our public philosophy—"liberal" here used in its oldest philosophical sense—is perhaps only a half century old. It contrasts sharply with our republican tradition (again, a reference to a broader and older set of ideas, not the political party) that sees liberty as depending on "sharing in self-government" and "deliberating with fellow citizens about the common good and helping to shape the destiny of the political community." Taking on the responsibilities of republican citizenship, Sandel writes, requires "a knowledge of public affairs and also a sense of belonging, a concern for the whole, a moral bond with the community whose fate is at stake."

Breaking with Hartz's view, many historians have concluded that the best way to understand the core American philosophy at the time of the Revolution and the Founding is to see it as both liberal *and* republican—in our terms, both individualistic *and* communitarian. The legal scholar Cass Sunstein, one of the pioneers in the republican revival that took hold among intellectuals in the 1980s, argued rightly that "one of the largest accomplishments of modern historical scholarship has been the illumination of the role of republican thought in the period before, during, and after the ratification of the American Constitution." Because of this new perspective on the old, it "is no longer possible to see a Lockean consensus in the founding period, or to treat the framers as modern pluralists believing that self-interest is the inevitable motivating force behind political behavior." Yet Sunstein does not deny that the American Founding's version of republicanism is inflected with liberal ideas. On the contrary, he says, "it incorporates central features of the liberal tradition." A proper understanding of our political trajectory, argues Kloppenberg, thus requires "a balanced view that sees the continuous presence of rights talk and the continuous presence of competing ideals of the common good." It is a story in which "arguments for freedom and arguments for community have jostled against each other." Precisely right.

I fold the republican idea, with its emphasis on civic virtue and the quest for a common good, under the rubric of "community," partly because this word is more familiar to us, and also because the idea of community encompasses contemporary concerns in ways that the old and honorable word "republicanism" does not. In his underappreciated book *The Dance with Community*, the political theorist Robert Booth Fowler sees the rediscovery of republicanism as "providing a language of restrained and chastened communitarianism," and he links the republican revival to the larger engagement with the idea of community that has blossomed over the last quarter century.

As Fowler notes, the new emphasis on the importance of republican ideas in our Founding has been contested by historians who continue to see brands of liberal individualism as predominant. (This, too, is part of the politics of history.) What cannot be contested is that the republican scholars have been sufficiently persuasive to allow us to conclude that the United States was born with a divided political heart. The Founders, as we'll see in more detail in Chapter 6, were seeking a balance between liberty and community (between liberalism and republicanism) because they understood that preserving the liberty they so prized depended upon virtues and forms of solidarity that an individualistic conception of freedom could not sustain on its own. As the philosopher William M. Sullivan, a key figure in the republican revival, put it: "The preservation of liberty, which is the preservation of individualism in its positive meaning of personal dignity, thus turns on the preservation of public life, and that is necessarily a cooperative work."

The Founders understood that self-interest is a fact of human nature, and *also that it is not the only fact.* They tried to build protections against the excesses of self-regarding behavior into their framework for our government. But they also sought to build a community that fostered the virtues self-government required. They wanted to promote prosperity but contain "luxury," which they saw as leading to corruption. (Today's anti–Wall Street demonstrators can draw inspiration from the importance many of the Founders ascribed to checking luxury's influence.) The revolutionaries of the 1770s and 1780s understood that the experiment in self-government on which they were embarking required a noble balancing act. So it was, and so it remains.

II

The quest for community that is always present in American life, if sometimes submerged, arose from what Tocqueville called "habits of the heart," and those familiar with the 1985 book inspired by that phrase will immediately see connections between my argument and that of Robert Bellah and his colleagues. (I also owe a debt to them for the title of this book, although the initial inspiration was more subconscious than conscious—a reflection, perhaps, that I had long ago internalized their observations.) In *Habits of the Heart: Individualism and Commitment in American Life*, Bellah and his coauthors—Richard Madsen, William M. Sullivan, Ann Swidler, and Steven M. Tipton—argued that American individualism was sustained by non-individualistic inclinations that allowed a free society to cohere. The *Habits of the Heart* authors feared (a quarter century before the rise of the Tea Party movement) that individualism "may have grown cancerous" and threatened to destroy the social connections Tocqueville saw as moderating individualism's "more destructive potentialities."

In tracing three formative strands in the American character—"biblical," "republican," and "modern individualist"—they did not deny the centrality of the individualistic inclination. Indeed, individualism came in two distinct varieties, one they associated with Benjamin Franklin, the other with Walt Whitman. Franklin, "the archetypal poor boy who made good," emphasized "what many felt in the eighteenth century—and many have felt ever since—to be the most important thing about America: the chance for the individual to get ahead on his own initiative." Franklin described the classic American path to upward mobility, long before the term became popular: "If they are poor, they begin first as Servants or Journeymen; and if they are sober, industrious and frugal, they soon become Masters, establish themselves in Business, marry, raise Families, and become respectable Citizens." Bellah and his colleagues call Franklin's approach "utilitarian individualism."

This classic, one might say bourgeois, approach provoked the rise of an entirely different form of individualism. Bellah and his coauthors refer to it as "expressive" and identify it with Walt Whitman, for whom "success had little to do with material acquisition." Whitman, they write, believed that "a successful life" was "rich in experience, open to all kinds of people, luxuriating in the sensual as well as the intellectual, above all a life of strong feeling." It is, of course, a mistake to offer a one-dimensional view of Whitman. He was not a hedonist, if hedonism is defined as putting personal pleasure above all other things. He was also highly political, active in the Democratic Party in the 1840s and 1850s and then an ardent anti-slavery Republican well known for his poetry saluting Abraham Lincoln. Bellah and his colleagues acknowledge that Whitman was inspired by the nation's republican tradition, noting that the "self-sufficient farmer or artisan capable of participation in the common life was Whitman's ideal as well as Franklin's and Jefferson's." Still, they are right to identify Whitman with a very particular strand of American individualism. For him, they argue, "the ultimate use of the American's independence was to cultivate and express the self and to explore its vast social and cosmic identities."

Tracing these two forms of individualism is especially instructive in understanding the 1960s and that era's contradictions. It produced, simultaneously, a counterculture that was seen as part of the left, and a New Right that celebrated capitalist individualism and gathered strength in the Goldwater movement and in organizations such as Young Americans for Freedom. The counterculture was heir to the romantic, Whitmanesque strain of individualism (even if parts of it occasionally and sometimes erratically celebrated small community, typified in the form of the commune or the ashram). The new conservatives stood up for the untrammeled freedom of entrepreneurs to rise and prosper, defending their efforts against the meddling of state bureaucrats and all who would redistribute their income and wealth. Both movements were as American as Whitman and Franklin.

It is common enough for historians and social critics to cite our republican tradition by way of contrast to our individualism. But the *Habits of the Heart* authors were right to place a particular emphasis on another communitarian strand in our story that they label as "biblical" and trace back to the first Puritan settlements in Massachusetts. It is ironic, perhaps, that while it was Ronald Reagan who repopularized John Winthrop's declaration that settlers in the New World would create "a city set upon a hill," the sermon in which the phrase appeared was, in its attitude toward individualism, anything but Reaganesque. Entitled "A Model of Christian Charity," Winthrop's address gave us what Bellah and coauthors identify as one "archetypal . . . understanding of what life in America was to be." Winthrop declared: "We must delight in each other, make others' conditions our own, rejoice together, mourn together, labor and suffer together, always having before our eyes our community as members of the same body." (Rush Limbaugh would certainly see Winthrop's words as "socialistic.") Winthrop also offered a classic—and counterintuitive—account of how our *differences* bind us together in community. God created differences, Winthrop argued, so that "every man might have need of other, and from hence they might all be knit more nearly together in the Bond of brotherly affection." (The philosopher Wilson Carey McWilliams nicely brought Winthrop's observation down to earth for our time: "A quarterback who begins to act as though he is better than the linemen who protect him is likely to receive a forceful reminder of the equality of teammates, despite the inequality of command.") The *Habits of the Heart* writers note that the seventeenth-century Puritan settlements "can be seen as the first of many efforts to create utopian communities in America. They gave the American experiment as a whole a utopian touch that it has never lost, despite all our failings." It is another side of American "exceptionalism."

There are tensions in this biblical inheritance that can be seen to this day in arguments between the Christian right and the Christian left. If the Christian left would emphasize a community that shares material gifts and burdens and makes "others' conditions our own," the Christian right stresses shared moral commitments that require each member of the community to live up to a strict personal moral code—what we now usually think of when we hear the word "Puritanism." For Winthrop, true freedom, which he called "moral freedom," was rooted in "the covenant between God and man" and involved giving liberty "to that only which is good, just and honest." Thus is our biblical inheritance itself torn between a stress on communal action and an emphasis on individual behavior—or, perhaps more precisely, between a belief in communal action aimed at transforming *personal* norms, and a faith in communal efforts to transform social and economic *structures*. One could argue that in contemporary times, Catholic social thought, with its emphasis on both individual behavior and social responsibility, most closely resembles this old biblical strain in American life. This would certainly surprise Winthrop's Puritans, given their rather dismal view of the Church of Rome.

The third strain identified by Bellah and his coauthors, the "republican" tradition, has, as we've already seen, enjoyed a broad intellectual revival over the past two decades, of which their book was part. The rediscovery of the republican tradition was crucial to the study of history because it challenged the widely held view that individualistic liberalism was the one and only American tradition. This also had powerful political implications.

III

The renewed interest in republicanism as an alternative to liberalism in explaining the origins of American politics was not initially part of some strategy to ransack the nation's story to find old justifications for current political positions. On the contrary, the two scholars first associated with the renewed emphasis on our republican past, Bernard Bailyn and Gordon Wood, were both resolutely committed to preserving a healthy distance between the historical enterprise and the politics of the present. Wood has been especially emphatic about separating the writing of history from the work of political agitation. "I suppose the most flagrant examples of present-mindedness in history writing come from trying to inject politics into history books," Wood has written. "I am reminded of Rebecca West's wise observation that when politics comes in the door, truth flies out the window." This only makes Wood's insistence on the centrality of republicanism to the American Founding all the more persuasive.

Wood transformed our understandings of our revolution in his pathbreaking 1969 book, *The Creation of the American Republic: 1776–1787*. Wood certainly did *not* claim that the idea of liberty was anything but foundational for the American rebels. But he argued that early American republicans believed that "liberty had been misunderstood and falsely equated with licentiousness." *True* liberty was something else entirely. As Wood wrote:

> True liberty was "natural liberty restrained in such a manner, as to render society one great family; where every one must consult his neighbour's happiness, as well as his own." In a republic "each individual gives up all private interest that is not consistent with the general good, the interest of the whole body." For the republican patriots of 1776 the commonweal was all-encompassing—a transcendent object with a unique moral worth that made partial considerations fade into insignificance. "Let regard be had only to the good of the whole" was the constant exhortation by publicists and clergy. Ideally, republicanism obliterated the individual. "A Citizen," said Samuel Adams, "owes everything to the Commonwealth." "Every man in a republic," declared Benjamin Rush, "is public property. His time and talents—his youth—his manhood—his old age—nay more, life, all belong to his country." "No man is a true republican," wrote a Pennsylvanian in 1776, "that will not give up his single voice to that of the public."

In a line of argument much invoked by republican revivalists in the 1970s and 1980s, Wood wrote that "ideally, republicanism obliterated the individual," and that "republicanism was essentially anti-capitalistic, a final attempt to come to terms with the emergent individualistic society that threatened to destroy once and for all the communion and benevolence that civilized men had always considered to be the ideal of human behavior." This

highly communal view of liberty—"each individual gives up all private interest that is not consistent with the general good"—is about as distant as
can be imagined from the contemporary right's view of the freedom for
which the Revolutionary patriots struggled. It is the aspect of our history
that has been buried under a mountain of misleading polemics.

Again, republicanism was just one strain, although a central one, in
Revolutionary ideology. Wood has been as alive as any historian to the complexity of the Revolution and its sweeping character, and also to how much
the country changed after our revolution was over. His most celebrated
book, *The Radicalism of the American Revolution*, published in 1991, insisted that ours was not a conservative revolution, but was "as radical and
as revolutionary as any in history." It overthrew old hierarchies and created
a far more egalitarian and democratic society. The Revolution, Wood wrote
in a lengthy essay on the rise of American capitalism, led to an "explosion
of entrepreneurial power," paving the way for the enterprising republic
Wood described in his recent work *Empire of Liberty*, a history covering
the period from Washington's inauguration to the aftermath of the War of
1812.

By the end of that war, Wood writes, "America's conception of its national character was becoming much more indebted to the middling people's go-getting involvement in commerce and enterprise. These ambitious,
risk-taking entrepreneurs, who were coming into their own by the second
decade of the nineteenth century, were the generation that imagined the
myth of the American dream." This take on American history, more to the
Tea Party's liking, is simply one part of the larger story, as Kloppenberg
observed. Republican and liberal ideas, communitarian and individualistic
inclinations, all interacted with each other to create a national character
not easily captured in a sound bite. Significantly, Wood cites the work of
Joyce Appleby, the contemporary historian most inclined to emphasize
the importance of capitalism and property in the early republic. The post-
Revolution generation, Appleby argues, brought forth "a new character
ideal." He was "the man who developed inner resources, acted indepen-
dently, lived virtuously, and bent his behavior to his personal goals." Appleby
argues that "the self-made man" appeared "as a recognizable type for the
first time in this era."

This productive maelstrom of entrepreneurship and energetic striving gave birth to American individualism. And notice, as the philosopher Steven Lukes did, that if the word "individualism" carried terribly negative meanings among the eighteenth- and nineteenth-century French philosophers, it came to be viewed as a triumphant concept on the other side of the Atlantic. "In France," Lukes wrote, the word "usually carried, and indeed still carries, a pejorative connotation, a strong suggestion that to concentrate on the individual is to harm the superior interests of society." It was a word associated with "social dissolution," "egoism," and "social or economic anarchy." In America, by contrast, individualism was associated with the "realization of the final stage of human progress in a spontaneously cohesive society of equal individual rights, limited government, *laissez-faire*, natural justice and equal opportunity, and individual freedom, moral development and dignity." Tocqueville, of course, was the partial exception among French writers who proved the rule. He used "individualism" less harshly than did most of his countrymen because he was referring to a tempered *American* individualism, which he saw as "a calm and considered feeling which disposes each citizen to isolate himself from the mass of his fellows and withdraw into the circle of family and friends."

The historian Yehoshua Arieli observed that American individualism "supplied the nation with a rationalization of its characteristic attitudes, behavior patterns and aspirations" and "expressed the universalism and idealism most characteristic of the national consciousness." In the 1880s, James Bryce anticipated Louis Hartz in privileging the idea. "Individualism, the love of enterprise, and the pride in personal freedom," Bryce wrote, "have been deemed by Americans not only their choicest, but [their] peculiar and exclusive possession."

It thus makes a mockery of the American story to deny the power of individualism in our history. But it is just as misleading to ignore our yearnings for a strong common life and our republican quest for civic virtue. Our skepticism of excessive state power arose from religious sources and classical traditions, and so did our doubts about pure individualism. "We hold these truths to be self-evident, that all men are created equal, that they are endowed by their Creator with certain unalienable Rights, that among these are Life, Liberty and the pursuit of Happiness." Thus began our Founding document. Yet its signers also forged a full-hearted communal bond in defense of those freedoms. "With a firm reliance on the protection of Divine Providence," they declared, "we mutually pledge to each other our Lives, our Fortunes, and our sacred Honor." Individual liberty and shared sacrifice are the bookends of our Declaration of Independence.

Because writers such as Bryce and Arieli were right in understanding individualism's hold on the American imagination, alternative traditions stressing community have often been cast as eccentric dissents from predominant currents of thought. The idea that Americans cherish individualism is so deeply embedded in the national consciousness that historians' rediscovery of our republican roots from the late 1960s forward came as something of a surprise. And the republican revival coincided with—and helped encourage—a flowering of communitarian thought on both the left and the right. The interplay between the rediscovery of American republicanism in our past and the reemergence of communitarian thinking in the 1980s and 1990s is an especially powerful example of how historical understandings shape and interact with our present.

Yet these ideas played quite differently on the left and on the right. Over time, communitarians gained substantial ground, politically and intellectually, among American liberals—and also among European labor and social democratic parties. But where communally oriented ideas had once exercised a powerful hold on the conservative mind, they receded in importance as individualism became steadily more important in the Reagan-Thatcher years. And in the United States (though not in Britain) the movement toward individualism accelerated in the first decade of the twenty-first century, culminating in the rise of the Tea Party. This further aggravated ideological and partisan polarization. Where once communitarians could make at least occasional common cause across ideological and partisan lines, the communitarian-individualist divide became, during the Obama years, yet another source of political discord and misunderstanding.

CHAPTER IV

Reinventing American Liberalism
Why the Left Embraced Community

T H E republican revival and the rise of communitarian thinking came in the nick of time for American liberals and the left. As New Dealism receded into history, progressives needed some new ideas, or at least a new gloss on old ones. A communitarianism rooted in republicanism provided an alternative framework to a socialism inflected by Marxist thinking and a progressive faith in centralized power at precisely the moment when the left was searching for new arguments. In more immediate political terms, it also offered a supplement to a rights-oriented liberalism that was popular in the upper middle class but aroused suspicion among working-class voters, who began straying from the old New Deal coalition in the late 1960s.

With the fall of the Soviet Union in 1991, rigid forms of state socialism were thoroughly discredited—and, in truth, Soviet practice had long before destroyed confidence in command economies that created oppressive states claiming to govern in the name of the proletariat. Communitarianism upheld traditional objectives of the left—on behalf of the environment, social justice, and an economy rooted in solidarity as well as competition—but in language that was less doctrinaire and more widely appealing. Some conservatives suspected that "community" was being used in a game of bait and switch, a way of disguising the same old goals of the left behind a lovely word. "Community" is, indeed, more attractive (in the United States especially) than "collective," and "building community" is a more broadly shared purpose than "expanding the state."

But the emergence of a communitarian disposition among American liberals and European social democrats also reflected their own second thoughts and self-criticisms. In *The Communitarian Persuasion*, Philip Selznick noted that communitarianism involved "the quest for a public philosophy that could take account of what liberalism failed to appreciate as well as what it could clearly see and rightly teach." He cited Rudolf Scharping, a leading German Social Democrat who lamented in the mid-1990s that his party had "created an overly regulated, overly bureaucratic and overly professionalized welfare state." Taking his own movement to task, Scharping observed acidly (and in positively Tocquevillian terms): "We did not believe in people's capacity for spontaneously helping and caring for others in the neighborhoods; we did not dare to hope that parents of schoolchildren would take care of the upkeep of classrooms; we did not believe that we could leave the running of a kindergarten to the parents." He and his allies had "succumbed to a blind faith in science and experts."

Amitai Etzioni (who can fairly be seen as the founder of Communitarianism as a political movement with a capital *C*) issued a manifesto in 1993, *The Spirit of Community*, stressing the need to accent the responsibilities of democratic citizens as well as their rights. This grew out of a broader interest among liberals in talk of "virtue," a concern more typically associated with contemporary conservatives. At stake were the civic and public-regarding virtues dear to the Revolutionary-era republicans, but also traditional virtues, including the importance of the family. The philosopher William Galston was both a founder of the Communitarian movement and an intellectual campaigner on behalf of the family as "the critical arena in which independence and a host of other virtues must be engendered." He wrote:

> The weakening of families is thus fraught with danger for liberal societies. In turn, strong families rest on specific virtues. Without fidelity, stable families cannot be maintained. Without a concern for children that extends well beyond the boundaries of adult self-regard, parents cannot effectively discharge their responsibility to help form secure, self-reliant young people. In short, the independence required for liberal social life rests on self-restraint and self-transcendence—the virtues of family solidarity.

For many conservatives, liberal communitarians were engaging in an urgent rescue job. "Communitarians do not seek to found a new school of thought on the ruins of liberalism," wrote Bruce Frohnen, a conservative scholar. "They seek to save liberalism from its own excessive hostility toward authority, to save liberalism from itself."

Liberals were, indeed, responding to peculiar cross-currents within their creed—and to substantial electoral problems, since the Democrats lost every presidential election but one between 1968 and 1992. Liberals came to be identified with the sweeping cultural changes of the 1960s, to both their benefit and their detriment. On one hand, Democrats could point to their battle for civil rights with pride, even if it came at the cost of electoral losses among whites in the South. And in political terms, the JFK and LBJ years helped turn African Americans into the party's most reliable electoral bloc. The party's support of equal rights for women created a new gender alignment, particularly among the middle and upper middle classes. In the past, women had been slightly more conservative in their voting patterns than men. This pattern was reversed beginning with the 1980 election as a coalition of younger and single women, poorer women, and upper-middle-class feminists came together behind liberal objectives and liberal candidates.

But the 1960s counterculture produced a decidedly mixed legacy. It was absurd, of course, to identify most actual liberal and Democratic politicians directly with countercultural norms. It was hard to find politicians who led more temperate and restrained family lives than Jimmy Carter, Walter Mondale, or Michael Dukakis. Yet beginning with the 1972 campaign and Richard Nixon's successful association of Democrat George McGovern with "acid, amnesty, and abortion"—the first referring to the drug culture, the second to amnesty for draft resisters—Democrats and liberals had to answer for forms of cultural liberation that were looked upon skeptically or with outright hostility by more traditionalist voters, particularly in the white working class. The great party of New Deal communalism seemed to have become the champion of individualism, Walt Whitman style.

That Whitmanesque individualism left over from the 1960s and 1970s came together with the more sober Ben Franklin individualism in the 1980s to produce what came to be known as the "Me Decade," the popular designator for the 1980s offered by the novelist Tom Wolfe. His best-selling novel *The Bonfire of the Vanities* brilliantly introduced and satirized the self-centered Wall Street "master of the universe" as a new social type. Critics on the left saw a crass "era of greed," and it certainly was a time of growing economic inequality in which power and wealth shifted toward the world of finance. Acronyms such as "M&A" and words such as "arbitrage" entered the popular lexicon. The loosening of sexual mores that began in the 1960s reached full flower. One of the most important sociological works on the era—even if its author poked fun at himself as a practitioner of "comic sociology"—was David Brooks's *Bobos in Paradise*. It described the rise of a new dominant class, "bourgeois bohemians," and it is hard to imagine a more individualistic pairing of words. Brooks's caffeinated epigram for the era made his point. "It was now impossible," he wrote, "to tell an espresso-sipping artist from a cappuccino-gulping banker."

Yet as Brooks's odd-couple marriage of the bourgeois and the bohemian also suggested, the politics of the 1980s and 1990s were the product of tensions and contradictions. Yes, there was Reagan in 1980 and the "Republican Revolution" of 1994. But there were also Bill Clinton's two victories and a sense, even after 1994, that conservatism was now short on ideas and reliant on anti-government nostrums that seemed stale after three decades of use. Reagan himself was always careful to show the side of himself that, rhetorically at least, embraced neighborhood, family, religion, and tradition. The country portrayed in Reagan's "Morning in America" advertising campaign in 1984 was warm, communitarian, and resolutely local. The words the announcer intoned were largely about improvements in the economy. The pictures were of fathers and sons working together, of warm and tidy neighborhoods, of weddings and family togetherness, of young campers earnestly saluting the flag. In a single minute, the ad captured the double-barreled message of Reagan-style conservatism: individualistic at its core, but communitarian in its affect. Reagan's political success owed a great deal to this brilliantly mixed message. His core supporters saw him as a resolute believer in conservative doctrine, and his harshest critics regarded him as an inflexible ideologue. But Reagan himself and those around him understood the dual yearnings of the rest of the country for an individualism tempered by a spirit of community.

Bill Clinton was paying attention to all this, and while his old dealings with his draft board and the sex scandal that shook his administration re-ignited some of the old 1960s culture wars, his political approach stressed community as an explicit part of his political appeal. He tried to integrate it into his program of government, as the story of the penny in the last chapter suggested.

Clinton, of course, is widely seen as the master of split-the-differences politics. The word "triangulation" was invented on his watch to describe his strategy of standing tall between parties and ideologies. His enemies saw only tactical cleverness and manipulation, calling him "Slick Willie." But Clinton, like Reagan, understood both sides of the American political character. And Clinton was far more explicit than Reagan was in seeking a new political synthesis that took the country's communitarian yearnings seriously. The "third way" that Clinton and Britain's Tony Blair proclaimed was much derided. It was certainly part of a political strategy to find the electoral middle. But it was also a serious enterprise, aimed at combining the individualism of the free market with a defense of a common-good politics that stressed government's obligations to the excluded and to those threatened by economic change.

In many ways, both Clinton and Tony Blair were harking back to the politics of the New Liberals—T. H. Green and L. T. Hobhouse were two of the movement's most important voices—who were writing in Brit-ain at the time Populism and Progressivism were taking hold in the United States. The philosophy of the New Liberals, as Avital Simhony and David Weinstein have written, took "community and common good seri-ously without abnegating liberalism's devotion to the cultivation of indi-viduality."

This captured the direction in which Clinton sought to move. The words that described his own personal goals, "opportunity, responsibility, community," served as the chapter headings in *Between Hope and History*, the book Clinton wrote while he was president. The first was individualis-tic, even if Clinton favored public measures to distribute opportunities more widely. The second had its individualistic and communitarian sides—Clinton stressed both "personal" and "mutual" responsibility. And Clinton's specific emphasis on community reflected his sense that the "Me Decade" had produced a counter-yearning for what the journalist Paul Taylor would label a "We Decade."

Clinton faced, as all politicians do, limits on government's capacity to create community. He pushed for an expansion of opportunities for voluntary service through his AmeriCorps program, a signature of his administration and one of his proudest achievements. He paid far more attention to communities of faith than had been customary for Democrats. He created alliances between government and faith-based charities and social action groups that predated those pursued more visibly by George W. Bush. And when Clinton spoke of his Christian faith, his language reflected his Southern Baptist roots and its inflections were those of the African American churches where he preached so often. It was far more the language of the "beloved community" inspired by civil rights Christianity than the individualistic stress found in so many white evangelical churches whose core promise emphasized individual conversation and salvation. The text he chose when he spoke at the Metropolitan Baptist Church in Washington in 1997, from Paul's letter to the Ephesians, was characteristic of his approach to Christianity: "We are all part of one another." It is one of the purest communitarian declarations in the New Testament.

Communitarianism was thus both a reaction to the weaknesses liberals perceived in their own doctrines and a response to the steady rise of individualism as the defining characteristic of conservatism, particularly in the United States and Britain. While conservatives continued to express their public fealty to Edmund Burke's "little platoons" of society as "the first principle . . . of public affections," contemporary conservatism was moving elsewhere. It was more and more inclined to defend large private economic organizations, the marketplace as the central instrument of (and metaphor for) social life, and investment and the acquisition of wealth as the most honored and socially productive activities. It was a brand of conservatism that swept aside other forms in both the United States and Britain. The very idea of the social, as against the individual, came in for increasing conservative disapproval. Margaret Thatcher captured this spirit when she declared: "There is no such thing as society. There are individual men and women, and there are families." In his successful effort to become the first Conservative prime minister since Thatcher, David

Cameron felt obligated to distance himself from some of the harsher aspects of Thatcherism, and her famous quotation provided him with an almost ideal foil. "There *is* such a thing as society," he declared after winning the Conservative Party leadership in 2005. "It's just not the same thing as the state." It has fallen to Cameron to reengage conservative communitarianism. Cameron made the idea of a "Big Society" based on voluntary action and local institutions a signature of his tenure after he assumed office in 2010, even if translating the slogan into policy proved difficult.

Cameron was responding to the long communitarian comeback, as was George W. Bush when he promoted "compassionate conservatism" and its "armies of compassion" as companions to Burke's little platoons. Both were reacting to the successes of Clinton and Blair, for whom "community" became a master word in their joint campaign to create their third way between the old left and the New Right. It enabled both to distance themselves from a right seen as excessively individualistic and socially indifferent, and from those aspects of the left criticized by Scharping as too statist, too critical of localism, and too beholden to social rights shorn of responsibilities.

For Blair's New Labour Party, community was a ready-made concept that provided an alternative to Thatcher's no-such-thing-as-society Conservatism *and* to the older forms of socialism that stressed state power and the "common ownership of the means of production, distribution and exchange." These were the words of Clause 4 of the old Labour Party constitution that Blair successfully fought to change. Adopted in 1918 and drafted by the Fabian socialist Sidney Webb, the original Clause 4 was regarded by Labour modernizers as a relic of doctrinaire thinking inappropriate to a dynamic market economy. It pledged the party

> to secure for the workers by hand or by brain the full fruits of their industry and the most equitable distribution thereof that may be possible upon the basis of the common ownership of the means of production, distribution and exchange, and the best obtainable system of popular administration and control of each industry or service.

The revision for which Blair successfully campaigned made one concession to the left, explicitly declaring Labour a "democratic socialist party."
But the specific socialist commitment to common ownership dissolved into
gauzier language highlighting community and solidarity. The new Clause 4
read:

> The Labour Party is a democratic socialist party. It believes that by
> the strength of our common endeavour we achieve more than we
> achieve alone, so as to create for each of us the means to realise our
> true potential and for all of us a community in which power, wealth
> and opportunity are in the hands of the many, not the few, where
> the rights we enjoy reflect the duties we owe, and where we live
> together, freely, in a spirit of solidarity, tolerance and respect.

Blair's own rhetoric constantly emphasized the effort of the new communitarian left to bring together traditionalists and modernizers:

> It allows us to unite old and new. The traditionalist is right to worry
> about the breakdown of family life. The moderniser is right to say
> that shouldn't prejudice us against single parent families, the
> majority of whom do not choose to be single parent families. The
> moderniser is right to say global markets are good not bad. The
> traditionalist is right to worry about the inequity that can arise from
> them. The moderniser needs values. The traditionalist needs
> modern reality.

Strong language about responsibility—familiar from the American communitarian movement, Etzioni's writings, and Bill Clinton's rhetoric—was
always central to Blairism. "You can't build a community on opportunity or
rights alone," Blair declared. "They need to be matched by responsibility
and duty. That is the bargain or covenant at the heart of modern civil society.
Frankly, I don't think you can make the case for Government, for spending
taxpayers' money on public services or social exclusion—in other words for
acting as a community—without this covenant of opportunities and responsibilities together."

This truly was a transatlantic movement, for so much of what Blair had to say, Clinton had said, too, sometimes—especially in the early years of their respective ascendancies—a year or two ahead of Blair. Consider Clinton's 1991 speech to the Democratic Leadership Council in Cleveland, Ohio, the address Clinton saw as his breakthrough moment. It was the speech that gave his trinity of values—"opportunity, responsibility, community"—its first test run:

> Our burden [Clinton declared] is to give the people a new choice, rooted in old values, a new choice that is simple, that offers opportunity, demands responsibility, gives citizens more say, provides them responsive government—all because we recognize that we are a community, we are all in this together, and we are going up or down together . . . we believe in community, in repairing a torn fabric of our country at its most fragile point, the millions and millions of children who are being robbed of their childhoods, because we really are all in this together. This is a new choice Democrats can ride to victory on: opportunity, responsibility, choice, a government that works, a belief in community.

And ride to victory they did.

There was a problem with "third way" communitarianism that would become obvious only with the economic implosion of 2008. Both Clinton and Blair championed a permissive view of the financial markets—Clinton signed the repeal of the New Deal–era restrictions separating investment banking from commercial banking—that was consistent with their effort to link progressive politics to a warm endorsement of modern capitalism. It turned out, as an earlier generation of progressives, New Dealers, and Labour Party social democrats understood, that there were good reasons for those of a communitarian temper to insist on a more socially minded and rule-bound marketplace. This had certainly been a lesson of the 1930s. But in the time of Clinton and Blair, the experience of the Great Depression was buried far in the past. The prospect of marrying a booming, globalizing, and loosely regulated capitalism with a decent level of public provision and public investment seemed dazzling.

The means of Communism's collapse in Eastern Europe also contributed to the communitarian turn by renewing interest in civil society, the institutions of social life that were independent of the state but also different from those of the marketplace. Living under dictatorships, the anti-Communist rebels of Eastern Europe discovered that even the most efficient and brutal police forces and intelligence services could not stamp out all vestiges of social life that survived in cafes, churches, workplaces, and families. The Eastern European dissidents used the enclaves of civil society to incubate free institutions that ultimately triumphed. The idea of "civil society" gained currency throughout the West, and it was, as the sociologist Adam Seligman observed, "used as a slogan to advance the cause of community" and to challenge radical individualism. In *Whose Keeper?*, one of the most important books advancing the civil society idea, Alan Wolfe criticized the conventional political debate for casting the state and the market as the main mechanisms of social organization. Doing so, he argued, ignored some of the most important institutions in the lives of most individuals. They included family, church, neighborhood, workplace, and a variety of voluntary associations ranging from sports clubs and youth groups to privately organized day care centers. They might even be seen to encompass the loose fellowships created in taverns such as Cheers, the fictional setting for what eventually became the most highly rated television show in the United States. The program's popularity—it ran eleven seasons, from 1982 to 1993—may have owed absolutely nothing either to politics or to academic philosophy and sociology. Yet its theme song celebrating a place "where everybody knows your name" spoke powerfully to a national mood that included a longing for face-to-face fellowship and a strengthening of community bonds.

If communitarian talk was taking hold in politics and even in TV sitcoms, it was also exerting a growing presence in academic philosophy. The philosophers associated with communitarianism were, like their counterparts in politics, responding simultaneously to currents on the left and the right—though, again, they were typically thinkers whose broad sympathies ran leftward. For example, Michael Walzer, a giant among the philosophers with communitarian leanings, has often found himself engaged in two-front arguments. He offered a powerful egalitarian case against the libertarianism of his Harvard colleague Robert Nozick, whose book *Anarchy, State, and Utopia* was his generation's most sweeping and thoughtful defense of libertarian individualism. But Walzer also questioned the form of egalitarian liberalism put forward by John Rawls, a fellow philosophical giant of the period, whose book *A Theory of Justice* was described by one philosopher as "the closest thing to a book that people are ashamed to admit that they have not read."

Rawls asked what principle of justice an individual would agree to if he operated behind a "veil of ignorance," not knowing whether he would find himself at the top of a society's class structure, at the bottom, or somewhere in between. Rawls argued that the only inequalities to which such a person would assent would be those that rendered *everyone* better off. Beyond that, Rawls's impartial observer behind the veil would lean toward egalitarianism, with the aim of protecting himself from the worst outcomes. It was a brilliant case for a generous welfare state within the framework of a capitalist economy. The rich could get richer as long as the activities that brought them wealth made everyone else richer, too. Beyond that, society would generously redistribute benefits to protect those who fell behind in the race for achievement.

Rawls's general defense of a more egalitarian society fit well with Walzer's social democratic leanings, and Walzer shared many of Rawls's liberal commitments. But in a direct response to Rawls, Walzer expressed skepticism of a philosophy of justice rooted in what "ideally rational men and women would choose if they were forced to choose impartially, knowing nothing of their own situation, barred from making particularist claims, confronting an abstract set of goods." The problem, Walzer argued, is that human beings are shaped by—and cannot escape—"the particularism of history, culture and membership." In his book *Spheres of Justice*, Walzer thus posed the core communitarian and pluralist challenge to Rawls:

> Even if they are committed to impartiality, the question most likely to arise in the minds of the members of a political community is not, What would rational individuals choose under universalizing conditions of such-and-such a sort? But rather, What would individuals like us choose, who are situated as we are, who share a

culture and are determined to go on sharing it? And this is a question that is readily transformed into, What choices have we already made in the course of our common life? What understandings do we (really) share?

Walzer concluded that "every substantive account of distributive justice is a local account." Following former House Speaker Tip O'Neill's famous quip, one might ask: if all politics is local, is all philosophy local, too? Not exactly, but then Tip wasn't entirely right about politics, either. But rootedness does matter, in philosophy no less than in politics.

The broadest critique of Rawls's view from a communitarian perspective came from Michael Sandel, the Harvard philosopher whose work we encountered earlier. Sandel has recently reached a wide audience through the PBS broadcast of his popular lecture course *Justice* and the publication of a best-selling companion book. But he made his initial mark in philosophy by asserting that there is no such thing as a free-floating self, "barren of essential aims and attachments," whose "values and relations" are simply "the products of choice." Sandel insisted that "we cannot regard ourselves as independent in this way without great cost to those loyalties and convictions whose moral force consists partly in the fact that living by them is inseparable from understanding ourselves as the particular persons we are." All of us, after all, are "members of this family or community or nation or people, as bearers of this history, as sons and daughters of that revolution, as citizens of this republic."

The republican revival was central both to Sandel's understanding of the American story and to his critique of the American present. His 1996 book, *Democracy's Discontent: America in Search of a Public Philosophy*, was a comprehensive compendium that married republican-inflected history with communitarian politics (even though Sandel himself has been wary of being labeled "communitarian"). He argued that our discontents flowed from our devotion to a very narrow view of freedom that had produced a "procedural republic" neutral on the question of what constitutes the "good life." The republican idea, by contrast, insists that "liberty depends on sharing in self-government," which in turn requires "a sense of belonging, a concern for the whole, a moral bond with the community whose fate is at stake." Sandel's critique of the procedural liberal state is fundamental: "The public philosophy by which we live cannot secure the liberty it promises, because it cannot inspire the sense of community and civic engagement that liberty requires."

A good portion of Sandel's book is an examination of moments in American history in which the republican strand of our tradition was at the forefront, and also an account of republicanism's steady decline. In the day-to-day political parlance of our time, Sandel is clearly a liberal or progressive because of the priority he places on civic concerns over those of mere market calculation. He thus highlights the struggles for the eight-hour day, the empowerment of labor, anti-trust laws, anti-chain-store legislation, and the early planning efforts of the New Deal. Yet in philosophical terms, he is a republican, not a liberal.

Writing about more recent times, Sandel finds inspiration in the "civic stirrings" of Robert F. Kennedy's rhetoric and RFK's emphasis on the importance of local community. "Nations or great cities are too huge to provide the values of community," Kennedy declared, offering a sentiment Sandel cites approvingly. "Community demands a place where people can see and know each other, where children can play and adults can work together and join in the pleasures and responsibilities of the place where they live." One senses an invitation to stop by Cheers. In a classic complaint against modernity's tendency to break down social bonds, Kennedy spoke of how "the world beyond the neighborhoods has become more impersonal and abstract," of housing developments that provided "no place for people to walk, for women and their children to meet, for common activities." The home "is a place to sleep and eat and watch television; but the community is not where we live. We live in many places, and so we live nowhere."

Communitarianism's critics point to such rhetoric as embodying a certain nostalgia and to a tendency to overlook modernity's liberating aspects. Were not the forms of community constructed in small towns and closely knit neighborhoods often experienced by those who lived in such places as sources of intimidation and informal but effective coercion? Not for nothing is the liberating flight to the most cosmopolitan parts of the big city a popular motif of American film and fiction. Moreover, capitalist critics of communitarians pointed to the rise of the "new urbanism" and other community-friendly forms of development. Thanks to the market's responsiveness, they argued, Americans who yearned for older forms of community in new places could now find them—and in homes that also featured granite countertops, vast and well-equipped kitchens, Jacuzzis, instant boiling water, and other amenities unknown in the old neighborhoods. This is a building block of Bill Bishop's "Big Sort."

The rise of communitarianism did not go unchallenged among liberals and on the left, either. Many of communitarianism's progressive critics agreed with the philosopher Richard Rorty in seeing in it a "terminal wistfulness." Liberals insistently asked *which* rights associated with liberalism communitarians would actually give up. They noted (correctly) that communitarians themselves were often divided on issues such as abortion or on exactly how to balance the rights of those accused of crime with the rights of those who are its victims. And given the sympathy of many liberals during the 1960s to more-relaxed attitudes about sexuality and divorce (and the rising importance of abortion rights as a core commitment of American liberalism and feminism), communitarianism seemed to some liberals a stealthy effort to reimpose more restrictive personal norms—a kind of creeping Puritanism. Thus the philosopher Amy Gutmann's quip that communitarians "want us to live in Salem but not believe in witches."

Stephen Holmes, a staunch philosophical defender of liberalism, argued that communitarians vacillated between claiming they were offering an "alternative" to liberal society and insisting they were suggesting only a "supplement." Holmes observed that "the first claim is unconvincing while the second claim is unexciting." His critique of communitarianism was biting:

Liberalism is dissatisfying, these critics contend, because it fails to provide what we yearn for most: fraternity, solidarity, harmony, and most magically, *community*. Communitarians invest this word with redemptive significance. When we hear it, all our critical faculties are meant to fall asleep. In the vocabulary of these antiliberals, "community" is used as an anesthetic, an amnesiac, an aphrodisiac.

Jeffrey Stout, the Princeton professor of religion, saw communitarian thinking as having "an implicitly utopian character," and he criticized its partisans for rarely offering "any clear sense of what to do about our misgivings aside from yearning pensively for conditions we are either unwilling or unable to bring about." He added: "When you unwrap the utopia, the batteries aren't included."

Certainly there was utopianism among the communitarians, as well as a bit of nostalgia—even if it's fair to ask how many political philosophies *ever* come with batteries included. And Holmes from the left noticed the same quality in communitarian thinking that Bruce Frohnen had noticed from the right: that it was indeed designed more as a corrective or "supplement" to liberalism than as a full-scale alternative.

Yet that was precisely its power. Communitarians enjoyed a growing influence on liberalism and the left because they were identifying problems that liberals and social democrats needed to solve. Even Sandel's critics had to acknowledge that liberalism has always struggled with the task of creating "the sense of community and civic engagement that liberty requires." A purely individualistic society cannot maintain the solidarity and social cohesion that are a prerequisite for preserving freedom. Free men and women have to feel some sense of obligation to defend *each other's* rights—the very requirement the founders embraced in the last line of the Declaration. It has been the American struggle from the outset.

The new quest for community could not be dismissed as mere nostalgia. It was also a rational response to social change, a protest against the gaps people were experiencing in sociability, communal solidarity, and civic formation. It was not so much a rebellion against the modern world as an attempt to deal with modernity's dislocations. If individuals managed to create new forms of attachment—from the rise of megachurches to the spread of youth sports leagues to the organization of mothers' circles and fathers' groups—they were doing so in response to a sense that our stock of "social capital" was diminishing, the central theme of Robert Putnam's brilliant, data-driven portrait of national disconnection, *Bowling Alone*.

All this helps explain why communitarian ideas played a growing role in the rhetoric and thinking of Democratic politicians. Bill Clinton's espousal of the idea of community was not a one-off. It was important both to Hillary Clinton's 2008 campaign for the Democratic presidential nomination and, as we have seen, to Barack Obama. Obama, who had attended many of the Harvard seminars Putnam organized around the theme of social capital, returned to the idea in one of his most important pre-campaign speeches in which he addressed the role of religion in American life, long a vexing issue for liberals. His 2006 address at the "Call to Renewal" conference coordinated by the progressive religious leader Jim Wallis even carried some faint echoes of a John Winthrop sermon:

> Our failure as progressives to tap into the moral underpinnings of the nation is not just rhetorical. . . . After all, the problems of poverty and racism, the uninsured and the unemployed, are not simply technical problems in search of the perfect ten point plan. They are rooted in both societal indifference and individual callousness—in the imperfections of man.
>
> Solving these problems will require changes in government policy, but it will also require changes in hearts and a change in minds. I believe in keeping guns out of our inner cities, and that our leaders must say so in the face of the gun manufacturers' lobby—but I also believe that when a gang-banger shoots indiscriminately into a crowd because he feels somebody disrespected him, we've got a moral problem. There's a hole in that young man's heart—a hole that the government alone cannot fix.

Like most liberals who are religious, Obama found a powerful demand for social justice embedded in the great faith traditions. He took a swipe at those who would repeal the estate tax, saying this entailed "a trillion dollars being taken out of social programs to go to a handful of folks who don't need and weren't even asking for it."

But Obama was not simply ransacking the scriptures to find support for his favorite social programs. His talk was saturated with values and virtues. Contraception can reduce teen pregnancy rates, Obama declared, but so can "faith and guidance," which "help fortify a young woman's sense of self, a young man's sense of responsibility and a sense of reverence that all young people should have for the act of sexual intimacy." And if all this sounded preachy, Obama had an answer: "Our fear of getting 'preachy' may also lead us to discount the role that values and culture play in some of our most urgent social problems."

Thus did a talented American politician find a way to marry America's biblical and republican traditions behind a robust call for community. It was to define his rise to the presidency—in ways that were not always noticed.

The growing liberal responsiveness to the communitarian imperative produced a series of paradoxes in American politics. At the very moment when American liberals and the left were rediscovering the power of community in both its local and national forms—and even acknowledging in the process a debt to conservatives who had long insisted upon religion's role in public life—conservatives themselves were moving away from their commitments to community. The power of a communitarian critique of individualism—in history, in philosophy, in politics, and in everyday life—called forth an increasingly militant defense of individualism that found a mass political outlet in the Tea Party movement and increasingly crowded out the more communal forms of conservatism. And rather than make common cause with their potential communitarian allies on the left, the conservative communitarians sharpened their differences with liberals by insisting that the forms of community built under the auspices of the national government could never fully claim legitimacy.

But there is a mystery here: how did conservatism, born in opposition to individualism, become the proud and unapologetic carrier of American individualism's most robust strain?

CHAPTER V

From Tradition to Revolt
How Conservatives Left
Community Behind

I N light of conservatism's history, it is odd that cultivating community and common values has so receded as a central conservative preoccupation. Conservatism was born, after all, not to defend individualism but in revolt against it. "Conservatism, as a distinguishable social philosophy, arose in direct response to the French Revolution," wrote Robert Nisbet, an influential old-school conservative. Standing "in reaction to the individualistic Enlightenment," conservatives "stressed the small social groups of society," seeing such clusters of humanity—and *not* individuals—as society's "irreducible unit."

Reacting to "economic change, moral secularism, and political centralization," conservatives "insisted upon the primacy of society to the individual—historically, logically, and ethically." They rejected the idea of society as "a mechanical aggregate of individual particles subject to whatever rearrangements may occur to the mind of the industrialist or the government official." Conservatives, Nisbet was arguing, spurned the very notion that Thatcher later embraced. True conservatives, he declared, are always alive to the "delicate interrelation of belief, habit, membership and institution in the life of any society." It's of some interest in light of what has happened to conservatism that the best one-volume collection of Nisbet's work is called *Tradition and Revolt*. Its subtitle now might be *From Edmund Burke to the Tea Party*.

Seeing conservatism as an anti-individualistic creed is not an antique notion from the attic of an eighteenth-century French aristocrat or the drawing room of a nineteenth-century Oxfordshire squire. George F. Will, who remained one of American conservatism's leading voices right through the Tea Party rebellion, published *Statecraft as Soulcraft* in 1983 to insist on the continuing relevance of the old conservatism of Burke. Will lamented that America's sense of community had become "thin gruel," and he chided fellow conservatives "caught in the web of their careless anti-government rhetoric."

"Just as all education is moral education because learning conditions conduct," Will wrote, "much legislation is moral legislation because it conditions the action and the thought of the nation in broad and important spheres in life." He followed Burke in highlighting the importance of "sentiments, manners and moral opinions," and argued that these were neither "private" nor "properly beyond the legitimate concern of public agencies."

"It is generally considered obvious that government should not, indeed cannot legislate morality," Will wrote at another point. "But in fact it does so, frequently; it should do so more often; and it never does anything more important." Conservatism, he said, "is about the cultivation and conservation of certain values, or it is nothing."

American conservatism, of course, had long been torn between libertarians and traditionalists, between those for whom the economic market was the primary object of their affections and those whose deepest commitments were to virtue, hierarchy, and Burke's "sentiments, manners and moral opinions." Russell Kirk, an intellectual leader of the traditionalist forces, spoke for many on his side in 1954 when he declared: "Conservatism is something more than mere solicitude for tidy incomes." It's not something many conservatives would say now. Kirk-style conservatives, such as Nisbet and George Will in his *Statecraft as Soulcraft* period, preferred values to profits, community to pure individualism, and self-discipline to consumerism.

The traditionalists and libertarian-leaning free market conservatives had feuded on the pages of William F. Buckley Jr.'s *National Review* magazine from the moment of its founding in 1955. If the traditionalists' conservatism had the deeper roots, the free market conservatives held powerful sway in the United States during the Gilded Age and came into their own as a coherent political force when they organized in opposition to Franklin

D. Roosevelt's New Deal in the 1930s. Kim Phillips-Fein, demonstrating how historians can shed unexpected light on the present, offered a persuasive case that the new conservatism—often seen as the creation of Buckley's *National Review* in the 1950s and 1960s and the neoconservatives and right-of-center think tanks in the 1970s—was actually born in opposition to Roosevelt. In *Invisible Hands*, she traced the rise of conservatism to the work of an "impassioned, committed" group of business leaders who saw in the New Deal "a fundamental challenge to their power and their place in American society." In the more than forty years before Ronald Reagan's victory, they worked with both politicians and intellectuals "to resist liberal institutions and ideas, and to persuade others to join in fighting back, until the liberal order began to falter." History certainly rhymes. Seventy years on, supporters of the Tea Party found ample financial help from wealthy conservative business leaders certain that Obama, like Roosevelt before him, was reopening the path to socialism. The Koch brothers had forebears, including their own father, who belonged to the Birch Society.

The central texts that inspired the Tea Party rebellion were also canonical to the anti–New Deal business leaders. None was more important than Friedrich A. Hayek's *The Road to Serfdom*, published in 1944. Hayek, an Austrian economist who decamped to the London School of Economics in 1931 and eventually found his way to the University of Chicago, provided the anti–New Deal conservatives with both an inspiring theory and a way of disentangling themselves from a right fringe that had sympathized with Nazism and fascism in the 1930s. At the time Hayek wrote, Nazism was widely seen as an extremist movement of the right, an aberrant species of capitalism. On the contrary, the Austrian economist insisted, "the rise of fascism and Nazism was not a reaction against the socialist trends of the preceding period but a necessary outcome of those tendencies." Hitler's party, after all, was committed to National *Socialism*. Viewed this way, even mild social democracy and forms of New Dealism could be charged with leading down the same "road to serfdom," if at a more measured pace, because state planning inevitably led to collectivism and dictatorship. "Economic control is not merely control of a sector of human life, which can be separated from the rest," Hayek wrote, "it is the control of the means for all our ends."

American progressives and European social democrats had long argued that government intervention provided a countervailing power to concentrated economic power. Government had the capacity to protect citizens from irrational and destructive market outcomes, and also to liberate them from subservience to monopolies, abusive employers, and the political power that accrued to large accumulations of wealth. But for Hayek, acquiescence to the market was preferable to stronger government, even strong democratic government. "Unless this complex society is to be destroyed," Hayek wrote of modern capitalism, "the only alternative to submission to the impersonal and seemingly irrational forces of the market is submission to an equally uncontrollable and therefore arbitrary power of other men." In 1930s America, the "other man" conservatives had in mind was FDR. After 2008, he was Barack Obama.

What's striking in retrospect is that Hayek injected into American conservatism a strain of thinking that was, at its heart, decidedly unconservative. As Phillips-Fein points out, Hayek himself strenuously rejected the idea that he was a conservative at all, insisting instead that he was a liberal in the nineteenth-century sense of the term. Conservatives, Hayek argued, were animated by "a fear of change, a timid distrust of the new as such." Lacking "faith in the spontaneous forces of adjustment," conservatives "cannot offer an alternative to the direction in which we are moving." Hayek, by contrast, presented himself as someone who "could accept changes without apprehension" and supported "a thorough sweeping away of the obstacles to free growth."

The tension between the traditionalists and the libertarians was thus fundamental. It went to the very definition of conservatism itself—and whether conservatism, as it was coming to be understood, was conservative at all. Confronting a contemporary liberalism that, in the 1950s at least, seemed to dominate the American consciousness and had sufficient influence in both political parties, William F. Buckley understood the need to broker an intellectual truce to keep his forces united against the liberal enemy—and, more important, in the battle against world Communism. His magazine gave birth to what came to be known as "fusionism," an amalgam of ideas that sought to unite libertarians and traditionalists. It accepted the centrality of liberty but also the need for virtue. Frank Meyer,

Buckley's chief ideologist, argued that traditionalists failed to appreciate that virtue was meaningful only if individuals arrived at it voluntarily. Libertarians, in turn, needed to accept a belief in an "objective moral order" as "the only firm foundation of freedom." Donald Devine, a political scientist who later worked for the Reagan administration, offered perhaps the neatest summary of fusionism. It involved "utilizing libertarian means in a conservative society for traditionalist ends." Because fusionists believed that American society was conservative to its core, libertarianism would allow the country's deepest traditionalist impulses free rein.

Fusionism was politically brilliant. It allowed the conservative movement to accommodate many tendencies, from libertarians who favored the legalization of drugs to Christian conservatives who focused on the spread of faith and individual virtue. But it was never intellectually stable. Fusionism worked better for conservatives when they found themselves in opposition (everyone could emphasize different reasons for opposing American liberalism) than when they held power. And it set up an ongoing contest over which wing of the movement would come to dominate the other. Which issues would actually take priority, tax cuts or a ban on abortion? Deregulation or the encouragement of religious faith? Was it more promising to wager on government's capacity as a moral educator (the younger George Will's emphasis) or on the likelihood that government would oppress and act foolishly (the thrust of much of Will's more recent writing)? And, as Nisbet might ask, must conservatism still insist upon "the primacy of society to the individual," or was Hayek's revolution on behalf of the sovereign self complete?

Although power within conservatism shifted inexorably toward its individualistic wing in the thirty years after Reagan's election, the communitarian strain died hard. As we've seen, Reagan himself understood the appeal of community, even if his economic policies were individualistic and had the effect of widening inequalities. "Reagan Democrats," particularly working-class voters in the Northeast and Midwest, were quintessential family-and-neighborhood people for whom "community" was not an abstraction but a concrete description of their way of life.

Among conservative intellectuals, the last great communitarian endeavor was the Mediating Structures project at the American Enterprise

Institute, which grew out of a manifesto issued in 1977 by the sociologist Peter Berger and the Lutheran pastor (later a Catholic priest) Richard John Neuhaus. The essay that inspired the project, "To Empower People," might be read in retrospect as providing the core philosophy for Reagan Democrats before they even existed. It's likely that Reagan was inspired by this forty-five-page pamphlet to add the value-laden trinity "family, work, neighborhood" to his broader promise of "peace and freedom." Using italics for emphasis, Berger and Neuhaus trumpeted the importance of *"those institutions standing between the individual in his private life and the large institutions of public life"* at a moment when citizens were experiencing a "historically unprecedented dichotomy between public and private life." Public life, they wrote, is ordered most importantly by "the modern state itself" but also by "the large economic conglomerates of capitalist enterprise, big labor, and the growing bureaucracies that administer wide sections of society, such as in education and the organized professions." On the other side was "that modern phenomenon called private life," which they saw as "a curious kind of preserve left over by the large institutions and in which individuals carry on a bewildering variety of activities with only fragile institutional support."

This dichotomy created a "double crisis"—a crisis for the individual "who must carry on a balancing act between the demands of the two spheres," and a "political crisis" because the large structures, including government itself, "come to be devoid of personal meaning and are therefore viewed as unreal or even malignant." The individuals who handled this crisis more successfully were those who "have access to institutions that *mediate* between the two spheres," thus "mediating structures." They wrote:

> Such institutions have a private face, giving private life a measure of stability, and they have a public face, transferring meaning and value to the megastructures. Thus, mediating structures alleviate each facet of the double crisis of modern society. Their strategic position derives from their reducing both the anomic precariousness of individual existence in isolation from society and the threat of alienation to the public order.

Berger and Neuhaus focused on four key mediating structures—neighborhood, family, church, and the voluntary association. They noted that such organizations had been blessed by the traditionalist intellectual heroes of the past, Burke and Tocqueville, and also by Nisbet, who, they noted, had "persuasively argued that the loss of community threatens the future of American democracy."

Intriguingly, in light of the harsh ideological polarization that came later, Berger and Neuhaus were critical of *both* liberals and conservatives for their lack of interest in—and even hostility to—these vital social institutions. "The concrete particularities of mediating structures find an inhospitable soil in the liberal garden," they wrote. "There the great concern is for the individual ('the rights of man') and for a just public order, but anything 'in between' is viewed as irrelevant, or even an obstacle, to the just ordering of society." The rationales for the institutions that lie "in between" were often dismissed, they wrote, "as superstition, bigotry, or (more recently) cultural lag."

But on the right, they also found "little that is helpful." They observed that "what is now called conservatism in America is in fact old-style liberalism . . . the laissez-faire ideology of the period before the New Deal, which is roughly the time when liberalism shifted its faith from the market to government." (They had probably read their Hayek.) Conservatism, they argued, "typically exhibits the weakness of the left in reverse: it is highly sensitive to the alienations of big government, but blind to the analogous effects of big business."

For good measure, they added: "We believe it proper and humane (as well as 'human') that there be areas of life, including public life, in which there is not a dollar sign on everything. It is debilitating to our sense of the polity to assume that only private life is to be governed by humane, nonpecuniary motives, while the rest of life is a matter of dog-eat-dog."

It's hard to imagine words of this sort issuing from a conservative think tank in the Obama era, given the hegemony of individualist thinking and a heightened reluctance on the right to criticize business. Indeed, Berger and Neuhaus were addressing both the left and the right in their polemic—a rarity these days in publications from ideological think tanks. They certainly influenced more communitarian liberals, and it's easy to hear echoes of Berger and Neuhaus in Barack Obama's "Call to Renewal" speech. When they wrote that "liberalism has a hard time coming to terms with the alienating effects of the abstract structures it has multiplied since the New Deal" and suggested this "may be the Achilles heel of the liberal state today," they were offering a view that many liberals had come to share. "The idea is not to revoke the New Deal," they wrote, "but to pursue its vision in ways more compatible with democratic governance." This was not a position held by the economic conservatives of their day, and it would be anathema to much of today's Tea Party, many of whom insist on the urgency of revoking both the New Deal and the reforms of the Progressive Era.

But if the mediating structures proposal began as an idea that bridged concerns on the left and the right—in part by criticizing both—it hardened over time into a concept used by conservative communitarians to distinguish themselves from their liberal counterparts. Liberals could and did speak a great deal about community, acknowledged William Schambra, a senior fellow at the Hudson Institute and a leading interpreter of Nisbet's thought. But they envisioned "a great American *national* community," which they saw as "vastly superior to the cacophony of petty *local* communities hitherto created by churches and voluntary associations." Tracing the national community idea back to Herbert Croly, the early twentieth-century thinker who provided the intellectual spark for Theodore Roosevelt's brand of Progressivism, Schambra argued that "the sense of community, belonging, and purpose that had once been supplied at the local level by Tocqueville's townships and voluntary associations . . . would now be centralized and nationalized." It would fall to the "federal government, and above all the American presidency," to "summon citizens out of their self-interested, parochial concerns, demanding that Americans instead commit their lives to the service of a larger national ideal: a noble, comprehensive national oneness."

Schambra, it should be said, is a serious conservative communitarian who grew frustrated with aspects of the Tea Party's politics, including its opposition to the Corporation for National and Community Service, a national enterprise that he believed *did* strengthen local community organizations. And his article chiding liberals for their efforts to create what he puckishly called "national oneness" also included a sharp warning to conservatives about the cost of indifference to local community-building efforts among the poor. "If conservatism's only idea of a civil-rights program is opposition to affirmative action, and if its only idea of a poverty program is opposition to welfare spending, then inevitably Americans will conclude that conservatives simply don't care about minorities or the poor," he wrote. "And if one critique of conservatism since the New Deal has proven to be particularly damaging, it is the proposition that conservatism is exclusively identified with the interests of the wealthy." It was just that criticism that the Occupy Wall Street protesters brought home.

Nonetheless, the energy of Schambra's critique was directed against liberal efforts to build community on a national level. This, he said, had "drained the strength and moral authority from local community institutions," while empowering "scientifically credentialed professionals and experts."

The question of whether national and local community-building efforts are at odds is central to our current debate. By ruling out the legitimacy of federal efforts to promote community, Schambra inadvertently undercuts the very national service programs he supports. They are, after all, much in keeping with America's Progressive tradition, as we'll see in more detail later. There are few clearer instances of how the federal government can support and strengthen *local* community groups. For all its failures (both perceived and real), the Community Action Program of Lyndon Johnson's war on poverty did succeed in expanding organizing in the nation's poorest neighborhoods and creating a new cadre of leadership, particularly in African American and Latino areas. The political scientist Theda Skocpol pointed to a long list of cases, going back to Civil War veterans groups, in which "popularly rooted voluntary organizations have often grown up in a mutually beneficial relationship with federal policies, including federal 'tax-and-spend' programs."

Where the politics of community is concerned, what's worth noticing is that while talk and argument about both national and local community continued on the left, the grand old idea of republicanism as enveloping the nation as well as the neighborhood was receding on the right. Schambra's rejection of the idea of building national community, which has won a wide hearing on the right, is antithetical to the conservatism of Alexander

Hamilton or Henry Clay—and to many of the achievements of the last three-quarters of a century of American life. "The domain of citizenship, which had expanded in the post–World War II years to bring in, for the first time, broader and broader ranges of Americans, began to shrink," wrote the historian Daniel T. Rodgers. "Talk of a social citizenship as extensive as the nation itself was less and less often to be heard."

Rodgers observed this phenomenon on the left as well as the right, but the redefinition of "virtue" was largely a conservative project. "For those working within the tradition of civic republicanism, virtue's essence was the sacrifice of the self for the public weal," he wrote. "In much of the conservative lexicon, the word 'virtue' simply became a synonym for ethical certainty, a slogan with which they set out to inject harder-edged morals into the schools [rather] than mere values clarification and to enlist families and teachers in pushing back the moral relativism of the times."

Rodgers noticed something else as well: the rise during the 1970s of a new metaphor that in ensuing years was invoked to explain practically every aspect of human life—the metaphor of the marketplace. Once we turned to religion, history, science, or philosophy to understand reality. But with ever growing confidence, advocates of the market claimed that rational economic choice could explain practically everything. "Most novel about the new market metaphors," he wrote, "was their detachment from history and institutions and from questions of power." We came to envision the world as "a socially detached array of economic actors, free to choose and optimize, unconstrained by power or inequalities, governed not by their common deliberative action but only by the impersonal laws of the market." In our ongoing conversations about politics and society, he wrote, "one heard less about society, history, and power and more about individuals, contingency, and choice."

II

But if conservatism was becoming more individualistic, more focused on the local than the national, and ever more entranced with the market metaphor, how does one explain the rise of the religious right, which certainly has a profound and authentic connection to America's biblical tradition?

In fact, the most important impact of the religious right on politics may have been less its ability to swell the Republican vote in specific elections—though it certainly did so—than its influence on Protestant evangelicalism more broadly.

For much of American history, evangelicalism was associated with movements of social reform, from the anti-slavery cause to William Jennings Bryan's Populism. But a funny thing happened to evangelicalism as the twentieth century dawned. Large parts of the Social Gospel movement, which inherited the evangelical reformist tradition at the turn of the last century, adopted increasingly liberal theological views that were, quite literally, heretical for traditionalist Christians. For the traditionalists among the evangelicals, the Social Gospel was more Social than Gospel, more interested in pursuing social reform than in spreading the Good News of salvation through Jesus Christ. In reaction, many evangelicals proudly adopted the label "fundamentalist" to highlight their defense of what they insisted were the "fundamentals" of Christian faith. Over time, many fundamentalists became what we now call evangelicals. The latter are often more relaxed in their theology than fundamentalists, but most remain far more conservative than the old Social Gospelers and their more liberal Protestant heirs. And with the rise of issues such as prescribed prayer in public schools, abortion, and the more diffuse question of "permissiveness" in the popular culture, these evangelicals and fundamentalists drifted further rightward, put off by what they saw as the liberals' embrace of less rigorous standards for private behavior.

The new evangelicalism also focused less on the prophetic aspects of the Christian faith and far more on personal—and thus individual—salvation. Their concern was less with the Sermon on the Mount or the Beatitudes than with the promise of eternal salvation to *individuals* who made highly personal decisions to embrace Jesus as their Lord and Savior. Their preferred passage in the New Testament is John 3:16: "For God so loved the world that he gave his only begotten Son, that whosoever believeth in Him should not perish, but have everlasting life." This is a Jesus who changes personal lives, not the Jesus who judged the rich, spoke up for the poor, and threw the moneychangers out of the Temple. This developing conservative evangelical faith focused more on "how Jesus changed my life" than on "how Jesus changed the world."

Not all evangelicals separated the two, of course, and one of the striking developments of recent years is the return of a prophetic sensibility among religious conservatives, particularly in the Millennial generation, which in turn has made younger evangelicals somewhat less conservative politically. But the long-term emphasis on an interior faith meant that in the main, outside their witness on abortion—which, again, had a close link to personal behavior and personal virtue—Christian conservatives developed a great deal more in common with libertarian individualists than their forebears would have imagined possible during William Jennings Bryan's era.

The effect was to further marginalize the traditionalist conservatives whose idea of faith, as Schambra pointed out, was quite different from the highly expressive and personally transformative religion of the evangelicals— and more different still from the spirited witness of the Pentecostals. It wasn't, as Schambra observed, "the sort of faith with which most traditionalists are comfortable."

> For those of the Russell Kirk persuasion [Schambra continued], religion tends to be a sober, staid, institutional affair; its value is not so much personal salvation as social stability. Religion is what ensures allegiance to permanent truths and established, quasi-aristocratic forms, thereby fortifying society against the onslaughts of radical innovation and democratic excess. In *Conservatism: Dream and Reality*, Robert Nisbet described the traditionalist posture toward faith this way: "Religion . . . was preeminently public and institutional, something to which loyalty and a decent regard for form were owing, a valuable pillar to both state and society, but not a profound and permeating doctrine, least of all a total experience."

For many of today's evangelicals, Schambra concluded, this "would have been a bit lukewarm." Indeed.

It's not surprising, then, that the last gasp of conservative communitarianism was George W. Bush's faith-based initiative, the heart and soul of his "compassionate conservatism." Bush, and especially his gifted chief speechwriter Michael Gerson, understood evangelicalism from the inside.

Both of them—and, again, Gerson in particular—realized that the longer American evangelical tradition had combined personal salvation with social witness. Gerson was also a close student of Catholic social thought and its emphasis on the common good. More than Bush himself, Gerson embraced the communitarian side of conservative thought.

Bush's faith-based initiative was thus an effort to unite the "wonder-working power" of personal conversion with a sense of social obligation to the poor. Bush, like the liberals, would cast himself as someone concerned for the less privileged. But unlike the liberals, he would understand the limits of the government and the importance of change in "the human heart." Bush's initiative would use *public* action to promote *personal* change.

His oratory was ringing. His view (and Gerson's) was expressed most fully and powerfully in his 1999 speech in Indianapolis entitled "The Duty of Hope." It was to be the manifesto of compassionate conservatism. Bush's break from pure free market conservatism was largely rhetorical, but it was still unusual rhetoric for a conservative to use. And Bush consciously set himself apart from what he called two "narrow mindsets." The first (predictably enough for a conservative)

> is that government provides the only real compassion. A belief that what is done by caring people through church and charity is secondary and marginal. Some Washington politicians call these efforts "crumbs of compassion." These aren't "crumbs" to people whose lives are changed, they are the hope of renewal and salvation. These are not the "crumbs of compassion," they are the bread of life. And they are the strength and soul of America.

But much less predictably, Bush pointed to a second "mindset" that he labeled "destructive":

> The idea that if government would only get out of our way, all our problems would be solved. An approach with no higher goal, no nobler purpose, than "Leave us alone."
>
> Yet this is not who we are as Americans. We have always found our better selves in sympathy and generosity, both in our lives and in

our laws. Americans will never write the epitaph of idealism. It emerges from our nature as a people, with a vision of the common good beyond profit and loss. Our national character shines in our compassion.

We are a nation of rugged individuals. But we are also the country of the second chance, tied together by bonds of friendship and community and solidarity.

At another point, Bush said: "This will not be the failed compassion of towering, distant bureaucracies. On the contrary, it will be government that serves those who are serving their neighbors. It will be government that directs help to the inspired and the effective. It will be government that both knows its limits, and shows its heart." And then came the clever invocation of the old fusionist conservative settlement in two short sentences. "The invisible hand works many miracles," Bush declared. "But it cannot touch the human heart."

There was a certain genius—of a political sort, but also, to some degree, in substance—behind Bush's initiative that should not be lost in the negative assessments of his presidency and in his failure to back up his rhetoric with sufficient resources. His approach seemed to demonstrate an understanding of the poverty of radical individualism. Indeed, it was a sophisticated attempt to embrace the duality of the American character ("We are a nation of rugged individuals. But we are also the country of the second chance") and to put its tensions to work on behalf of conservative politics. Bush sought to embrace the idea of the "common good," but gave this venerable community-minded idea an individualistic tilt. Bush hardly ever said a word about systemic injustice or economic inequality. Instead, he issued call after call for individuals to set their lives straight and for the country to solve social problems by converting people (behaviorally but also spiritually) one soul at a time. His approach was made clear in a single passage of his first inaugural address in 2001:

In the quiet of American conscience, we know that deep, persistent poverty is unworthy of our nation's promise. And whatever our views of its cause, we can agree that children at risk are not at fault. Abandonment and abuse are not acts of God, they are failures of love. And the proliferation of prisons, however necessary, is no substitute for hope and order in our souls. Where there is suffering, there is duty. Americans in need are not strangers, they are citizens; not problems, but priorities; and all of us are diminished when any are hopeless.

The socially minded could only applaud Bush's declaration that "children at risk are not at fault" and that those in need are "not problems, but priorities." It seemed a very liberal sentiment, and it was certainly compassionate. Yet Bush located the problems of the poorest not in the injustices of the society or in the structural failures of the economy but in the shortcomings of individuals: "abandonment and abuse" by parents, the failure of criminal offenders to find "hope and order in their souls." Compassionate conservatism involved a constant effort to square circles, to sand the rough edges off individualism, to build community by focusing on the reform of personal behavior.

It is impossible to know for certain whether Bush had the capacity—given the views of his party and of many within his own administration—to make compassionate conservatism into a coherent, community-minded creed for the right. In light of Bush's heavy spending on his initiative to combat AIDS in Africa and his investment of substantial political capital in his education reform program, compassionate conservatism cannot be wholly dismissed as a political gimmick. And Gerson believes in the effort to this day.

Yet compassionate conservatism suffered from both intellectual and political contradictions. Even before 9/11, the faith-based initiative had run into trouble in Congress, partly because many on the right end of Bush's party, including some Christian evangelicals, mistrusted it as a kind of Community Action Program in religious garb—big government carried out in God's name. Among liberals, on the other hand, there was both fear of obliterating the line between church and state and a skepticism bred by comparisons between the size of Bush's tax cuts and the comparatively paltry spending on his compassion agenda (again, with the exception of his AIDS initiative abroad). The cynicism was deepened by reports that federal money for faith-based programs was used on behalf of religious groups politically friendly to the White House. When it came to his domestic priorities, Bush's solicitude for those with tidy incomes (and for elderly voters who benefitted from his prescription drug benefit) seemed to outweigh his devotion to the armies of compassion.

In any event, compassionate conservatism receded into the shadows created by the attacks of September 11, 2001. It was replaced by the active martial conservatism of the broader "war on terror" and the specific wars in Afghanistan and Iraq. The growing unpopularity of both conflicts, the federal government's failures after Hurricane Katrina—an occasion that might have provided a true test of compassionate conservatism—the economic collapse of 2008, and the heavy spending on the subsequent financial bailout all sent Bush's popularity plummeting. Within Republican circles, these events gave new life to the party's libertarian wing and helped unleash the Tea Party. And the obituaries for Bush's idea poured in from the right. The most succinct came from the hard-right columnist Michelle Malkin. " 'Compassionate conservatism' and fiscal conservatism were never compatible," she wrote. "Never will be." And that is what the Tea Party came to believe—devoutly.

In many ways, Gerson (whom, I should acknowledge here, I both like and respect, despite our political disagreements) became the last torchbearer for compassionate conservatism. His 2007 book, *Heroic Conservatism*, was an effort to keep the disposition alive and to insist that of all the brands of conservatism on offer, it had the greatest chance of political success.

"Traditional conservatism has a piece missing—a piece that is shaped like conscience," Gerson wrote. For too many conservatives, he said, "any idea of the common good is viewed as a dangerous myth." Seeking to revive the alliance between evangelicalism and social justice so prominent in the American past, Gerson asked: "Where does someone belong who is pro-life *and* pro-poor? Someone who supports the traditional family *and* increased spending to fight AIDS? Someone who is passionate about the rights of handicapped children in America *and* the lives of displaced children in Darfur? I know that I have often felt homeless in the traditional camps of American politics."

And he was unrelenting in warning conservatives about the implications of pure individualism. "If Republicans run in future elections with a simplistic anti-government message, ignoring the poor, the addicted, and children at risk, they will lose, and they will deserve to lose," Gerson wrote. The heroic conservatism Gerson championed, by contrast, "can appeal to the conscience, inspire the nation, and change the world."

Yet the response of many conservatives to Gerson's effort demonstrated just how far the Republican Party was straying from the creed he was preaching. That *National Review* magazine, the arbiter of conservative orthodoxy, chose David Frum to review the book was itself significant. Frum, who served in the Bush White House with Gerson, was known to have had deep personal differences with his former colleague, and he began his review challenging Gerson on both his facts and his self-presentation.

But more significant for our purposes was Frum's critique of Gerson's core claims. Coming from a Republican who later became a sharp and brave critic of Tea Party conservatism, Frum's observations were especially revealing. Writing while Bush was still in office and before the financial meltdown, Frum asked:

> If heroic conservatism really can rally the nation, why has seven years of it left the nation so very conspicuously unrallied? If present trends continue, George W. Bush will exit the White House as the most continuously unpopular president since Harry Truman. The Bush-led GOP is widely condemned as corrupt, arrogant, and incompetent. In generic polls, voters prefer Democrats over Republicans on almost every issue.
>
> The troubles go beyond polls. Although America has prospered under George W. Bush, many of the social indicators that ought to concern a heroic conservatism have trended in the wrong direction. Poverty has increased, and in many American cities crime is worsening. As best we can tell, there has been no sustained increase in volunteering. The international democracy agenda that opened with

such promise has lost its momentum. Gerson himself has to admit that the trends are against him, or (as he puts it) "the darker impulses of conservatism have become more assertive, more public, and more pronounced."

What went wrong?

Frum answered that while "Americans are deeply compassionate people . . . they are also deeply pragmatic people. They want results, not a politics of moral gestures. And all too often, moral gestures are all that the Bush administration has offered." Again, it needs to be emphasized that by conventional measures, Frum found himself well to the left of conservatism in the Obama years. Nonetheless, his sense that the Bush administration had failed on the most basic levels of performance matched not only the views of many liberals but also the conclusions reached by a great many Tea Party supporters, who put a more ideological spin on Bush's shortcomings. They decided that Bush foundered not because he had moved too far to the right—and not because his compassion involved mostly moral gestures—but, on the contrary, because he had strayed too far from the individualistic and anti-government core of their brand of conservatism.

Another conservative critic, more sympathetically inclined to Gerson personally and more drawn to his overarching hopes, nonetheless captured the right's central objection to his ideas with precision. Writing in *Slate*, Ross Douthat, later a *New York Times* columnist, observed:

> It's a stirring vision in its way, but there's little that's conservative about it. What Gerson proposes is an imitation of Great Society liberalism, in which noble, high-minded elites like himself use the levers of government on behalf of "the poor, the addicted, and children at risk." He employs the phrase *limited government* here and there, but never suggests any concrete limits on what government should do. Whether he's writing about poverty or foreign policy, immigration, or health care, his prescription for the right is all heroism and no conservatism; indeed, save for its pro-life sympathies, his vision seems indistinguishable from the liberalism of an LBJ—or a Jimmy Carter.

Douthat added that Gerson's view "both politically and philosophically" represented "a betrayal of conservatism's proper role in a welfare-state society." He explained:

> From the 1970s onward, the Republican Party built its majority by running *against* a politics that seemed to privilege the interests of the poor over those of working- and middle-class taxpayers. This is not a legacy that should be lightly abandoned, not least because America already has a party that envisions the federal bureaucracy as alternatively compassionate and heroic. In the long run, you can't out-liberal liberalism; the Democratic Party will always offer voters the higher bid.

In truth, of course, few liberals ever saw Bush's agenda as remotely close to liberalism or progressivism as they understood it. And Gerson had entirely legitimate ground on which to stand. He was not trying to destroy conservatism. His purpose was to reconnect the contemporary right to earlier forms of conservatism that *did* encompass an idea of the common good and *did* stress community obligations as well as protections for individual rights. But in part because the Bush administration *did* fail, in part because Gerson was a more enthusiastic promoter of his version of conservatism than many of his colleagues, and in part because the right had steadily moved away from anything resembling communitarian conservatism, Gerson increasingly found himself a believer without a congregation—even as he also discovered that many who shared some of his strongest convictions were now making their political home on the moderate left.

Gerson certainly understood the direction of the political winds. In a *Washington Post* column headlined "Why the Tea Party Is Toxic for the GOP," he challenged the Tea Party's view of the Constitution and embraced a Republican and conservative past that the Tea Party was largely disowning. Many in the Tea Party, he said, believed "the federal government has only those powers specifically enumerated in the Constitution—which doesn't mention retirement insurance or health care." This assertion, he acknowledged, "was logically consistent." It was also "historically uninformed, morally irresponsible and politically disastrous."

"The Constitution," Gerson insisted, "in contrast to the Articles of Confederation, granted broad power to the federal government to impose taxes and spend funds to 'provide for . . . the general welfare'—at least if Alexander Hamilton and a number of Supreme Court rulings are to be believed. In practice, Social Security abolition would push perhaps 13 million elderly Americans into destitution, blurring the line between conservative idealism and Social Darwinism." Gerson's conclusion:

> Most Americans who identify with the tea party movement are understandably concerned about the size and reach of government. Their enthusiasm is a clear Republican advantage. But tea party populism is just as clearly incompatible with some conservative and Republican beliefs. It is at odds with Abraham Lincoln's inclusive tone and his conviction that government policies could empower individuals. It is inconsistent with religious teaching on government's responsibility to seek the common good and to care for the weak. It does not reflect a Burkean suspicion of radical social change.

He was right: it didn't—and doesn't.

Gerson's agony was based in realism. Individualistic, small-government conservatism was in the saddle. The Tea Party became the loudest voice on the right. More and more, conservatism became a creed devoted to low taxes and less business regulation—and little else. Conservatives of a traditionalist, communitarian, and small-*r* republican leanings were scattered and defeated. Community building was to be a task of the left and of Barack Obama. All this has had some very peculiar effects on American politics.

III

It goes without saying, but perhaps a progressive should say it: every nation needs an intelligent and constructive form of conservatism. At its best, conservatism challenges the progressive worldview in at least three indispensable ways.

First, conservatives are suspicious of innovation and therefore subject all grand plans to merciless interrogation. Their core inquiry goes something like this: Maybe this new health (or education or environmental) plan is a great idea, but will it really work? What are its unintended consequences? Can our governmental institutions carry it off? Not all progressive ideas pass the test. In the debate over Obama's health care proposal, conservatives were at their best when they shelved demagoguery and ideology and asked practical, focused questions.

Second, conservatives respect old things and old habits. They are not always right in this. Racial segregation and discrimination are good examples of old ways that were morally wrong. But Russell Kirk's admiration for custom and convention speaks to something deep in the human heart. Our habits are the product of time, based on the slowly accumulated wisdom of our ancestors. That's why tradition should not be discarded lightly. Many who are not in the least conservative can acknowledge, with Kirk, that custom and convention "are checks both upon man's anarchic impulse and upon the innovator's lust for power." It's worth remembering that Hitler's staunch opponents included not only the German left, but also, as the historian John Lukacs has insisted, conservative traditionalists horrified by the ways in which the Nazis were ripping apart German society—and slaughtering fellow human beings.

Related to this is the third great contribution of conservatism: a suspicion of human nature and a belief that people cannot be remolded like plastic. Conservatives see a fallen side of human nature, often described as "original sin." When utopians propose to create New Men or New Women, the conservative will cry: *Stop!* From generation to generation, human nature doesn't change radically—even in a world of technologies that were unimaginable just a decade or two earlier. Efforts to alter human nature, the conservative is right to insist, can risk descent into totalitarian catastrophe. A society that fails to keep these conservative warnings in mind is likely to run into trouble.

But in its current incarnation, conservatism has taken on an angry crankiness. It finds itself in the grips of a pseudo-populism that true conservatism instinctively mistrusts. What on earth would William F. Buckley Jr. have made of "death panels"?

Conservatives of the Edmund Burke stripe always understood the necessity of reform, yet the creed is now caught up in a suspicion of all reform. Conservatives who once asked if a particular proposal was practical are now inclined to look at *all* proposals involving *any* expansion of government's responsibility as unconstitutional. Our current forms of conservatism seem thoroughly unconservative or, to use dissident conservative Peter Viereck's term from the 1950s, "pseudo-conservative," which is a close cousin to "pseudo-populist." The mob that gathered outside the Capitol in the winter of 2010 to shout epithets at Democratic lawmakers before they voted on the health care bill was disrespectful of the very norms that conservatism preaches. Utopianism, typically a danger on the left, now runs rampant on the right.

Many who call themselves conservative propose to cast aside even government programs that have stood the test of time. They seem to imagine a world in which government "withers away"—a phrase that comes from Friedrich Engels, not Buckley or Burke. Or else conservative politicians trying to hang on to the votes of the elderly tie themselves up in unruly contradictions, declaring—for the purposes of the 2010 election—that they are simultaneously opponents of government-run health care and passionate defenders of Medicare against the cuts contained in "Obamacare." Their case on Medicare became more problematic after the House of Representatives passed Representative Paul Ryan's 2011 budget, which included deep Medicare cuts and a plan to turn the program into a kind of voucher system. Ryan's plan was consistent with the underlying position of the new conservatism, but in utter contradiction to the campaigns that had just been run by many of those who voted for it.

Modern conservatism has usually supported the market against the state. But its oldest and most durable strains insisted that the market was an imperfect instrument. True conservatives may give "two cheers for capitalism," as Irving Kristol put it in the title of one of his books, but never three.

Conservatism has always made its greatest contribution as a corrective force that seeks to preserve the best of what we have. It has always understood that weaving the fabric of community and instilling a respect for the commons both involve painstaking work over time.

But post-Bush conservatism, as the 2012 Republican primary campaign made clear, has abandoned its communitarian sympathies for a defense of a pure and radical individualism. It has constricted its program-matic imagination to cuts in taxes, regulation, and government. It has thus broken with its own long tradition of respect for government's contribution to a free and prosperous society. It has placed much rhetorical emphasis on a robust patriotism, yet it treats our national government as an interloper, echoing extreme states' rights and even secessionist doctrines discredited long ago in the fires of the Civil War and in the peaceful revolution of the civil rights movement. In so doing, it has relegated Alexander Hamilton, Henry Clay, and Abraham Lincoln to second-class status in the conserva-tive pantheon.

As Gerson suggested in his pained response to the Tea Party, this new conservatism claims the mandate of American history, but it can do so only by rewriting the American story to the point where it ceases to be recogniz-able. The true American trajectory is defined by balance—by a belief in the importance of both the local and the national, and by an understanding of the indispensability of both the individual and the community.

Because our current political debate is over fundamentals—about who we have been, who we are, and who we should be—it's natural that it includes a robust argument over the meaning of American history. For this very reason, it's important to get our national story right, even while acknowledging, as the debate over the meaning of Reconstruction suggests, that many aspects of our history have always been contested. We have spent more than two centuries working to build a government that is at once energetic and limited, effective but not overpowering, mindful of both our rights and our obligations in a republic that has grown steadily more democratic. Many of these arguments—sometimes tragically, sometimes triumphantly—touched on the question of race. Our Constitution begins with the words "We, the people," and so it's natural that we have argued over the meaning of Populism. We have been, from the beginning, a racially and culturally diverse nation, and have grown only more diverse since our Found-ing. So we have argued about how a nation of nations, a community of com-munities, could create "out of many, one."

In the midst of all the contention, no issues have been as vexing or as important as the meaning of the Constitution and what our Founders had in mind for the republic they created.

Part Two

What History Teaches Us

CHAPTER VI

One Nation, Conceived in Argument
The Revolution, the Constitution, and the Origins of the American Debate

THE federal government was created by the states to be an agent for the states, not the other way around," Rick Perry, the Republican governor of Texas, told his party's leaders at a meeting in the spring of 2011, before he mounted his unsuccessful presidential campaign.

That would have come as a great surprise to a rather important Republican president named Abraham Lincoln. "The Union is older than any of the States; and, in fact, it created them as States," Lincoln declared in his July 4, 1861, message to Congress. "Having never been States, either in substance or in name, outside of the Union, whence this magical omnipotence of 'State rights' . . . Much is said about the 'sovereignty' of the States; but the word, even, is not in the national Constitution."

Indeed, those first words of the Constitution are not "We the states," but "We the people." And the Constitution's Preamble speaks of promoting "a more perfect union," "Justice," "tranquility," "the common defense," "the General Welfare," and, of course, "the Blessings of Liberty." These are national goals. True, the Constitution required ratification by the states. But when the word "states" appears in the document, it is usually in a compound word, "United States," or in reference to how the states (and the people of the states) will be represented in the national government. It's a civics-book notion now often forgotten, but the Constitution was written with the express purpose of replacing the Articles of Confederation with a framework for a much stronger national government. We are the "United States," not the "Confederate States," the latter having entered history in an act of *rebellion*—as Lincoln pointed out in that July 4 oration—against the government designed by the Founders. Yet those most inclined to speak of their devotion to the Constitution are far more likely to quote the vague language of the brief Tenth Amendment ("The powers not delegated to the United States by the Constitution, nor prohibited by it to the States, are reserved to the States respectively, or to the people") than to cite the rest of the document. Rarely do they quote the Preamble, which is presumably the best summary of the Constitution's purposes.

It is a peculiarity of the United States, and one particularly powerful at this moment, that our Constitution is not just honored but venerated. And one could fairly ask: Why not? It's worthy of admiration as the most enduring constitution in the world. Yet that very point of agreement provokes immediate discord. Did it endure because we have chosen to live by every word, strictly interpreted, or did it work because its language was elastic enough to accommodate the great transformations that have occurred since 1787? Was its meaning altered and reinterpreted at regular intervals—with the Civil War amendments, the Progressive Era amendments, and the interpretative revolutions of the New Deal and the Warren Court? Or are we required, in light of the document's greatness, to discern the "original" meanings and purposes of the Founders? This, of course, presumes that these are fully knowable and that the Founders spoke with one voice.

Such questions do not deter today's Tea Party constitutionalists, who are quite certain that the Constitution clearly points down the political path they have already decided to take. At the 2010 Conservative Political Action Conference, speaker after speaker explained how the Constitution—especially as originally written, and as they interpreted it—provided an infallible guide to contemporary politics.

"If we remove the foundations for our principles and our policies, America will fall," declared Senator Jim DeMint of South Carolina. "Those principles were written into a contract with the American people that promised to limit the federal government's power. We call that contract the Constitution and when it [was] signed it didn't even allow a federal income tax and that sounds like a good way to limit the size of the federal government to me."

Referring to a brief declaration of conservative principles signed by a group of longtime leaders on the right, former Minnesota governor Tim Pawlenty sought to rally the convention by turning the Constitution into a mandate for every item on the conservative wish list for that year's midterm elections. The signers, he said, were

> recommitting themselves and their organizations to the constitutional framework, the constitutional principles and the constitutional values that made this nation great. They are the values of limited government. They are the values of the rule of law. They are the values of limited, excuse me, individual responsibility. They are the values of free markets. They are the values of respect for the sanctity of life. They are the values of respecting traditional marriages and families and down the list. Those are the kinds of principles that this nation was founded on. Those are the principles that made this nation great. Those are the principles that will lead us forward as a conservative movement.

Presumably, right-to-work laws, the elimination of the estate tax, a return to don't-ask-don't-tell, and the urgency of keeping the prison at Guantánamo open are also in the Constitution somewhere, if only we look hard enough. And of course conservatives were absolutely certain that the measure they disliked most, President Obama's health care reform, was passed in absolute defiance of the Founders' wishes. They counted on an increasingly conservative Supreme Court to ratify their judgment.

It fell to Representative Mike Pence of Indiana to summarize with admirable compactness the faith that all the answers could be discovered in our Founding documents. "There's nothing that ails this country," Pence insisted, "that couldn't be fixed by paying more careful attention to the principles enshrined in the Declaration of Independence and the Constitution of the United States of America."

I I

As these orations suggest, we often treat the Founders of our country not as the gifted statesmen and politicians they were, but as religious prophets and heroes akin to Moses or St. Paul. They are revered as the carriers of tablets that, if not divinely inspired, come close to being sacred. The Constitution, as Gordon Wood has noted, is regarded as "fundamental scripture."

The Revolutionary generation certainly did count in its ranks outstanding men and women. (And yes, as historians such as Rosemarie Zagarri have taught us, there *were* important women in the ranks.) But treating the Founders as quasi-religious prophets who produced texts equivalent to the Bible or the Talmud clouds our view of who they were and what they did. It plays down the profound and important disputes among them. Our nation was founded not on a grand consensus but on a series of arguments. The Constitution reflects not a single definitive judgment but a series of compromises, some of them designed—notably in the case of slavery—to paper over rather than resolve conflicts. "Historians today can recognize the extraordinary character of the Founding Fathers while also knowing that those eighteenth-century political leaders were not outside history," Wood wrote. "They were as enmeshed in historical circumstances as we are, they had no special divine insight into politics, and their thinking was certainly not free of passion, ignorance, and foolishness." What may be most impressive about them, in fact, is that in so many cases "they did their creative thinking on their feet . . . in the heat and urgency of debate." Thus, Wood notes, many of "our most cherished principles of constitutionalism associated with the Founding were in fact created inadvertently. They were the products not of closet philosophizing but of contentious political polemics."

If our nation was conceived in argument and dedicated to the proposition that life and politics regularly present us with difficult choices among competing goods, our current discontents and divisions become less mysterious and less threatening. Our forebears were engaged in balancing acts no less intricate and difficult than our own. Their approach was not unprincipled. On the contrary, their efforts can be seen as heroic because they held to principles that often conflicted one with another. They tried as best they could to achieve balance. The values of liberty, equality, republicanism, democratic sovereignty, and the common good each posed demands that were not easy to reconcile.

To make this discovery is liberating. It means that our approach to the past should not be defined by a quest for old certainties that must be applied to all circumstances. Instead, we should turn to the past for enlightenment and encouragement. Earlier generations were seeking to find an appropriate equilibrium among competing commitments, just as we are. We should be no less willing than they were to revise past arrangements and understandings. Our revolution, as Wood argued in *The Radicalism of the American Revolution*, was not the "conservative" affair that some have called it in retrospect when they compared it with the revolutions in France in 1789 and Russia in 1917. It was, for its own time, radical. "In our eyes the American revolutionaries appear to be absorbed in changing only their governments, not their society," Wood wrote. "But in destroying monarchy and establishing republics they were changing their society as well as their governments, and they knew it." Because of the Revolution, "Americans had become, almost overnight, the most liberal, the most democratic, the most commercially minded, and the most modern people in the world."

The Revolution, he said, "made possible the anti-slavery and women's rights movements of the nineteenth century and in fact all our current egalitarian thinking." It was followed by a second revolution—our Civil War. The Civil War generation was bound to the Founders' underlying principles, but not to their flawed and temporary resolution of the issue of slavery. Indeed, they urged radical change in the name of our Founding principles; this was the key to Abraham Lincoln's political career and the heart of his rhetorical strategy. And they were prepared to enshrine those changes in the Constitution itself through the Civil War amendments.

During the 1930s, the New Deal generation upheld the freedom promised by the Founders at a moment when much of Europe was turning its back on democracy and individual liberty. Yet the saviors of democracy during the Great Depression achieved their ends by embarking on innovations in the economy and in government that many conservatives resisted as unconstitutional and inconsistent with the design of the Founders. The New Dealers did not amend the Constitution itself (except for the repeal of the Prohibition amendment, which had little bearing on their larger program). Instead, they encouraged a revolution in constitutional interpretation that for nearly three generations beat back conservative efforts to use the Constitution as a straitjacket and a cudgel against reform. In the 1930s and 1940s, they saved the freedoms and the republican institutions that were at the heart of the Founders' achievement. They also laid the groundwork for the preservation and expansion of those achievements during the Cold War and the civil rights revolution that finally fulfilled the promises of the Civil War.

It's hard to think of any area where our understanding of history is more relevant to the present than our battles over how to interpret the words and goals of the document at the foundation of our government. If our politics reflects an underlying tension between individualism and community (and between republicanism and liberalism), this view has important implications for whether it's even possible, as Justices Antonin Scalia and Clarence Thomas and other contemporary conservatives have argued, to root constitutional decisions in "originalism" or the "original intent" of our Founders.

A classic alternative to originalism was the view expressed by the late Justice William Brennan. "The genius of the Constitution," Brennan declared, "rests not in any static meaning it might have had in a world that is dead and gone, but in the adaptability of its great principles to cope with current problems and current needs."

Brennan's view has won substantial support from some of the best historians of the period of the Revolution and the Constitutional Convention, not because they shared Brennan's politics (though in many cases they might have) but because they rejected what the historian Joseph J. Ellis has called "a set of implicit assumptions about the framers as a breed apart, momentarily allowed access to a set of timeless and transcendent truths."

"You don't have to believe that tongues of fire appeared over their heads during the debates," Ellis declared. "But the doctrine requires you to believe that the 'miracle at Philadelphia' was a uniquely omniscient occasion when 55 mere mortals were permitted a glimpse of the eternal verities and then embalmed their insights in the document." In fact, he writes, "the original framers of the Constitution harbored deep disagreements over the document's core provisions." The "debates in the state ratifying conventions further exposed the divisions of opinion on such seminal issues as federal vs. state jurisdiction, the powers of the executive branch, even whether there was—or should be—an ultimate arbiter of the purposefully ambiguous language of the document."

Treating the Founders as a breed apart, as people uniquely able to rise above their own circumstances and concerns, is a short step from denying the possibility that later generations can be trusted to make wise decisions and sound judgments. As Wood has argued, we "unnecessarily denigrate ourselves if we think of the Founding Fathers as heroes, as something other than men like ourselves with interests and social positions to promote."

More recently, in his 2010 commencement address at Harvard University, retired Supreme Court justice David Souter offered a quietly devastating critique of the originalist approach to judging associated with Justice Antonin Scalia and other contemporary Court conservatives. Souter avoided the word "originalist" and did not mention Scalia. Instead he described their method as the "fair reading" model, summarizing it as a belief that "deciding constitutional cases should be a straightforward exercise of reading fairly and viewing facts objectively."

The problem is that the Constitution is rooted not in any single value but in "a pantheon of values" and that "a lot of hard cases are hard because the Constitution gives no simple rule of decision for the cases in which one of the values is truly at odds with another." Souter went on:

> Not even its most uncompromising and unconditional language
> can resolve the potential tension of one provision with another,
> tensions the Constitution's Framers left to be resolved another
> day; and another day after that, *for our cases can give no answers
> that fit all conflicts, and no resolutions immune to rethinking
> when the significance of old facts may have changed in the
> changing world.* . . . For the tensions that are the stuff of judging
> in so many hard constitutional cases are, after all, the products
> of our aspirations to value liberty, as well as order, and fairness
> and equality, as well as liberty. *And the very opportunity for
> conflict between the good and the good reflects our confidence that
> a way may be found to resolve it when a conflict arises.* That is
> why the simplistic view of the Constitution devalues those aspira-
> tions, and attacks that confidence, and diminishes us. [Emphasis
> added]

The prophetic role ascribed to the Founders grants their ideas an authority that is denied to the insights of later generations. Typically, each side in a contemporary debate insists that one value (liberty *or* community, order *or* equality) overrode all others in the judgment of the organizers of our Revolution and the authors of our Constitution.

Appeals to an authoritative past are not confined to any one side of our ongoing debate. Progressives and reformers are no less alive than conservatives to the Founders' hold on the national imagination. But it has typically been the opponents of innovation who proclaimed themselves constitutionalists hewing to the "real," "original" meaning of the document. In many cases, these appeals to the past were based either on a defense of the rights of property—including, until the Civil War, property in slaves—or in the name of "individual liberty," or on an insistence that the states had the right to resist national legislation. These appeals become problematic when the Founders themselves are seen to have held conflicting views, when the Constitution is understood to uphold multiple values that sometimes conflict with one another, and when some of its provisions are understood to embody not timeless truths but sensitive compromises aimed at resolving (or getting around) pressing disagreements of the moment.

Such a view animated Souter's critique of the "fair reading" model, and it contrasts sharply with the quasi-religious view of the Founding that is by no means unique to our time. Richard Hofstadter notes that "naïve providential interpretations" of the nation's origins go back at least to George Bancroft's historical work in the mid-nineteenth century. Abraham Lincoln, as we've seen, built his case against slavery in his Cooper Union speech by insisting that the preponderance of the nation's Founders shared his view, not that of slavery's defenders. Harold Holzer noted that if Lincoln invoked the Bible in crafting his most famous utterance to that point—"a house divided against itself cannot stand"—he turned at Cooper Union "to the word of the secular gods of the American dream: the founding fathers." Again, the smell of incense seems to engulf the constitutional moment.

Yet a far less reverential view of the Founding document began gaining ground after the Civil War. The new realism was aroused by Supreme Court decisions in the Gilded Age that turned the Constitution—even the due process and equal protection clauses in the Fourteenth Amendment, which were great progressive breakthroughs—into a warrant for constraining the reforms and new departures being demanded by a rapidly industrializing nation. In *Congressional Government*, the classic work of political science that he wrote when he was a professor, Woodrow Wilson argued that Americans had turned the Constitution into an object of "an undiscriminating and almost blind worship." He urged that his fellow citizens become instead more "open-eyed . . . to its defects," to emancipate themselves from "timidity and false pride" in how they read it, and to be willing to engage in "a fearless criticism."

Wilson was reflecting a broad revolt against the idea of turning the Constitution into a rigid constraint. This revolt reached a peak during the Progressive Era and the New Deal. We think of the idea of a "living Constitution" as an invention of the last half century, offered in defense of the liberalism of Earl Warren's Supreme Court in the 1950s and 1960s. The idea is much older. In his keynote address at the 1912 Progressive Party convention that nominated Theodore Roosevelt, Albert Beveridge declared his party's belief that "the constitution is a living thing, growing with the people's growth, strengthening with the people's strength, aiding the people in their struggle for life, liberty and the pursuit of happiness, permitting the people to meet all their needs as conditions change."

A year later, Charles Beard published *An Economic Interpretation of the Constitution*. It was one of the great acts of debunking in American historical writing. Far from being saints, the Founders, in Beard's telling, were not much different from the plutocrats against whom Populists and Progressives raged in their time. Long before Marxism began exerting an important influence on historical writing, Beard was a hard economic determinist. He offered this relentless chain of logic:

> Different degrees and kinds of property inevitably exist in modern society; party doctrines and "principles" originate in the sentiments and views which the possession of various kinds of property creates in the minds of the possessors; class and group divisions based on property lie at the basis of modern government; and politics and constitutional law are inevitably a reflex of these contending interests.

Beard might simply have said, *Follow the money.*

In Beard's hands, the Constitution was not holy writ but, as he put it, "essentially an economic document based upon the concept that the fundamental rights of property are anterior to government and morally beyond the reach of popular majorities." The Constitutional Convention was not the product of a popular vote or a popular mass movement. Indeed, the "large propertyless mass" was largely excluded from the Convention. And in the voting to ratify the document, only a quarter of adult males actually cast ballots. The rest were either indifferent or excluded from the electoral rolls by property requirements. The Constitution was thus the work neither of the "whole people" nor of the states but "of a consolidated group whose interests knew no state boundaries and were truly national in their scope."

It is bracing to think about Beard again, even if his narrow economic view of the Constitution's origins left out large parts of the story. As Wood notes, Beard's theory "has been torn to shreds and no one pays attention to it anymore." Beard himself backed away from his own conclusions later in life. "An economic interpretation," he wrote in 1935, "is merely what it professes to be—a version, not the absolute truth, of history." This was a long way from the sweeping accusatory vigor of his original thesis. The Beard of 1914 fell victim to a tendency that afflicts all who tie history too closely to the present. He was overly eager to turn the Founders into the robber barons so familiar in his time. And he was so insistent on debunking the false sanctification of the Founding by the conservatives of his day who were intent on foiling reform that he oversimplified the tale he had to tell. Wood proposes a more nuanced understanding of the Founders. They did indeed accept "the reality of interests and commerce"—and they were no doubt attuned to their own interests. But they "were not modern men" and therefore had not abandoned the classical traditions of "civic humanism" and "republicanism."

Yet as Wood points out, Beard's larger aim, "that the Constitution ought to be seen as the consequence of historical circumstances and contending interests," has not "had the attraction for historians that it should have had." Seeing the Founding in its historical context and paying close attention to the divergences as well as the points of agreement within the

Revolutionary and immediate post-Revolutionary generations can enlighten us about tensions in our political life that we still confront.

And at the very moment Beard was softening his position, the constitutional skepticism he had promoted was rejuvenated by another round of Supreme Court decisions in the early 1930s voiding large parts of the New Deal. Small-*d* democrats and progressives believed that the Constitution was being used to frustrate the popular will and to block measures necessary to the country's recovery from economic calamity. It was foolish, the New Dealers argued, to imagine that the Founders had anticipated the social and economic changes that would alter the nation's needs 150 years later.

The Constitution, Franklin Roosevelt insisted, was "a layman's document, not a lawyer's contract." Its ambiguities had created "an unending struggle between those who would preserve this original broad concept of the Constitution" and those who "cry 'unconstitutional' at every effort to better the condition of our people." The United States, FDR insisted, could not afford "to sacrifice each generation in turn while the law catches up with life." Underlying his view was a sense of urgency: "The millions who are in want will not stand by silently forever while the things to satisfy their needs are within easy reach."

In his day, Theodore Roosevelt had suggested that voters be given the right to petition to force referenda on "whether or not judges' interpretation of the Constitution is to be sustained." In the 1930s, TR's cousin pursued what he thought was a less radical proposal: rather than overturn the idea of judicial review, FDR simply asked Congress to expand the size of the Supreme Court so he could appoint liberal judges who would interpret the Constitution with, as his attorney general put it, "a lively sense of the importance of the social problems *which have now spilled over state lines.*" This, of course, led to one of the most controversial episodes of the New Deal era, FDR's "court packing" plan, which set off the most important legislative fight that Roosevelt lost. Jeff Shesol, the author of the definitive account of the court battle, concluded that it was "the catalyst that helped fracture the New Deal coalition." It also served to "reawaken the GOP; unite conservatives across party lines; and shatter the myth of Roosevelt's omnipotence."

But something else happened as well. Over time, the Court adopted a more liberal view and became far more hospitable to the New Deal's way of thinking. Some conservatives on the Court backed off their hard line, though there is much debate among historians over whether Roosevelt's initiative played a role in this or not. Roosevelt eventually had the opportunity to appoint justices of his own who altered the Court's political balance.

This shift, later labeled the "Revolution of 1937," inaugurated a long period in which Court decisions reflected what came to be known as the "New Deal Settlement." From 1937 through the years of Earl Warren's leadership as chief justice, the Supreme Court gave Congress broad latitude to legislate on economic and social matters and intervened primarily on behalf of individual rights, particularly—the *Brown v. Board of Education* decision is emblematic—the rights of minority groups. This led the Court away from the emphasis on states' rights so central to earlier conservative decisions. In its series of rulings incorporating the Bill of Rights into state constitutions, the Court placed individual rights above the claims of state governments. This had the effect of broadening the federal government's power to enforce individual claims against the states. These decisions unleashed ferocious opposition in a segregated South that had relied on states' rights theories from the beginning of the republic to enforce white supremacy. Richard Nixon's replacement of Earl Warren as chief justice by Warren Burger slowed the liberal judicial revolution but didn't stop it entirely.

"To recall the great cases of the Warren and Burger Courts today is like reading off the heroic battles of a war still fresh in living memory," the legal scholar Cass Sunstein wrote in 1990. The catalogue of liberal triumphs Sunstein then reeled off is impressive:

> Beginning with *Brown v. Board of Education*, the Court invalidated racial segregation in schools, public transportation, even golf courses. In *Baker v. Carr* and *Reynolds v. Simms*, it called for reapportionment of state legislatures in line with the principle of one person, one vote. In *Harper v. Board of Elections*, it struck down the poll tax. In *Mapp v. Ohio* and *Miranda v. Arizona*, among many cases, it granted a multitude of new rights to criminal defen-

dants. In *Griswold v. Connecticut* and *Roe v. Wade*, it recognized rights of sexual and reproductive privacy, including the right to obtain an abortion. In other cases, only slightly less well known, it banished prayer from the public schools, struck down many laws as impermissible sex discrimination, gave nonmarital children and aliens the right to be free from official discrimination, and offered extraordinarily broad protection to speech, including advocacy of crime, false statements about public officials, commercial advertising, and pornography.

Sunstein added: "Many of the rights affirmed by the Court, though actually quite new, are now taken for granted, as if they had always been part of our constitutional heritage."

But this was not the only part of history that liberals forgot as the Court advanced individual rights across a broad front. Liberals also came to see the Supreme Court as the driving agent of change and progress, overlooking the horror their philosophical and political forebears experienced when the right invoked constitutionalism to block reform. Cries of "judicial activism" that became, in the Warren years and after, a staple of conservative sloganeering had, as Sunstein noted, "played a major role during the New Deal" when *liberals* were enraged at the Court's eagerness to strike down Roosevelt's reforms. For New Dealers, Sunstein noted, it "would have seemed peculiar . . . to suggest that social reform on behalf of the disadvantaged should come from the courts."

And so for years, our nation's debate over what the Supreme Court should do has been distorted by a kind of willful blindness to history on both sides. Conservatives who criticized judicial activism were, in fact, simply seeking a different kind of judicial activism. They disliked the political direction of the Warren Court's decisions but were not at all opposed to an activism aimed at restricting Congress's ability to pass regulatory legislation, the executive's capacity to enforce those regulations, the power of government at various levels to place some constraints on private property rights, and the federal government's purview to take actions that conservatives insisted should be the prerogative of the states.

Yet as increasingly conservative Supreme Courts exercised broad

power to strip away the ability of progressives to legislate on matters ranging from the environment to disability rights, liberals were slow to shift
their rhetoric and their public arguments to make clear that judicial activism was now, as it had been so often in the past, a practice of the legal
right. Sunstein was one of the first judicial scholars to understand that history was repeating itself in ways liberals needed to acknowledge. "In many
respects," he wrote in 1990, "the current position of the Supreme Court is
akin to that of its predecessor in the New Deal. As then, constitutional
politics through the judiciary is unlikely to advance liberal causes." It was
a powerful and wholly accurate bit of understatement.

But facts, as Ronald Reagan said, are stubborn things, and reality is
finally catching up with the public argument. The columnist George Will
was one of the few popular commentators on the right to admit with admirable candor that conservatives needed to abandon their critique of judicial activism. He didn't have to add that the old argument was inconvenient
now that conservatives controlled the Court. "Conservatives spoiling for a
fight should watch their language," he wrote in 2010, and "rethink their
rhetoric about 'judicial activism.'" Will argued that the "proper question"
for conservatives in assessing Supreme Court nominees was: "Will the nominee be actively enough engaged in protecting liberty from depredations
perpetrated by popular sovereignty?" This, of course, is exactly the sort of
question that the conservative Court asked in the days before the New
Deal settlement, to the great consternation of progressives.

Note Will's skepticism of "popular sovereignty"—a mistrust of democracy itself. As the new millennium began, a conservative Supreme Court
would make clear that it indeed viewed democracy as far less important
than other ideas and commitments in the American intellectual pantheon.
It was ready to use whatever notions of constitutionalism were convenient
to bolster the power of conservatives to protect property and an individualistic view of public life.

III

It is risky to speculate about what future historians will say, but two Supreme Court decisions, one at the beginning and one at the end of the first

decade of the twenty-first century, are almost certainly destined to define a tipping point in our constitutional debate. Both reminded liberals there were limits to the idea that, in Sunstein's phrase, "social reform on behalf of the disadvantaged should come from the courts." In fact, the decisions in *Bush v. Gore* in 2000 and *Citizens United v. Federal Election Commission* in 2010 definitively put an end to the era of liberal confidence in the high court as a fair arbiter of justice. Both decisions challenged the Court's legitimacy. For conservatives who had battled liberal "judicial activism" for a half century, both decisions were gratifying. They signaled the right's victory in the judicial wars and pointed to the new era that George Will had described. The Court would be as activist as it had ever been in the Warren era, perhaps more so, but on the conservative side. The Court's definition of constitutionalism would lead it with great consistency to decisions congenial to the ideological right.

The *Bush v. Gore* decision on December 12, 2000, came after a long argument over how and whether to recount popular votes in Florida, the outcome of which would determine the winner of that year's presidential election. That Democrat Al Gore had received 500,000 more popular votes nationwide than George W. Bush never entered the calculations. The fact that faulty ballot design in several Florida counties robbed Gore of thousands of votes that would have given him the state and the presidency was not part of the case, either.

These considerations loomed large in the minds of many of Gore's supporters, but they were not even the most troublesome aspect of controversy. And in and of itself, the fact that the five most conservative appointees on the Court ruled in favor of the Republican presidential candidate did not explain the long-term damage the decision did to the Court. Truly astonishing was the fact that the five justices who chose to intrude in Florida's election process were the same ones who had always claimed to be champions of the rights of states and foes of "judicial activism" and "judicial overreach."

Worse, to reach the result most convenient for the conservative candidate, the conservative justices invoked liberal principles they had previously disdained. In general, conservative justices had long been wary of what they saw as the overuse by liberals of the equal protection doctrine to extend rights to minorities and women. Yet it was that very commitment to equal protection that the Court invoked to protect Bush from defeat. Weirdly, the doctrine was used to stop a recount whose purpose was to move *closer* toward equal protection of all those voters—many of them poor and members of minority groups—who might have lost their ballots because of unreliable voting equipment. And conservative justices who had long advocated for states' rights felt perfectly free to cast aside the decision of a *state* court acting on a *state* matter and impose their will by fiat. States' rights were fine unless they led to an inconvenient political result.

To make the decision as bitter as possible for its critics, the majority that had abruptly stopped the recounting of ballots on the theory that Al Gore would suffer no "irreparable harm" from a delay said just a few days later that it was now too late to have a recount that "comports with minimal constitutional standards," directly contradicting what they had said in the first place.

Never in history has a Court made as clear as this one did that it didn't really believe in the principles it was using to get to the result it wanted. "Our consideration is limited to the present circumstances," the justices in the majority wrote, "for the problem of equal protection in election processes generally presents many complexities." Such complexities didn't bother them in this particular case, of course, but they were telling all future courts never to apply their reasoning in *Bush v. Gore* to any other case. It was a reasoning process designed to produce one outcome, one time.

One theme of this book has been how contemporary conservatism has shed many of the doctrines and principles that have allowed it to contribute so much to the inherent balance of American political life. The resort to brute judicial force to settle the 2000 election seemed decidedly unconservative. It was, after all, Robert Nisbet who offered the classic conservative distinction between "power" and "authority." Power, he noted, was based upon force. Authority is "based ultimately upon the consent of those under it." In a democracy, we recognize the authority even of leaders with whom we disagree because we accept the legitimacy of the process that got them there. The Supreme Court ruling gave Bush power without the authority that would have come from legitimacy. This would only aggravate the political problems he faced once the feelings of national unity bred by

the terrorist attacks of September 11, 2001, faded and the war in Iraq went
sour.

Understanding the radicalism of *Bush v. Gore* and the way the Court
had mimicked the very "results-oriented" jurisprudence that conservatives
had long condemned is essential to understanding the deep polarization of
recent years and the rise of an increasingly embattled and angry liberalism. There was lasting fury over what liberals could only see as the ruth-
less use of judicial power—and also over the highly disciplined and often
vicious attacks on Gore for the simple act of seeking what candidates in
close races had always demanded: a recount.

But a decade on, and in the wake of the Tea Party rebellion, *Bush v.
Gore* is also illustrative of how the invocation of the Constitution by conservatives had become a routine way of achieving their political goals. It
involved harking back to the Constitution as it was written in 1787, down-
playing the impact of the Civil War and Progressive Era amendments, and
ignoring the steady democratization of the country in the intervening two
and a quarter centuries.

Recall that when the recount of the ballots in Florida threatened to
put Gore in the lead—and this seemed a strong possibility before the Supreme Court abruptly halted the recount—many conservatives insisted
that the Florida legislature, under Republican control, should ignore the
actual count of the popular vote in the state and simply impose a slate of
Bush electors. This was defended as "the constitutional option," since the
Constitution vested in state legislatures the right to choose presidential
electors as they wished. Writing in the *New York Times* in late November
2000, William Kristol, the conservative editor and commentator, made the
case for going around the vote count:

> The Florida Legislature has to be ready to assert its own constitu-
> tional prerogative against the Florida courts' intervention in the
> electoral process. The United States Constitution provides that
> presidential electors may be appointed in such manner as the state
> legislatures may direct.
>
> On or before Dec. 12, the Florida legislature may have to
> choose to ratify the slate of electors certified by the secretary of

state against the wishes of the Florida Supreme Court. That decision would then have to be upheld by the United States Congress. This would be a constitutional crisis, to be sure—but forcing such a "crisis" is preferable to supine yielding to an imperial judiciary.

Put aside that conservatives were relentlessly accusing Al Gore at the time of selfishly provoking a "crisis" simply by demanding a recount. Creating a "crisis," it seemed, was acceptable as long as it was provoked on behalf of George W. Bush. But the key word here is "Constitution," used as a vehicle for moving the election away from the counting of ballots, that is to say, away from democracy.

During oral arguments, Justice Antonin Scalia made clear he read the situation exactly as Kristol did. "There's a right of suffrage in voting for the legislature," he told Lawrence Tribe, Gore's lawyer, "but Article II makes it very clear that the legislature can, itself, appoint the electors."

John Yoo, who later became famous for his Bush administration memos on torture and his defense of rather unbridled notions of presidential power, wanted to make sure the people knew their place. "Contrary to Democratic rhetoric," he asserted in the *Wall Street Journal*, "the people have no right to vote for president or even the Electoral College; that power is only delegated to them by the grace of the legislature. In appointing the electors itself, the legislature would be directly taking up its constitutional functions again." A move away from democracy is thus recast nobly as a legislature "taking up its constitutional functions again," as if the states had been lazy in letting the people decide who their presidential electors would be. And the Supreme Court majority vigorously asserted precisely this point in *Bush v. Gore*, stating flatly: "The individual citizen has no federal constitutional right to vote for electors for the President of the United States unless and until the state legislature chooses a statewide election as the means to implement its power to appoint members of the Electoral College." It was instructive for the people to learn how circumscribed their right to choose the president really is.

Striking throughout the controversy was how the Constitution was invoked over and over as a means of reversing democratic advances that the nation had taken for granted for decades. At the time the Founders wrote the Constitution, they imagined that all electors would be chosen by legislatures. There were many restrictions on the right to vote, including those of property. Over the years, while retaining the Founders' framework, the nation steadily extended the right to vote to white men without property and eventually to African American men and then to women. Popular election of those who would select our president was part of this democratic advance. To step back from the idea that voters should name electors—and to step back from a fair count of Florida's votes—was to retreat into a less democratic world, to a time when the people's will was thought to need buffering by those, including state legislators, who claimed to know better. "Many of our original structures of government plod along unaltered to this day, though they are rooted in assumptions and biases that have been not only rejected, but in many instances forgotten," wrote the columnist Harold Meyerson. "Today, conservatives like Scalia and Yoo cheerfully defend the rights of legislatures over people, but prudently decline to invoke the demophobic and aristocratic beliefs that led to the establishment of these rights."

The legal scholar Peter Shane offered a devastating analysis of the decision that is worth citing at length because of his emphasis on "the conspicuous trajectory of our constitutional development toward more democracy" throughout our country's history:

> Never before in the history of democratic government has an unelected judicial organ chosen the head of state by preventing the counting of votes. Such an event cuts entirely against the grain of our political history. The past 200 years have witnessed a broadening of the franchise in the United States (and throughout the world) in terms of both eligibility and applicability. The right to vote has become central to our conception of citizenship. It is hard to imagine any modern-day Western theory of governmental legitimacy that does not rest in some essential aspect on "the electoral connection." Thus, it was startling to witness the Supreme Court's incautious embrace of a theory of the world's most important elected office that treats its democratic character as merely discretionary.

Bush v. Gore is antidemocratic in more than its ordination of a particular electoral outcome. It is oblivious to the democratic character of our Constitution in every aspect of its analysis. Its very starting point—the asserted authority of the states to disenfranchise voters altogether from participation in the selection of presidential electors—is unpersuasive in the face of the text and history of the Fourteenth Amendment . . . The majority's premise takes no serious account of the text of the Fourteenth Amendment, its history, nearly universal practice since 1868, and the conspicuous deepening of our constitutional commitment to democracy in the ensuing 132 years. The failure even to address these issues mocks the majority's supposed commitments to textualism and originalism in other contexts.

Bush v. Gore set a pattern for the coming decade. The Founders of our nation would be brought into play, but not to remind us of how advanced their conception of government was for its time and how their republican commitments expanded our rights. Rather, they would be invoked as after-the-fact advocates for reimposing on our nation the *least* democratic aspects of the era in which they lived.

If the new decade began with *Bush v. Gore*, it ended with another decision that was also, to use Shane's word, conspicuous as a departure from long democratic precedent. And like *Bush v. Gore*, it was a case of judicial activism tilting the electoral system toward conservative interests and outcomes. The Court's five-to-four decision in *Citizens United v. Federal Election Commission* on January 21, 2010, allowed the use of corporate and union money in unlimited sums to influence election campaigns. *Citizens United* was, all at once, a truly remarkable piece of judicial activism, a precedent-shattering evisceration of a century-long tradition of limiting corporate power in American politics, a break with the republican tradition's well-founded fear of political corruption, and a direct interference with the electoral rules in a way that favored those who had put the conservative justices in a position to make the ruling in the first place. In a peculiar turn of history, given that President Bush's appointees were decisive to this outcome, *Bush v. Gore* made *Citizens United* possible.

The case arose when Citizens United, a conservative group, brought suit arguing that it should be exempt from the restrictions of the 2002 McCain-Feingold campaign finance law for a movie it made that was sharply critical of Hillary Clinton, at the time a presidential candidate. The organization argued that as a First Amendment matter, it should not be required by law to disclose who financed the film.

The conservative majority's determination to go far beyond the case before it became clear in June 2009 when the Court, in a remarkable act of overreach, postponed a decision and called for new briefs and a highly unusual new hearing. It chose to consider an issue only tangentially raised in the original case by calling into question a 1990 decision that upheld the long-standing ban on the use of corporate money in campaigns. As Justice John Paul Stevens noted later in his scalding dissent, "Essentially, five justices were unhappy with the limited nature of the case before us, so they changed the case to give themselves an opportunity to change the law."

The broad idea of keeping corporate money separate from politics went back to the 1907 Tillman Act, and all the precedents were on the side of insisting that corporations did not have the same rights as actual, live human beings, even if, as a legal fiction, corporations were often treated as "persons."

The entire episode came as something of a shock to those who had insisted that Chief Justice John Roberts was a moderate sort of conservative and that he would pay close attention to precedent. After all, Roberts had promised exactly this when he appeared before the Senate Judiciary Committee at his confirmation hearings.

"I do think that it is a jolt to the legal system when you overrule a precedent," Roberts had said back in 2005. "Precedent plays an important role in promoting stability and evenhandedness. It is not enough—and the court has emphasized this on several occasions—it is not enough that you may think the prior decision was wrongly decided. That really doesn't answer the question, it just poses the question."

"And you do look at these other factors," Roberts went on, "like settled expectations, like the legitimacy of the court, like whether a particular precedent is workable or not, whether a precedent has been eroded by subsequent developments." He paraphrased Alexander Hamilton as saying in

"Federalist #78," "To avoid an arbitrary discretion in the judges, they need to be bound down by rules and precedents." This was, one might say, a thoughtful, *conservative* view.

By Roberts's own standards, *Citizens United* should have gone the other way. Tossing out an established system whose construction went back to 1907 was indeed an act of "arbitrary discretion." The ban on corporate money in politics had been upheld over many years by justices of various philosophical leanings. It was not the product of a single decision by a temporarily activist Court. And the precedents were clearly workable, since no one was asking the Court to change them, and parties and candidates had long lived by them. They had not been eroded. The corporate ban had been upheld in case after case, no matter where particular court majorities stood on other campaign finance provisions. The ban on corporate contributions was simply taken for granted. As the court had stated just six years earlier, Congress's power to prohibit direct corporate and union political spending "has been firmly embedded in our law."

Rarely has a case so clearly pitted republican notions of self-government and the community's right to keep the political system free of corruption against a radical kind of individualism conveying to corporations the same rights as those guaranteed citizens. The Founders played a key role in the dueling opinions of Justice Scalia, who supported the ruling, and Justice Stevens, who denounced the result as threatening "to undermine the integrity of elected institutions across the Nation." The fact that each read the Founders differently pointed to the limits of a jurisprudence based on "original intention," given the complexity of the Founders' views and the habit of originalists to be absolutely confident in their ability to read the Founders' minds.

The Framers, Stevens argued, "took it as a given that corporations could be comprehensively regulated in the service of the public welfare." The conservative majority "enlists the Framers in its defense without seriously grappling with their understandings of corporations or the free speech right, or with the republican principles that underlay those understandings . . . To the contrary, this history helps illuminate just how extraordinarily dissonant the decision is."

Citing the work of legal scholar Zephyr Teachout, Stevens noted that "it is fair to say" that the Framers "were obsessed with corruption." They understood this "to encompass the dependency of public officeholders on private interests . . . They discussed corruption 'more often in the Constitutional Convention than factions, violence, or instability.' . . . When they brought our constitutional order into being, the Framers had their minds trained on a threat to republican self-government that this Court has lost sight of."

Scalia barely took Stevens's argument seriously:

> The Framers didn't like corporations, the dissent concludes, and therefore it follows (as night the day) that corporations had no rights of free speech. Of course the Framers' personal affection or disaffection for corporations is relevant only insofar as it can be thought to be reflected in the understood meaning of the text they enacted. . . . Even if we thought it proper to apply the dissent's approach of excluding from First Amendment coverage what the Founders disliked, and even if we agreed that the Founders disliked founding-era corporations; modern corporations might not qualify for exclusion. Most of the Founders' resentment towards corporations was directed at the state-granted monopoly privileges that individually chartered corporations enjoyed. Modern corporations do not have such privileges, and would probably have been favored by most of our enterprising Founders—excluding, perhaps, Thomas Jefferson and others favoring perpetuation of an agrarian society.

There is something breathtaking about defending a Court decision that overturned decades of precedent with the remarkably weak assertion that modern corporations "would *probably* have been favored by most of our enterprising Founders," as if it were possible to know what the Founders would have made of Microsoft, Apple, General Motors, or ExxonMobil. All involved forms of economic organization unknown in 1787 and products that Hamilton, Madison, or Franklin could not have imagined. On the matter of fearing corruption, Stevens was surely closer to the Founders' republican principles. And the very effort to convert a corporation into an actual person would have been as alien to the Founders as it was to Stevens. He wrote:

Although they make enormous contributions to our society, corporations are not actually members of it. They cannot vote or run for office. Because they may be managed and controlled by nonresidents, their interests may conflict in fundamental respects with the interests of eligible voters . . . It might also be added that corporations have no consciences, no beliefs, no feelings, no thoughts, no desires. Corporations help structure and facilitate the activities of human beings, to be sure, and their "personhood" often serves as a useful legal fiction. But they are not themselves members of "We the People" by whom and for whom our Constitution was established.

The dissenting justice added a bit of common sense that seemed to escape the Court that day. "A democracy cannot function effectively," he wrote, "when its constituent members believe laws are being bought and sold."

Thus did conservative originalism help produce a decision about a set of institutions that the Founders would have found peculiar, involving an election campaign process totally unknown to them, on the basis of a theory that they would have considered bizarre.

IV

Arguing that "originalism is hardly the only way to abide by the Constitution," the historian Jill Lepore made the essential point. "Setting aside the question of whether it makes good law," she wrote in her delightful book *The Whites of Their Eyes*, "it is, generally, lousy history." It's possible, she insisted, "to cherish the stability of the law and the durability of the Constitution, as amended over two and a half centuries of change and one civil war, and tested in the courts, without dragging the Founding Fathers from their graves."

Lepore described the impossibility of placing ourselves in the minds (or the smocks) of our eighteenth-century forebears in about as memorable a way as any writer I have come across:

In eighteenth-century America, I wouldn't have been able to vote. I wouldn't have been able to own property, either. I'd very likely have been unable to write, and, if I survived childhood, chances are that I'd have died in childbirth. And, no matter how long or short my life, I'd almost certainly have died without having once ventured a political opinion preserved in any historical record, except that none of these factors has any meaning or bearing whatsoever on whether an imaginary eighteenth-century me would have supported the Obama administration's stimulus package or laws allowing the carrying of concealed weapons or the war in Iraq, because I did not live in eighteenth-century America, and no amount of thinking that I could, not even wearing petticoats, a linsey-woolsey calico smock, and a homespun mobcap, can make it so.

Respect for the Founders and for the words of our Constitution cannot be allowed to become a mandate for trying to turn the twenty-first century into the eighteenth. It cannot become an all-purpose veto of any idea, any advance, any change, any innovation that seems appropriate and just in our times. It cannot become an excuse for skipping over everything that happened since 1787 and ignoring the expansion of democratic rights to previously excluded groups. It cannot ignore the Civil War amendments, which opened the way for full participation of African Americans in our public life. It cannot ignore the Progressive Era amendments, which sought to update our government for the challenges of a new economy and a very different world—and also began the process of recognizing women as full partners in public life.

We should honor the history of what actually happened in 1787 by acknowledging that the writers of the Constitution were gifted men with interests, ideas, and even prejudices. They were human beings like us. They were also visionaries quite prepared to break with the conventions of their times and to push the boundaries of what was then considered possible.

And surely we must get the history of the period right. Rick Perry's view, cited at the beginning of this chapter, suggests that the Constitution was all about states' rights. This is flatly wrong. As the legal scholar Garrett Epps has written, conservatives "claim that the Constitution was set up to restrain the federal government. If so, there's precious little evidence of it.

The actual text of the Constitution is overwhelmingly concerned with making sure the new government had enough power; the framers thought the old Articles of Confederation were fatally weak."

Of course, Epps added, the Constitution also protected rights. The Founders "didn't want to set up a government that could throw people in jail without a good reason, or steal their property, or do away with free elections. The original Constitution prohibited oppressive practices, and the Bill of Rights added other restrictions." But anyone who reads the 5,000 words agreed upon in Philadelphia cannot escape Epps's conclusion: that "the document as a whole is much more concerned with what the government *can* do—not with what it can't."

Originalism itself also needs to be challenged on its own grounds. As the colloquy between Justices Scalia and Stevens on *Citizens United* suggested, there is a serious argument to be had over what the Constitution actually says, and what the Founders actually intended. By many lights, Stevens could be said to have won the argument in the case on originalist grounds alone with his emphasis on corruption and the republican tradition that shaped the Founders' view. He was pointing to the distance between the Framers' understandings and the majority's decision. As Epps points out, originalists not only want to claim that "what the framers said governs." They also "want to control what counts as what the founders said." With tongue in cheek—but only partly—Epps argued that Scalia's originalism often seems inspired by the thought: "Trust me, I knew the framers and here's what they would have said."

It is thus a salutary development that a new school of originalism has arisen among liberals. It insists that the Framers' Constitution is a far more progressive document than conservatives have claimed. "Progressives are losing the fight over the courts and the Constitution because conservatives have maneuvered us into running from, rather than embracing, the text and history of the Constitution," argued Doug Kendall and Jim Ryan, legal scholars who are pioneering a progressive originalism. They also pointed to the key flaw in the conservatives' argument: their desire to focus only on "the original Constitution" while ignoring "the whole Constitution as amended throughout the nineteenth and twentieth centuries," changes that "have often been the result of liberal and progressive reform efforts." Kendall and Ryan cite the distinguished legal scholar Akhil Amar, the author of *America's Constitution: A Biography*, who argued that rather than abandon constitutional history, liberals should "claim it as their own."

Kendall, Ryan, and Amar are key figures in a broad debate among legal progressives over how to reclaim ground that has been ceded to conservative originalists by default. It is an urgent task, even if there are limits to this new liberal originalism. In a 2011 exchange with Kendall and Ryan in *Democracy* journal, legal scholars Geoffrey Stone and William Marshall insisted that "liberals should not pretend that honest answers to vexing constitutional questions can be gleaned simply by staring hard at an ambiguous text." This is true.

It's also true, as William E. Forbath has argued, that the "public appeal" of the conservative originalists is not based on widespread confidence that their reading of the Constitution is right. Rather, it has "aroused citizens, lawmakers, and judges" because it offers a "narrative of a 'traditional' nation that it promises to restore: an America dedicated to personal responsibility and limited government, private property and godliness." There is, Forbath argues, an alternative narrative also deeply embedded in our history: that "you can't have what the Framers called a 'republican form of government,' and certainly not a constitutional democracy, in the context of gross material inequality among citizens." Our tradition has resisted such inequalities because they produce oligarchy; because they destroy "the material independence and security that citizens must have in order to think and act on their own behalf and participate on a roughly equal footing in the polity and society;" and because they impede "access to basic goods that are the foundation of dignity and standing in one's own eyes and in the eyes of the community." In sum: "The Framers believed that personal liberty and political equality required a measure of economic independence and material security." Protecting our constitutional democracy thus demands that we address "our unequal and unfair society."

Where Kendall, Ryan, Stone, Marshall, and Forbath all agree is that progressives must rejoin the battle for American history. The time has come for a more accurate and less mythologized view of the Founding. We need both a more respectful *and* a more realistic view of the Founders that honors them for their efforts to balance their philosophical principles and their practical concerns. In particular, as I have been arguing throughout this book, they were republicans *and* liberals, they understood the possibilities *and* limits of government, and they honored individual rights *and* the imperative of building a durable sense of community, nationally as well as locally.

Only by appreciating the Founders' sense of balance can we put an end to the practice of reading the Constitution in a highly partisan way that always seems to place it on one side of our debate. More decisions along the lines of *Bush v. Gore* and *Citizens United* will, as Justice Stevens argued in both cases, undermine the legitimacy of the Supreme Court and trust in the Constitution as a document that transcends party and interest. Stevens articulated this with particular power in his dissent on *Bush v. Gore:* "Although we may never know with complete certainty the identity of the winner of this year's Presidential election, the identity of the loser is perfectly clear. It is the Nation's confidence in the judge as an impartial guardian of the rule of law."

Misreading our past is especially troublesome with respect to the Founding period because of the centrality of the Constitution to all of our debates. But it is also a problem when it comes to our attitude toward the role of government itself. Our contemporary arguments seem to assume that government played only a minor role in the development of our nation, and that laissez-faire was the rule in America until the Progressives and New Dealers entered the scene. This view is badly mistaken, and it will have a pernicious impact on our future if it goes unchallenged.

CHAPTER VII

The American System
How Strong Government, Strong Individuals, and Strong Communities Have Supported Each Other

SPEND some time with the Republican presidential candidates who gathered to debate at St. Anselm's College in New Hampshire in June 2011—or any of the many, later GOP debates—and you'll encounter a powerful consensus about the federal government and its proper role in American life: shrink it and get it out of the way. One after another, each in his or her own way, the candidates declared that productive citizens and private companies would bring back prosperity and solve the nation's problems on their own.

"This economy is stalled," declared businessman Herman Cain, who briefly rose to the top of the GOP lists before being pushed out by accusations related to his sexual past. "It's like a train on the tracks with no engine." And he offered a rather striking metaphor for President Obama's policies. "The administration has simply been putting all of this money in the caboose," he said. "We need an engine called the private sector. That means lower taxes, lower the capital gains tax rate to zero, suspend taxes on repatriated profits, then make them permanent." Thus was the government of the United States of America reduced to a lowly caboose.

Next came former senator Rick Santorum of Pennsylvania, who proved to be a more formidable candidate than his competitors or most of the media expected. "What we need," he declared, "is an economy that's unshackled." The Obama administration had "passed one oppressive policy and oppressive regulation after another," with the president's health care plan "being first and foremost."

The answer, said (or, perhaps more accurately, reiterated) former governor Tim Pawlenty of Minnesota, who dropped out of the race two months later, was a government that "cuts taxes" and "also dramatically cuts spending." He went on with the litany so favored that evening: "We need to fix regulation. We need to have a pro-American energy policy. We need to fix health care policy. And if you do those things, as I've proposed, including cut spending, you'll get this economy moving and growing the private economy by shrinking government." Note that again, "growing the economy" and "shrinking government" were seen as synonymous.

"Every time the liberals get into office," declared Representative Michele Bachmann, whose campaign ended after the Iowa caucuses in January of 2012, "they pass an omnibus bill of big spending projects. What we need to do is pass the mother of all repeal bills, but it's the repeal bill that will get a job killing regulations. And I would begin with the EPA, because there is no other agency like the EPA. It should really be renamed the job-killing organization of America." Her extraordinary proposal to abolish the Environmental Protection Agency, created under Republican president Richard Nixon, was met with nary a dissent from any of the Republicans onstage.

Representative Ron Paul, the purest libertarian of the bunch, offered the most direct answers. Asked what standards there should be for government assistance to private enterprise, Paul flatly rejected the premise of the question. "There shouldn't be any government assistance to private enterprise," he said. "It's not morally correct, it's [il]legal, it's bad economics. It's not part of the Constitution . . . when the politicians get in and direct things, you get the malinvestment. They do the dumb things." Government equals politicians equals dumb. That was that.

Former House Speaker Newt Gingrich had once talked with some sympathy about a mandate to require all Americans to buy health insurance. Not anymore. "If you explore the mandate, which even the Heritage Foundation at one time looked at," he said, seeking cover from the staunchly conservative think tank, "the fact is, when you get into a mandate, it ultimately ends up with unconstitutional powers. It allows the government to define virtually everything. And if you can do it for health care, you can do it for everything in your life, and, therefore, we should not have a mandate."

A slippery slope, indeed, from health insurance to "everything in your life"—though he did not explain whether Medicare or long-standing government mandates for drivers to buy car insurance were also way stations to oppression.

Former governor Mitt Romney of Massachusetts recited from the same catechism when asked about the federal government's rescue of the American auto industry. A bad idea, he insisted. "There is a perception in this country that government knows better than the private sector, that Washington and President Obama have a better view for how an industry ought to be run," Romney said. "Well, they're wrong. The right way for America to create jobs is . . . to keep government in its place and to allow the private sector and . . . the energy and passion of the American people create a brighter future for our kids and for ourselves."

Just a week earlier, Romney had provided an even sharper definition of the country's struggle over government in what was almost a throwaway line in the formal speech announcing his candidacy. "Did you know," Romney asked, "that government—federal, state, and local—under President Obama has grown to consume almost 40 percent of our economy? We're only inches away from ceasing to be a free economy."

For the record, the federal government of which Obama was in charge "consumed" about a quarter of the economy at the moment Romney spoke—and this after a severe recession, when government's share naturally goes up as the private economy shrinks.

But even granting Romney his addition of spending by all levels of government, the notion that we are "inches away from ceasing to be a free economy" was remarkable. It suggested that the only way to measure freedom was by toting up how much government spent and comparing it with the rest of the nation's activity.

It implied, whether Romney intended to do so or not, that we were less "free" because we spent money on public schools and student loans, Medicare and Social Security, police and firefighters, roads and transit, national defense and environmental protection. It also implied that we would be more free if government spent zero percent of the economy on such things.

If freedom, as Romney seemed to be insisting, came down primarily to the quantity of government spending, then a country such as Sweden, where government spends quite a lot, would be less free than a right-wing dictatorship that had no welfare state and no public schools—but also didn't allow its people to speak, pray, write, or organize as they wish. It was a peculiar way to measure freedom.

This was the nearly unanimous view across the conservative spectrum in 2011. Former Utah governor Jon Huntsman wasn't at St. Anselm's that night because he entered the contest afterward. But in an interview given to the *Wall Street Journal* a few weeks later, he pledged fealty to the same doctrine as his rivals had, even if he was milder-spoken and more given to talking about civility. "I think the appropriate role of the federal government is to carefully measure out the nation's competitiveness," he said. "When are taxes too high and making us less competitive than our major trading partners? When do we reach the point of onerous regulation and have to throttle back so we can maintain a competitive posture?" Note again: Huntsman (who dropped out during the 2012 South Carolina primary) defined no positive role for government in this interview, just more tax cutting and deregulating.

And if this field of candidates was not sufficiently anti-government, it was augmented in August 2011 by the entry of Texas governor Rick Perry, whose views about federal power were more akin to those of mid-nineteenth-century nullifiers or even secessionists than to Lincoln's. Compared with Perry, Mitt Romney looked far more like his liberal father, George Romney, the governor of Michigan who during the 1960s had been a champion of civil rights and progressive government. Indeed, Mitt Romney made much of Perry's argument in his right-wing libertarian manifesto *Fed Up!* that Social Security was a "failure" and an "illegal Ponzi scheme," and might even be unconstitutional. It was, Perry had written, "by far the best example" of a program "violently tossing aside any respect for our founding principles."

Perry also questioned judicial interpretations of the Constitution's commerce clause that permitted "federal laws regulating the environment, regulating guns, protecting civil rights, establishing the massive programs and Medicare and Medicaid, creating national minimum wage laws, [and] establishing national labor laws." He even suggested that the direct election of United States senators had been a mistake because taking the power to pick senators away from the state legislatures had undermined states' rights. He had gone even further in 2009 when he declared: "We've got a great union. There's absolutely no reason to dissolve it. But, if Washington continues to thumb their nose at the American people, you know, who knows what might come out of that?" Secession had come back to life. Perry's campaign failed after a series of debate gaffes. But he, along with Paul, offered Tea Party thinking in its most unvarnished form.

The notion that Republicans believe in less government and lower taxes—and nothing more or less—is so ingrained that we often forget the Republican Party was not always defined this way, and neither was the tradition from which the party sprang. Once upon a time, the Republicans proudly and unabashedly constituted the party of national action.

So let us go a bit further back, to a 1964 book by a then prominent Republican named Jacob K. Javits. It's inconceivable today that a Republican would even consider expressing the views Javits put forward then.

New York's senior senator, it should be acknowledged, was unabashedly in the party's liberal wing—and it tells us something that liberal Republicans in those days embraced the words "liberal" and "progressive," feeling no need to retreat meekly behind the more anodyne moniker "moderate." In *Order of Battle: A Republican's Call to Reason*, Javits argued that his progressive views were more in keeping with his party's tradition than those of the then ascendant conservatives. He did so by explaining his "choice of ancestors," casting his political approach as standing in a direct line from Alexander Hamilton, Henry Clay, Abraham Lincoln, and Theodore Roosevelt. There was nothing eccentric about his view. Historians have usually traced the lineage of the Republican Party this way. Hamilton was a federalist devoted to a stronger national government. Clay started political life as a Jeffersonian Republican but became an ardent nationalist. Javits was right to argue that Clay "revitalized the federalist strain in the one-party politics of his day and made it the basis of the newly formed Whig Party." Lincoln, in turn, was an ardent follower of Clay and a loyal Whig who only reluctantly joined the new Republican Party after the collapse of his old party had become plain and the issue of slavery and its extension had been forced to the forefront of American politics by the Kansas-Nebraska Act. And Teddy Roosevelt was squarely in the Lincoln tradition and entered politics at a moment when the cult of Lincoln was strongest in the Republican Party and the country.

Javits then proceeded to offer brief intellectual biographies of his four heroes showing how each cut against the grain of the kind of conservatism he was battling inside his party in his day.

Because of "the loose and barren rule under the Articles of Confederation," Javits wrote, Hamilton came to understand the need for a strong federal government "free of the incubus of states' rights." Absolute power corrupts absolutely, but "Hamilton's experience with the semianarchic states' rights and individualism released by the Revolution brought home to him the reverse truth—that the absence of power can corrupt just as thoroughly as its overbearing presence." Javits offered lavish praise for Hamilton's 1791 *Report on Manufactures*, which foresaw a commercial and industrial future for the United States. "If published today," Javits said, "part of that report would find the Radical Right—and even some authentic 'conservatives'—anathematizing Hamilton as a 'left winger.'" In particular, he noted they would reject Hamilton's claim that "the inspection of manufacturers by agencies of government" was sanctioned by the Constitution's clause allowing Congress to regulate interstate commerce.

Javits found much to like in Henry Clay's "American System," which sought to use protective tariffs to build American manufacturing, and used the revenues from the tariffs for "internal improvements" in the form of roads and canals. Under Clay's leadership, Javits argued, the Whigs "had a coherent public-land policy, a coherent tariff policy, a coherent fiscal and monetary policy and a coherent policy on public education—all of which had as their point of departure and point of return the internal improvement of the American Commonwealth."

Lincoln is every Republican's hero, of course, and Javits quoted him extensively on the evils of slavery and the imperative of saving the Union. He stressed Lincoln's moderation in trying to balance these two objectives, noting that in trying to keep the Union together, Lincoln demanded that slavery not be extended to new territories even as he avoided calls for its immediate abolition in states where it already existed. Above all, Javits highlighted Lincoln's Clay-inspired commitment to national action in a host of areas. As Obama would often do more than four decades later, Javits cited Lincoln's classic defense of public action: "The legitimate object of government is to do for a community of people whatever they need to have done, but cannot do at all, or cannot so well do for themselves, in their separate and individual capacities." Javits went on to praise Lincoln's innovative uses of federal power through the Homestead Act, to provide free land for would-be farmers; the Morrill Act, which granted federal land to the states for the establishment of "agricultural and mechanical colleges"; and the creation of the National Academy of Sciences under a federal charter. Javits also noted approvingly the 1860 Republican Party platform's continuing commitment to internal improvements—which, the platform insisted, "are authorized by the Constitution"—and its pledge to "immediate and efficient aid" from the federal government to build a transcontinental railroad.

As for Theodore Roosevelt, he was the natural hero to liberal Republicans as the politician who embraced and popularized the word "progressive" while endorsing a far more expansive federal role in controlling monopolies, regulating the trusts, protecting the nation's natural resources, and conserving the environment. Javits noted both TR's critique of corporations ("artificial individuals called corporations, become so very big that the ordinary individual . . . cannot deal with them on terms of equality") and his relative sympathy for labor unions. He also cited, approvingly and at length, Roosevelt's 1910 "New Nationalism" speech, in many ways TR's most radical public address. Again, Obama would echo Javits in drawing on Roosevelt's example and inspiration in a December 2011 speech in Osawatomie, Kansas, the site of the original New Nationalism speech. "The citizens of the United States must effectively control the mighty commercial forces which they themselves called into being," Roosevelt had declared. "This, I know, implies a policy of far more active government interference with social and economic conditions in the country than we have yet had, but I think we have got to face the fact that such an increase in governmental control is now necessary."

It's worth remembering that *Order of Battle*, while on the whole genially written, was a shot fired in the war for the future of the Republican Party—a war Javits's side would lose within months of his book's publication. At the 1964 Republican National Convention in San Francisco's Cow Palace, the conservative forces gathered behind Barry Goldwater routed the moderate and liberal wings of the party and began the party's long march toward the anti-government right. Its culmination was reflected on that 2011 debate stage in New Hampshire—and on many more stages in the coming months—where there was no room for ideas even remotely approximating those Javits had championed nearly fifty years before.

At the very end of his book, Javits took Goldwater on directly, declaring that the conservatives' hero "tends to disconnect himself from, and would have others disconnect themselves from, the traditions of the Republican Party and its historic role in American life." Goldwater, he argued, had backed away from the "internal improvements" tradition of Hamilton, Clay, Lincoln, and TR by proposing to sell off the Tennessee Valley Authority (one of the New Deal's most extensive public planning endeavors), to make Social Security voluntary, and to weaken labor unions. Goldwater, he noted, also called the progressive income tax into question and opposed civil rights laws. And Javits was scalding when it came to the "Radical Right" in general and the John Birch Society in particular. The far right's political approach, he said, was "extremist" and not authentically conservative. "It is the rancorous enemy of the politics of civility that marks the authentic conservative temperament."

Goldwater would have none of this. When he finally secured the nomination, the likable but steely Arizonan did nothing to conciliate the wing of the party he had just defeated. On the contrary, in his acceptance speech on July 16, Goldwater signaled that the likes of Javits could just take a walk (an invitation, it turned out, that many of the more liberal Republicans, including Javits, were happy to accept). "Anyone who joins us in all sincerity, we welcome," Goldwater said. "Those who do not care for our cause, we don't expect to enter our ranks in any case."

Then, just to make things unambiguous, Goldwater took his famous stand on "extremism" and "moderation" by declaring: "And let our Republicanism, so focused and so dedicated, not be made fuzzy and futile by unthinking and stupid labels. I would remind you that extremism in the defense of liberty is no vice. And let me remind you also that moderation in the pursuit of justice is no virtue." The John Birch Society members who found themselves among Goldwater's delegates cheered wildly. The moderates and liberals sat in stunned, stony silence.

There was an odd affirmation later that night of Javits's sense of history and his fear that the Republican Party was abandoning the Hamilton-

Clay-Lincoln tradition of national action in favor of states' rights doctrines that had been advanced by Lincoln's enemies in the Deep South. Theodore H. White, the legendary chronicler of presidential elections, ended his account of the evening by recalling his last memory of a momentous day. "This reporter went to sleep in the darkness of the early morning after Goldwater's nomination, bothered by the victorious singing beneath his windows," White wrote in *The Making of the President 1964*. "The strains were familiar but cacophonous until he separated them. Some of the Goldwater jubilants were singing the 'Battle Hymn of the Republic' and others were singing 'Dixie.'" The song of Lincoln's enemies threatened to drown out the anthem of his friends.

The revolution in Republican thinking that Goldwater began that night in the Cow Palace continued apace. In the coming years, Republicans of Javits's persuasion would either leave the party or be purged by conservatives in primaries. Javits's turn came in 1980, when Ronald Reagan's election sealed the victory of the Goldwater revolution. Just two months before Reagan's triumph, Javits was defeated in a Republican primary by a conservative county official named Alphonse D'Amato, who went on to serve eighteen years in the Senate. Even in New York, the putative citadel of liberalism, a progressive Republican claiming the lineage of Hamilton, Clay, Lincoln, and Teddy Roosevelt could not survive.

II

The great transformation of the Republicans from the party of national action to the party of states' rights and a restricted view of what the Constitution allows the federal government to achieve is simultaneously well known and underappreciated.

The party's shift toward conservatism is certainly a given in our discourse. Javits himself conceded as much when he acknowledged in his book how often he was asked: "Isn't it illogical for you to be a Republican?" What's missed is how profound this shift in the Republican worldview actually was, how much of a break it represented from the party's history, and how radically the definition of what constitutes "conservatism" had changed and narrowed. Liberal though he was in conventional terms, Javits was not wrong to insist that the conservative's task in politics always involves "explaining why the complexities of existence stand in the way of utopian solutions to all problems, and why in so many hard cases the best we can hope for is a succession of provisional compromises or accommodations, subject to change as circumstances change." This is the conservatism of prudence and complexity that acknowledges human imperfection.

But I have offered Javits his say here for a larger reason. By emphasizing the ideas of Hamilton and Clay and their role in the early American story, his account underscores the flaws in currently popular historical understandings. Those understandings go something like this: The United States spent its first century or so after the Founding as a nation in which the federal government played an exceedingly limited role in public life. The Constitution was read as placing severe limits on government action. Economic life was left in the hands of individuals and entrepreneurs. Government "got out of the way" and let the market operate freely in a nation where individualism was the single, dominant American characteristic.

According to this view, it was only during the Progressive Era administrations of Theodore Roosevelt and Woodrow Wilson—and then, more dramatically, under Franklin Roosevelt's New Deal—that the federal government became an active player in American economic life. And it was only with the Supreme Court decisions of the later New Deal years and after that this rapid growth of government was sanctioned as constitutional. Not for nothing have judicial conservatives spoken of "the Constitution in exile," by which they mean the Constitution as it was understood before New Deal jurisprudence opened the way for federal power to exert itself.

As in most conventional accounts, this one is based on certain important truths. The Progressive and New Deal Eras *were* breakthroughs, as I will be arguing later. Progressives signaled this when they amended the Constitution to allow for an income tax, to provide for the direct popular election of senators—overturning the system of elections by state legislatures that was both elitist and deferential to states' rights—and also by extending the right to vote to women. The FDR years changed the country profoundly as the federal government assumed a much larger role in regulating the workings of banking and commerce and the relations between employers and employees. It also found itself being held ever more accountable for the economy's overall performance. Through Social Security, the federal government assumed a decisive role in protecting older Americans from poverty, and widows and orphans from penury. Unemployment insurance, public power, and rural electrification expanded government's writ. And so, most drastically, did all the exertions required to win the vast war against Hitler's Germany and imperial Japan. Harry Truman's Fair Deal built on the New Deal's achievements, notably by expanding Social Security to the program we now recognize. The Great Society went further still. Medicare and Medicaid were large down payments on Truman's hopes for a national health system. LBJ's War on Poverty and the civil rights bills were aimed at lifting up Americans who had not fully shared in the New Deal's bounty.

This is all true enough. What it misses is the extent to which government—including the federal government—was deeply involved in the American economy *from the beginning of the republic.* The very idea that there is a sharp and clear divide between "public" and "private" spheres was a creation not of the Founders but of Gilded Age Supreme Courts in the 1870s and 1880s. In the country's earlier years, the idea of mixed public-private corporations was common and taken for granted. Javits's brief history of the initiatives undertaken by Hamilton, Clay, and Lincoln is instructive precisely because it illustrates the many ways in which Americans looked to government at all levels for both economic innovation and relief from chronic social problems. The latest historical scholarship underscores how active the federal government was long before the arrival of the two Roosevelts. "So familiar is the historical narrative that pits America's conversion from nineteenth-century *laissez-faire* to twentieth-century big government that the multiple, well-noted exceptions to this familiar story have been ignored," wrote University of Virginia historian Brian Balogh in his breakthrough 2009 book, *A Government Out of Sight.*

The federal government's involvement with health care, for example, did not begin with Medicare or even with the public health initiatives of the Progressive Era. The Federal Marine Hospital System was created under a law signed by President John Adams in 1798. As Balogh points out, it "funded hospitals located throughout the nation to treat seamen who fell ill or were injured on the job," and the number of mariners treated grew from 4,000 in 1823 to 13,000 by 1858. It might be said that the nation instituted a program of socialized medicine for seamen just a decade after the ratification of the Constitution. Federal disaster relief was a common practice from the beginning of the republic, Balogh notes, and it was resisted only when southerners began fearing that federal assistance of this sort might provide "a precedent for national intervention on the slavery question." (It is a recurrent theme in American history: opposition to federal intervention on issues related to race leads to a wholesale attack on federal action in other spheres.) It is rarely noted, Balogh added, that Americans "who supposedly feared distant government subsidized a national postal service that dwarfed its European counterparts in its scope and capacity to carry news at bargain prices." As the communications scholar Richard John noted, "No other branch of the central government penetrated so deeply into the hinterland or played such a conspicuous role in shaping the pattern of everyday life."

Even at the peak of laissez-faire thinking during the Gilded Age, the federal government was engaged in a massive social welfare program that foreshadowed the enactment of Social Security, a fact that the historical sociologist Theda Skocpol brought to wider attention in her 1992 book *Protecting Soldiers and Mothers.* Our long-forgotten system of Civil War pensions was established in February 1862 and grew steadily as successive Congresses expanded access. By 1910, noted Larry DeWitt, a historian of Social Security, "about 28 percent of all men age 65 and older in the country were receiving Civil War pensions—making the pension system in effect a national retirement program for at least one major cohort of citizens." Another 300,000 widows, orphans, and other dependents "were also on the pension rolls at that point." In its peak cost year, 1894, "the Civil War pension system accounted for 37 percent of all federal expenditures." The Social Security program, by contrast, has never come close to that share. And even during the laissez-faire Gilded Age, government provided important support to railroad construction and protected private industries behind protective tariffs.

Balogh also points to one of the most sweeping actions ever undertaken by an American president—one, as it happens, who was deeply critical of federal power in principle. The Louisiana Purchase under Thomas

Jefferson doubled the size of the United States at the stroke of a pen (and with the expenditure of $11.5 million and the forgiveness of another $3.5 million in French debt). There "was little debate about the constitutionality of Jefferson's actions," Balogh wrote, even though in theory, "doubling the size of the republic through one executive action should have raised howls of protest from those who feared government consolidation." When they actually took the executive reins, Balogh noted, the Jeffersonians turned out to be "more amenable to using the latent authority of the federal government than they had been when not in power." George Will's dictum that "Americans talk like Jeffersonians but expect to be governed by Hamiltonians" seemed to apply to Jefferson himself.

Government activity and private endeavor were intermingled throughout our early history precisely because the stark division between public and private sectors that we now take as "normal" was not normal at all in the United States of that time. As Balogh notes, corporations in the early republic were "publicly crafted organizations granted special privileges in order to meet public service requirements." But the Supreme Court in the late nineteenth century sought "to establish strict boundaries between the public and private spheres" and turn corporations "into natural outcroppings of the economy, protected under the constitution from state interference with Fourteenth Amendment due process rights."

"Although most historical accounts extrapolate America's modern history from its supposed *laissez-faire* origins in the Gilded Age," Balogh argues, "no period in America's history was *less* representative of America's past than the brief era that stretched from the end of Reconstruction in 1877 through the panic of 1893." We assume that the Gilded Age's highly individualistic notions of property defined by a sharp distinction between public and private were with us from the very beginning. They were not.

As Michael Sandel has noted, economic arguments before the Gilded Age were largely republican in character. They stressed a common good, not just laissez-faire. Describing the contest between Democrats and the Whigs in the Jacksonian era, Sandel wrote: "In different ways, both parties shared Jefferson's conviction that the economic life of the nation should be judged for its capacity to cultivate in citizens the qualities of character that self-government requires."

True, Sandel noted, by the 1830s "few assumed, as Jefferson once did, that the agrarian life was the only way to civic competence. But even as the parties turned their attention to the national bank, protective tariffs, land policy and internal improvements, both Democrats and Whigs retained contact with the formative ambition of the republican tradition."

Contemporary conservatives are certainly not wrong in seeing enterprise and individual achievement as cornerstones of the early American republic. The Jeffersonians and the Federalists, the Jacksonian Democrats and the Whigs celebrated both, albeit in different ways, on behalf of different constituencies, and toward different policy ends. What today's conservatives overlook is that these were not the only values, or even the primary values, that our republic celebrated, and that government—at the federal, state, and local levels—was an active agent in promoting national development and shared prosperity. To believe otherwise, they need to wish both Alexander Hamilton and Henry Clay out of existence.

III

Conservatives are fond of quoting *The Federalist* as an almost infallible guide to national self-understanding. They are especially fond of citing Federalist 10, which stressed the importance of "curing the mischiefs of faction," and Federalist 51, on the importance of checks and balances. They are less given to citing Federalist 27, Hamilton's call for a robust federal government that touched the lives of individual citizens. Hamilton understood human nature and believed that unless the new national government became part of everyday life, it would either wither away or be sustained only through the use of brute force.

Thus, he argued in Federalist 27 that "the more the operations of the national authority are intermingled in the ordinary exercise of government, the more the citizens are accustomed to meet with it in the common occurrences of their political life, the more it is familiarized to their sight and to their feelings, the further it enters into those objects which touch the most sensible chords and put in motion the most active springs of the human heart, the greater will be the probability that it will conciliate the respect and attachment of the community." Hamilton continued:

Man is very much a creature of habit. A thing that rarely strikes his senses will generally have but little influence upon his mind. A government continually at a distance and out of sight can hardly be expected to interest the sensations of the people. The inference is, that the authority of the Union, and the affections of the citizens towards it, will be strengthened, rather than weakened, by its extension to what are called matters of internal concern; and will have less occasion to recur to force, in proportion to the familiarity and comprehensiveness of its agency. The more it circulates through those channels and currents in which the passions of mankind naturally flow, the less will it require the aid of the violent and perilous expedients of compulsion.

This is not a vision of the national government as merely "an agent for the states," as Rick Perry would claim, nor is it consonant with a national authority that would simply "leave us alone," the anti-tax activist Grover Norquist's favorite slogan. Hamilton favored a national government that would be "intermingled in the ordinary exercise of government" and be engaged in "matters of internal concern." Today, you might say that he saw the federal government as a partner and a problem solver.

The battles between Hamilton and Jefferson over federal authority and states' rights during George Washington's presidency revealed differences not only over philosophy and policy but also over the proper interpretation of the Constitution the nation had just adopted. For those who insist that originalism is an easy matter of discovering the Founders' intentions and applying them, one of the earliest battles in our democracy should give pause. Within just three years of the Constitution's ratification, two of its leading authors and interpreters, Hamilton and James Madison, were deeply at odds over Hamilton's proposal to create a national bank.

Hamilton put forward the idea for a bank in a report to Congress on December 14, 1790. As Gordon Wood notes, Hamilton's "bold and novel" plan called for a bank that would be capitalized at $10 million, "which was far more than all the specie, that is, gold and silver, in the country." A fifth of the capital would come from the government, the rest from stock that would be sold to private investors. Thus did the new republic begin its long experience with public-private partnerships. Investors could "pay for up to three-fourths of the shares with government securities," a way of liquidating the nation's debt. In what might be seen as our earliest argument over the merits of a gold standard, Hamilton wanted notes from the Bank of the United States to become "the principal circulating medium of money for a society that lacked an adequate supply of gold and silver coin." Only "a fraction of their worth was available in specie at any one time," which made even some Federalists nervous. John Adams worried that "every dollar of a bank bill that is issued beyond the value of gold and silver in the vaults, represents nothing, and is therefore a cheat upon somebody." (One can imagine Ron Paul citing Adams approvingly.)

Wood pointed to the great shortcoming of Hamilton's design, which would prove to be a larger problem in the Federalist worldview. The bank "would make money available only to large merchants and others who wanted short-term loans, ninety days or less." This, as Wood noted, reflected "Hamilton's insensitivity to the entrepreneurial needs of . . . ordinary farmers and small businessmen" and suggested "how little he and other Federalists appreciated the real sources of the capitalist future of America." A basic elitism would always be a difficulty for Hamiltonians and, later, for many Whigs, however visionary their programs.

But Hamilton's proposal *was* both visionary and imaginative—and it was too much for Madison. He "launched a passionate attack," Wood wrote, arguing "that the bank bill was a misguided imitation of England's monarchical practice of concentrating wealth and influence in the metropolitan capital, and, more important, that it was an unconstitutional assertion of federal power. The Constitution, he claimed, did not expressly grant the federal government the authority to charter a bank." Within Washington's cabinet, Thomas Jefferson, the secretary of state, and Edmund Randolph, the attorney general, sided with Madison.

Washington asked Hamilton to reply to his critics. Wood's description of Hamilton's argument is profoundly enlightening, since Hamilton struck chords that can still be heard in our time. Hamilton, said Wood,

> carefully refuted the arguments of Randolph and Jefferson and
> made a powerful case for a broad construction of the Constitution

that resounded through subsequent decades of American history. He argued that Congress's authority to charter a bank was implied by the clause in Article I, Section 8 of the Constitution that gave Congress the right to make all laws "necessary and proper" to carry out its delegated powers. Without such implied powers, Hamilton wrote, "the United States would furnish the singular spectacle of a *political society* without *sovereignty*, or of a people *governed* without *government*." That may have been Jefferson's ideal, but it was not Washington's. On February 25, 1791, the president signed the bank bill into law.

The fight over the bank involved the first shots fired in the creation of a new party system. Jefferson "began urging friends to support the agricultural interest and pure 'republicanism' against the 'stock-jobbers' in Congress." Madison accused Hamilton's supporters of being not only "speculators" but also "Tories," a loaded word so soon after the Revolution.

The project for which Hamilton is best known, even though it had less immediate significance in his time, was the *Report on Manufactures*, so admired by Javits, issued on December 5, 1791. Hamilton has since come to be regarded as a prophet for understanding that the future of the United States lay in manufacturing and that a nation could not be great, either in wealth or in political influence, if it remained reliant solely on agriculture. Jeffersonian Republicans were genuinely fearful that transforming the country from a land of independent yeoman farmers to one dominated by manufacturing employees would be less hospitable to republican virtue and self-rule. So Hamilton shrewdly insisted that the health of agriculture and the health of manufacturing went hand in hand, despite perceptions to the contrary. "Particular encouragements of particular manufactures may be of a Nature to sacrifice the interests of landholders to those of manufacturers," he wrote; "but it is nevertheless a maxim well established by experience, and generally acknowledged, where there has been sufficient experience, that the aggregate prosperity of manufactures, and the aggregate prosperity of Agriculture are intimately connected."

The encouragement of manufacturing, he argued, would lead to a healthier economy because it would be diversified. "When all the different kinds of industry obtain in a community, each individual can find his proper element, and can call into activity the whole vigour of his nature," Hamilton argued.

But he did not make the case for manufacturing on abstract grounds alone. In the world as it was, European nations were encouraging their own manufacturing while hoping that the United States would be confined to agriculture. Hamilton asked what would happen if Europe eventually closed itself off to American farm products. If European nations were organizing closed markets, the United States was required to do the same:

> The regulations of several countries, with which we have the most extensive intercourse, throw serious obstructions in the way of the principal staples of the United States. In such a position of things, the United States cannot exchange with Europe on equal terms; and the want of reciprocity would render them the victim of a system, which should induce them to confine their views to Agriculture and refrain from Manufactures . . . If Europe will not take from us the products of our soil, upon terms consistent with our interest, the natural remedy is to contract as fast as possible our wants of her.

Hamilton proposed to turn the United States into a manufacturing nation through extensive intervention in the marketplace:

> Certain nations grant bounties on the exportation of particular commodities, to enable their own workmen to undersell and supplant all competitors, in the countries to which those commodities are sent. Hence the undertakers of a new manufacture have to contend not only with the natural disadvantages of a new undertaking, but with the gratuities and remunerations which other governments bestow. To be enabled to contend with success, it is evident, that the interference and aid of their own government are indispensable.

The historian John C. Miller described the assistance Hamilton was prepared to extend to promote manufacturing as "calculated to stir the blood of even the most lethargic and self-satisfied businessman." Hamilton proposed "protective tariffs; bounties for the establishment of new industries; premiums for improvements in quality; awards for the encouragement of inventions, particularly labor-saving machinery; and exemptions from duty of essential raw materials imported from abroad." If this sounds like industrial policy, eighteenth-century style, it was. And Hamilton was unapologetic. "In countries where there is great private wealth, much may be effected by the voluntary contributions of patriotic individuals," he wrote, "but in a community situated like that of the United States, the public purse must supply the deficiency of private resource. In what can it be so useful, as in prompting and improving the efforts of industry?"

There were limits to what Hamilton's *Report on Manufactures* achieved during his time as Treasury secretary, as Gordon Wood has noted. Nonetheless, his *Report* was prophetic. It was a guide for policy makers in the Whig Party and among Republicans before the Great Depression. Both Progressives and New Dealers looked back to Hamilton's methods with approval, even if their ends were different—and even if Democrats such as FDR continued to proclaim themselves heirs to Jefferson. And our first Treasury Secretary was right on his central points: turning the United States into a manufacturing giant did ultimately turn the nation into a power with global influence; and government action was essential to securing this end.

Hamilton's experience makes clear that arguments over the federal government's role in our national development did not suddenly break out in the 1910s, 1930s, or 1960s. Government economic intervention on behalf of a common or national good has long been viewed as legitimate, even if it has almost always been contested. It's instructive that within just a few years of the adoption of the Constitution, its very authors were engaged in a high-stakes contest over what its words actually meant. It might be said that the originators of the Constitution were not themselves originalists, since they did not pretend to share a common understanding of what all of its provisions implied.

I V

What Hamilton started, Henry Clay continued. Clay, the three-time presidential candidate, Speaker of the House, secretary of state, and United

States senator, graced American politics for forty-nine years, winning his first election, to the Kentucky state legislature, at age twenty-six. He was controversial in his day. Andrew Jackson called his main adversary "the Judas of the West" and a "profligate demagogue." John Quincy Adams, his ally at many moments, called Clay "essentially a gamester" in his political and private lives. But Abraham Lincoln revered him as a political idol. When he eulogized the man in 1852, Lincoln saw in Clay virtues he hoped Americans would later see in him. Clay's lack of formal education, Lincoln said, "teaches that in this country, one can scarcely be so poor, but that, if he *will*, he *can* acquire sufficient education to get through the world respectably." Clay died at 11:17 A.M. on June 29, 1853. "The telegraph made the news of Clay's death instant and therefore indelible," wrote his biographers David S. Heidler and Jeanne T. Heidler. "Only hours passed before cities from Maine to Missouri began draping themselves in crepe and men from Savannah to St. Louis began pulling on black armbands. Washington, already slowed by summer's heat, came to a halt. President Millard Fillmore shut down the government, and Congress immediately adjourned."

Clay's importance, so obvious in 1853, is largely lost to us. Only recently have we begun paying attention to him again. Robert V. Remini, the great chronicler of the age of Jackson, noted that his *Henry Clay: Statesman for the Union*, published in 1991, was the first "modern, scholarly biography" of Clay in fifty years. Clay also received recognition in Merrill D. Peterson's *The Great Triumvirate*, a collective biography of Clay, Daniel Webster, and John C. Calhoun, published in 1987. The Heidlers' biography came out in 2010, to considerable acclaim.

This contemporary rediscovery of Clay may speak to our moment's longing for politicians capable of reaching compromises. The 1820 Missouri Compromise and the Compromise of 1850 both postponed—though could not permanently forestall—the nation's day of reckoning over slavery. But Clay's confidence in the federal government's capacity to bind and build the nation is also a tonic at this moment of doubt about collective action.

Many politicians have offered programs with catchy titles. We have seen New, Fair, and Square Deals, a New Frontier, a New Freedom, and a Great Society. Only Clay had the audacity to name his program the *Amer-*

ican System. It offered, Remini wrote, "a vision of progress," and "a bold reformulation of the relationship between government and society." The American System, Peterson wrote, "was not so much a philosophy seeking embodiment in public policy as it was a set of policies, with distinct interests behind them, seeking the dignity of a philosophy." He added:

> Yet the ideas, whatever their sources, were important. Viewed as a theory of political economy, the American System disputed the fundamental "free market" premises of the classical school. It believed that a youthful economy, like the American, required the fostering hand of government; it believed a republican government responsive to the interests of the people ought to promote employment, productivity, and wealth; it believed that national government, in particular, should assume a positive role in opening up promising lines of economic growth in advance of market forces. . . . In the philosophy of the American System, national wealth was an aggregate interest, paramount to the interests of individuals or of other nations; and in the United States its prospects were wonderful to behold.

Michael F. Holt, the author of the most comprehensive recent history of the Whig Party, described the party's program in words that applied precisely to Clay, the party's chief ideologist. The Whigs achieved their greatest political success, Holt wrote, when they invoked "the commonwealth tradition of using the state actively for the benefit of the people." Holt also rescues Clay from the claim of his enemies (and some of his friends) that he was merely trying to revive the old elitist Federalist Party. On the contrary, Holt insists, Clay married Jeffersonian Republican principles to a nationalist economic agenda.

"Of all major figures in American political history," wrote Daniel Walker Howe in *The Political Culture of the American Whigs*, "Clay had the most systematic and multifaceted program. If he had been able to implement it (that is, if he had been as capable a politician as he was an ideologist) he would have changed the course of United States history in the nineteenth century." Adoption of Clay's program would have created "much more precedent for government intervention in the economy and for planned response to social problems in general."

The very name "American System," Howe notes, was designed to distinguish "Clay's economic nationalism from the 'British system' of laissez-faire." There is an irony here in light of the United States' present-day association with laissez-faire, particularly as it is seen from developing countries. Third World nations often bridle at American free-market prescriptions as they seek their own paths for development, just as Clay did for the United States.

The American System's first plank involved federal spending for "internal improvements," the roads and canals the new nation required to bind it together. In January 1824, Clay rose in the House to defend a bill appropriating $30,000 for a survey of those roads and canals the president might deem militarily or commercially essential. At issue then, as it had been earlier with Hamilton and the Bank of the United States, was whether such a proposal was constitutional. Clay argued that the constitutional mandate authorizing the creation of the post office was enough to justify spending on roads. As Remini nicely summarized his argument: "Mails imply roads; roads imply their preservation; their preservation implies the power to repair them."

Clay also insisted that if the Constitution's grant of power to the federal government to regulate commerce had "any meaning," it surely implied "the power to foster it, to promote it, to bestow on it facilities similar to those which have been conceded to our foreign trade . . . All the powers of this government should be interpreted in reference to its first, its best, its greatest object, the union of these States."

Clay even anticipated an innovation that Richard Nixon was to sponsor more than a century later—and that Barack Obama would make part of his stimulus plan. "Before long," writes Howe, "Clay figured out how to circumvent the scruples of the strict constructionists. He hit upon the device of revenue-sharing, or, as he called it, 'distribution' of federal money to the states for specified purposes. This would have the added benefit of forestalling the state bankruptcies and repudiation of bonds that were playing havoc with investors at the time."

A second part of Clay's system was a protective tariff to spur the development of American industry. As Remini noted, its purpose was "not simply the protection of specific items to assist certain industries or particular raw materials. For Clay the tariff was a means of assisting all sections and classes through the dynamics of increased national wealth and power benefiting all Americans and uniting them in a common purpose and identity." Remini saw Clay as offering nothing short of "a planned national economy responsive to the new industrial age that had just begun to emerge within the United States."

Clay echoed Hamilton on the impact of Europe's policies on the United States, Speaking in 1824, he declared: "The policy of Europe refuses to receive from us any thing but those raw materials of smaller value, essential to their manufactures, to which they can give a higher value, with the exception of tobacco and rice, which they cannot produce." And he was reproachful of those who insisted that the government lacked the authority to do what he saw as necessary:

> Is there no remedy within the reach of the government? Are we doomed to behold our industry languish and decay yet more and more? But there is a remedy, and that remedy consists in modifying our foreign policy, and in adopting a genuine AMERICAN SYSTEM. We must naturalize the arts in our country, and we must naturalize them by the only means which the wisdom of nations has yet discovered to be effective—by adequate protection against the otherwise overwhelming influence of foreigners.

Clay underscored this point by distinguishing between political and economic freedom. "The truth is, and it is in vain to disguise it, that we are a sort of independent colonies of England—politically free, commercially slaves." And Clay was disdainful of those who said the Constitution did not authorize protective tariffs. "This constitution must be a singular instrument!" he declared. "It seems to be made for any other people than our own."

Two other components rounded out the Clay program: the sale of government-held western lands to settlers to finance his internal improvement plans, and the maintenance of a strong Bank of the United States. As

Sean Wilentz points out in his monumental political history *The Rise of American Democracy*, Clay, like other "commercially oriented Republicans," had "opposed recharter" of Hamilton's bank in 1811 "on the grounds that the national bank unfairly constrained the operations of state banks, which had proliferated throughout the country." Clay later became its champion. The Bank of the United States was consistent with Clay's national vision, but there was also political opportunism in Clay's decision to pick a fight with Jackson over rechartering the bank in the presidential election year of 1832, when Clay was Jackson's main opponent. Clay was confident he had a winning issue. "Should Jackson veto it," Clay proclaimed, "I shall veto him!" As Remini noted, Clay's move "was a blatant act of political self-interest."

And it misfired badly. Jackson swept the election, crushing Clay in the Electoral College 219–49. Clay had one more try at the presidency, in 1844, when he lost narrowly to James K. Polk. He would die disappointed in his failure to achieve his larger political ambition. Yet he and the Whig Party, of which he was the foremost figure, bequeathed the country a powerful political legacy. Daniel Walker Howe offered this epitaph to the Whigs:

> The common characterization of this period as "the age of Jackson" has obscured the contribution of the Whigs. Yet, as economic modernizers, as supporters of strong national government, and as humanitarians more receptive than their rivals to talent regardless of race or gender, the Whigs deserve to be remembered. They facilitated the transformation of the United States from a collection of parochial agricultural communities into a cosmopolitan nation integrated by commerce, industry, information, and voluntary associations as well as by political ties. From the vantage point of the twenty-first century, we can see that the Whigs, though not the dominant party of their own time, were the party of America's future.

V

My account here, though sympathetic in large part, is not intended as a "vote" for Hamilton or Clay, for the Federalists or the Whigs. Writing about history that way is foolish in any event. "I don't believe that historians should take sides with contestants of the past, whether Anti-Federalists versus Federalists or Republicans versus Federalists," Gordon Wood argued in introducing his recent book *The Idea of America*. "The responsibility of the historian, it seems to me, is not to decide who in the past was right or who was wrong but to explain why the different contestants thought and behaved as they did."

Indeed, a twenty-first-century progressive choosing to side unreservedly with Hamilton and Clay would be required to ignore fundamental issues at stake in the republic's early years. Within both Federalism and the more conservative wing of Whiggery lurked a profound resistance to the democratization of society and powerful strains of elitism. It fell to their opponents among the Anti-Federalists, the Jeffersonians, and the Jacksonians to make America more democratic—and the democrats largely won. Over time, as Wood notes, the Federalists were required to abandon aristocratic ideas in favor of "popular and democratic rhetoric." This rhetorical shift became a substantive concession to a far more democratic approach to politics.

Similarly, the political energy behind the Jacksonian movement came in large part from the energy of the middle classes, the yeoman, and a rising working class opposed to economic dominance by the financiers and merchants of Philadelphia, New York, and Boston. As is usually the case in elections, such class dynamics do not explain everything. Howe has noted sharp differences in party support along religious lines, with a rising, reformist evangelical movement in the North being central to the rise of Whiggery. ("If the Church of England was the Tory party at prayer," he wrote, "the Whig party in the United States was in many ways the evangelical united front at the polling place.") And revisionist historians have argued that both the Jacksonians and the Whigs were at heart parties of capitalism representing different wings of the business class.

Yet the democratizing character of the Jacksonian movement is unmistakable. Jackson's rhetoric in his bank veto message was a plain appeal to the nation's egalitarian ethos that today's critics of Wall Street might echo:

Equality of talents, of education, or of wealth can not be produced by human institutions. In the full enjoyment of the gifts of Heaven and the fruits of superior industry, economy, and virtue, every man is equally entitled to protection by law; but when the laws undertake to add to these natural and just advantages artificial distinctions, to grant titles, gratuities, and exclusive privileges, to make the rich richer and the potent more powerful, the humble members of society, the farmers, mechanics, and laborers who have neither the time nor the means of securing like favors to themselves, have a right to complain of the injustice of their Government.

Thurlow Weed, the gifted Whig political maestro, saw the bank veto message as allowing the Democrats "to enlist the laboring classes against a 'monster bank' or 'moneyed aristocracy.'" The surest proof of the Jacksonians' success in democratizing American politics was the extent to which the Whigs, disdainful at first of mass party politics, came to imitate their opposition's democratic ways. They did so with near perfection in their 1840 "Tippecanoe and Tyler, Too" campaign, routing Martin Van Buren, Jackson's successor and the master builder of his political organization. One Whig campaigner who acknowledged how the Democrats' approach to elections had transformed the Whigs was a young Abraham Lincoln. "*They* set us the example of organization," Lincoln said, "and we, in self-defense, are driven to it." Or, as the historian Harry L. Watson observed, "paradoxically . . . the Whigs fought to establish their vision of a properly hierarchical society by using fervently egalitarian rhetoric." Sean Wilentz is surely right in seeing "the flawed Jackson Democracy" as the successor to the Jeffersonians in being "the largest vehicle for expanding democracy." They were organized "as a movement of reform to eliminate a perceived recrudescence of privilege" and "created a new kind of political party, more egalitarian in its institutions and its ideals than any that had preceded it, unabashed in its disciplined pursuit of power, dedicated to securing the sovereignty that, as its chief architect Martin Van Buren observed, 'belongs inalienably to the people.'"

Yet the ambiguities of the age of Jackson do not stop there. The Whigs have gotten a better run from historians in recent years, as historical studies have focused more and more on race and gender than they did in the Roosevelt era. If the Jacksonians were the party championing class equality among white men, the Whigs (and before them the Federalists) paid more heed to equalities of race and gender—even if, by our contemporary standards, very imperfectly. "Throughout the South, the Whigs showed significantly less enthusiasm for the expansion of slavery than the Democrats," Howe noted. "In the North, Whigs, who tended to accept social differentiation, could easily adopt a condescending paternalism toward nonwhites. Ironically, the Democrats' great insistence on the natural equality of all white men prompted them to make a more glaring exception of non-whites. Taking seriously the motto 'all men are created equal,' Democrats called into question the very humanity of nonwhites in order to keep them unequal." And while the Whigs were hardly protofeminists, they were more open than the Jacksonians to women's education and began including women in their campaigns in 1840—even if, as the historian Harry L. Watson notes, their presence also reflected "the burgeoning cult of domesticity." Wilentz observes that "by the time of the 1844 election, Whig women would speak regularly at rallies and hold their own meetings." The Whigs, on the whole, opposed the brutality of Jackson's program of Indian removal—again, an indication of the peculiar interaction between race and class in the politics of the period. The Jacksonian policies were aimed at providing land for landless white men; the Whigs, less egalitarian in class terms, were more humanitarian in the treatment of native people.

And the politics of the period make clear that states' rights doctrines have always had an intimate connection to the politics of race. This is true not just in the obvious sense, that southern conservatives invoked the rights of states to protect slavery (and, later, segregation). More important, fear that *any* expansion of federal power would eventually allow Washington to abolish slavery led the southern defenders of bondage to oppose national initiatives, including the internal improvements championed by Clay. Two years after he was defeated for reelection, John Quincy Adams was elected to Congress, and he spent the last seventeen years of his life as a brave and consequential member of the House. An ardent foe of slavery and a proponent of federal action, Adams explained to his constituents why slavery's defenders opposed internal improvements:

> If the internal improvement of the country should be left to the
> management of the federal government, and the proceeds of the sale

of public lands should be applied as a perpetual and self-accumulating fund for that purpose, the blessings unceasingly showered upon the people by this process would so grapple the affections of the people to the national authority that it would, in the process of time, overshadow that of state governments, and settle the preponderancy of power in the free states; and then the undying worm of conscience twinges with terror for the fate of *the peculiar institution.* Slavery stands aghast at the prospective promotion of the general welfare.

Nathaniel Macon, a stout defender of slavery from North Carolina, succinctly corroborated Adams's point when he declared: "If Congress can make canals, it can with more propriety emancipate."

In one sense, the Whigs are very familiar to today's progressives. They can be seen, as the historian Lee Benson has suggested, as advocates of "the positive liberal state" whose aim was "to promote the general welfare, raise the level of opportunity for all men, and aid all individuals to develop their full potentialities." The Jacksonians, by contrast, favored "the negative liberal state" that left people free to pursue their own ends.

The Whigs were certainly institution builders in ways that today's progressives can only admire. As Watson noted, the Whigs "lent active government support to a wide range of useful or benevolent private enterprises: banks; corporations; transportation projects; public hospitals; prisons; institutions for the blind, the deaf, and the insane; public schools; and temperance crusades."

While there is something to Benson's view, its problem, as Howe has argued, is that it makes the Whigs sound "too much like twentieth-century liberals." Whig policies "did not have the object of redistributing wealth or diminishing the influence of the privileged." Although they were innovative, the Whigs "usually thought of themselves as conservatives, as custodians of an identifiable political and cultural heritage."

And the Whigs were deeply associated with evangelical religion and with projects—including temperance—aimed at improving the moral lives of individuals. What most profoundly separates Whiggery from today's liberalism were the Whigs' "moral absolutism, their paternalism, and their concern with imposing discipline." The Whigs may have been the most purely communitarian party in our country's history, drawing on our republican and biblical traditions to promote both public improvement and self-improvement. "Though they championed the opportunities of the marketplace as the ideal vehicles of self-improvement," Watson wrote, "they looked to family and faith for the moral inspiration that would lift the pursuit of wealth above the sordid level of mere greed."

There are lessons from the Whigs for today's conservatives and liberals alike. The linking of politics to religious faith that became common after the rise of the Christian conservative movement in the late 1970s and early 1980s is often seen as a profound break with a long tradition of church-state separation. But the Whigs demonstrate that strong religious and evangelical impulses have played a central role in our politics since at least the 1830s. Separation of church and state is not the same as the separation of religion from politics, and the Whigs' unapologetic moralism would be quite congenial to many religious conservatives of our era.

But today's religious right might also note that the Whigs did not confine their moralizing efforts to personal behavior. Their calls for more compassionate treatment of the blind, the deaf, and the insane and the expansion of public education and public hospitals all entailed public action, including government spending, aimed at giving substance to their talk about morality. And as time went on, evangelicals joined with less religious radicals in slowly moving the North's political center against slavery. In some cases, the evangelicals *were* the radicals. When the personal becomes political, it cannot successfully remain personal for long. When individual piety and private moral commitments spill over into social action, the work of community building begins.

In a certain sense, it is heartening that our current political debate, which seems so savage and so resistant to compromise, would in many respects feel familiar to those on opposite sides of politics in the era before the Civil War. We have been arguing since the beginning of the republic over what the Constitution does and does not allow the federal government to do and also over government involvement in the marketplace, federal spending on "internal improvements," and federal intervention in the affairs of the states. Our partisan traditions have crisscrossed each other.

Contemporary Democrats can claim in good conscience to be true to the egalitarian traditions of Jefferson and Jackson even as they endorse Hamiltonian and Whiggish notions of federal action on the economy, education, health care, and welfare. It is no wonder that Franklin Roosevelt came to be associated with the prescription of the Progressive Era prophet Herbert Croly that the nation needed to employ Hamiltonian means to Jeffersonian ends. FDR and his successors have been, like Hamilton and Clay, nation builders. But their nation building was always influenced by Jacksonian egalitarianism.

Republicans and conservatives can look back with sympathy toward Clay and Hamilton's projects of promoting American business and defending the legitimacy of existing economic hierarchies. Like Clay and Hamilton, they believe that the prosperity of the well-off will spill over and enrich the rest of the nation. Yet since their remedy involves a smaller federal government, conservative Republicans draw regularly on the rhetoric of Jefferson and Jackson. One might say they are using Jeffersonian means to Hamiltonian ends.

Above all, the history of the early republic reminds us that so many of the commonplace assertions in our current discourse are simply wrong. The idea that the Constitution leaves room for substantial government action in the marketplace and in the affairs of the states is not a novel concept invented by twentieth-century progressives or liberal jurists. Clay, Hamilton, and their allies battled fiercely on behalf of a robust federal government authorized to intervene in the nation's economic life by the very commerce clause that New Dealers and latter-day progressives would cite so often. The opponents of the Hamilton-Clay project were just as fierce in insisting on its unconstitutionality, the same claim made by conservatives in the New Deal era and today. But the partisans in our earlier fights were more candid about what they were doing. They accepted that in the new republic, battles over policies and battles over the Constitution elided into each other. They were arguing, after all, about a document many of them had shaped, and which all of them knew they were shaping still. In our day, those who cry about the constitutionality of particular programs reach back into a murky past and insist that its lessons and strictures are far clearer than they are. They pretend that there were no fundamental disagreements among the founders or in the generations that immediately followed them. Alexander Hamilton and Henry Clay—and Thomas Jefferson and Andrew Jackson—would tell them otherwise.

And both the Whigs and the Jacksonians operated within a republican tradition that took for granted the idea that public life and private economic life interacted with each other in a dynamic way. They did not see market economics as the sole or even primary determinant of the common good. "Although Jacksonians and Whigs did invoke arguments about economic growth and distributive justice," wrote Michael Sandel, "these considerations figured less as ends in themselves than as means to competing visions of a self-governing republic." The devotion of the Whigs to an activist, nationalist, and republican conception of economics is obvious enough in Clay's American System. As Sandel argues, "The Whig case for promoting economic development had less to do with increasing the standard of living or maximizing consumption than with cultivating national community and strengthening the bonds of the union."

But the Jacksonians were no less committed to republicanism. Their fear of the Whigs' hierarchical development schemes, Sandel observed, was rooted in worries over "the threat to self-government posed by large concentrations of wealth and power." And the more radical among the Jacksonians cultivated a strong sense of community among the laboring men of the nation's cities, particularly in New York. As Michael H. Frisch and Daniel J. Walkowitz argued, "republican ideology served perhaps longer than any other dimension of American culture as a legitimization of working-class values . . . [and] a bulwark against the corrosive power of capitalism." The early workingmen's associations, wrote Harry Watson, defended "a republican vision that stressed the centrality of labor in defending the common good, and the need for mutual respect . . . of all interests in society, masters and journeymen joined together in craft associations to assert their common role in public life." In his classic book *The Jacksonian Persuasion*, Marvin Meyers pointed to the great paradox that while Jackson's followers "cleared the path for the triumph of laissez-faire capitalism and its culture in America," they "held nevertheless in their conscience an image of a chaste republican order, resisting the seductions of risk and novelty, greed and extravagance, rapid motion and complex dealings."

VI

I have laid heavy stress on the stories of Hamilton, Clay, and the arguments of their time to underscore that in the republican tradition to which both the Whigs and the Jacksonians sought to be faithful, the lines between the public and private sectors were neither as clear nor as sharp as they are today. This is important because what advocates of laissez-faire and radical individualism claim as the "American way" does not go back to the country's origins. It was an innovation of the 1870s, 1880s, and 1890s.

As the historian Sidney Fine has noted, it was in the "period between Appomattox and the accession of Theodore Roosevelt to the presidency, in 1901," that "laissez-faire was championed in America as it never was before and has never been since." Conservative individualists are thus trying to convert a 35-year interlude into the norm for 235 years of American history. Brian Balogh is persuasive in seeing the Gilded Age, which gave birth to the nation's great corporations, as unusual both in the intellectual influences that held sway in society and in the legal theories put forth by the era's Supreme Court. Both were enormously influenced by the social Darwinism of Herbert Spence and William Graham Sumner, which extended the idea of "survival of the fittest" into social and economic life. One reason for the great Populist William Jennings Bryan's objection to Darwinism in general was his proper moral revulsion at social Darwinism in particular.

The Supreme Court, under the intellectual leadership of Justice Stephen J. Field, pioneered theories that today's economic libertarians now revere. As Balogh explains, Field "insisted that restraining government action in spheres best left to the market would ensure the integrity of both public and private spheres." This truly was judicial activism, since "the very effort to parse private and public was itself an historic intervention into social relations by the court, and a groundbreaking expansion of the national judiciary's penetration into matters previously left to state and local government."

Two decisions in particular marked a jarring break from the old republicanism. In its 1886 *Santa Clara v. Southern Pacific Railroad* decision, the Court held that "corporations are persons within the meaning of the Fourteenth Amendment." This extended unprecedented rights to corpora-

tions (which would have horrified rank-and-file Jacksonians) and vastly restricted the ability of government to regulate what the corporations did
(which would have bothered many activist Whigs). As Balogh writes, the
decision left public concerns in "a distinctly subordinate position" to private concerns. And in the 1905 *Lochner* decision, the justices invalidated a
New York labor law that limited the workday of bakers to ten hours. The
Court, as Balogh wrote, "rejected the argument that unequal bargaining
strength justified state interference with the sacred freedom of contract
principle." *Lochner* was effectively overturned by the Supreme Court in
1937, but we are still living with the strange doctrine of corporations as
persons, as the *Citizens United* case so recently reminded us.

Another sign that the Gilded Age, not the Founding period, had become the true north of conservatives in the second decade of the twenty-
first century was that *Lochner* had became the object of what George Will
called "a robust new defense" during the Obama years. Will cheered this
development, arguing that *Lochner* was "the liberals' least favorite decision because its premises pose a threat to their aspiration, which is to provide an emancipation proclamation for regulatory government." He added:
"The rehabilitation of *Lochner* is another step in the disarmament of such
thinking."

The *Lochner* and *Santa Clara* decisions were more, however, than
a blow to progressive liberalism. They were also a departure from a much
older American republicanism. They represented, as the historian James
Kloppenberg argued, "the eventual replacement of ethics by economics in
liberalism."

"Although vestiges of civic humanism continued to surface in the
rhetoric of Jacksonians chastising corruption, Whigs clamoring for order,
and Republicans denouncing slavery," he wrote, "the ideal of the virtuous
republic was sacrificed in exchange for the 'main chance.'"

Yet almost as soon as the United States had broken with the republican tradition, the country began to sense what it had lost. Those who organized against this counterrevolution worked under many labels, but they
ultimately came to be known as Populists. And if we are now confronting the reemergence of radical individualism and our own version of the
Gilded Age, the way home will inevitably require a new engagement with

our nation's Populist tradition. At its best, this tradition has always pointed us toward a politics that takes seriously both the dignity of every individual and the majesty of a democratic commonwealth that looks after the interests of the community.

CHAPTER VIII

What's the Matter with Populism?
Why Everybody Loves It,
Except When They Don't

POPULISM" is one of the most overused, and misused, terms in American politics. It is invoked with great passion, the subject of both lavish praise and a fearsome skepticism. Many claim for themselves populism's mandate from heaven, knowing—as George Bancroft observed early on—that legitimacy and even sanctification in American politics arise first from identification with "the people." In *The Populist Persuasion*, the historian Michael Kazin cites Ralph Waldo Emerson: "March without the people, and you march into the night." Kazin argues that "the language of populism in the United States expressed a kind of idealistic discontent" and "a profound outrage with elites who ignored, corrupted, and/or betrayed the core ideal of American democracy." American progressives have succeeded in improving the "common welfare" only when they "talked in populist ways—hopeful, expansive, even romantic."

Yet "populism" is also regularly used as an epithet to accuse politicians of pandering to popular prejudices. It is often linked to a politics of unreason rooted not in thought and analysis but in feelings and impulses, often arising from prejudice. The mid-twentieth-century conservative writer Peter Viereck saw American populism in the darkest terms, and he was joined in his view by many other intellectuals, liberal as well as conservative, during the 1950s. "Beneath the sane economic demands of the populists of 1880 to 1900," Viereck wrote, "seethed a mania of xenophobia, Jew-baiting, intellectual-baiting, and thought-controlling lynch-spirit."

Part of the problem is that as a free-floating concept—as distinguished from its origins in the particular historical movement associated with the People's Party of the 1890s—populism has no discernable ideological direction. Right-wingers, left-wingers, and centrists have all, at different moments, labeled themselves "populists." The historian Leo Ribuffo reports that William Z. Foster, one of the earliest leaders of the American Communist Party, traced his progression "from [William Jennings] Bryan to Stalin." Perhaps only in America is the idea of a populist Stalinist even possible. "Tradition lies in the eye of the beholder," Ribuffo noted dryly, "and politicians across the spectrum claim posthumous endorsements from departed statesmen."

George Wallace, in his longest phase as a rabble-rouser on race in the 1960s and early 1970s, used the thoroughly populist slogan "Trust the people." Wallace could be a confusing figure. At times he spoke in a New Deal idiom of class solidarity, and by the end of his life he had renounced racism. Yet it was as a tribune for white racial backlash that Wallace found his greatest political success.

Many contemporary figures of the left have embraced the populist label, including Jim Hightower in Texas, former senator Fred Harris of Oklahoma—when he ran for president in 1976, Harris's slogan was "The issue is privilege"—and, more recently, senators such as Sherrod Brown of Ohio and Byron Dorgan of North Dakota. The Occupy Wall Street movement is unmistakably populist, pitting the top 1 percent of Americans against the remaining 99 percent. Television and radio host Ed Schultz, a man of the left, thinks of himself as a populist, and so does Pat Buchanan on the right. Schultz and Buchanan can sound quite alike in their intonation at times and even occasionally—as when they discuss trade—in their substantive views. In the late 1970s and early 1980s, such leaders of the New Right as Richard Viguerie and Howard Phillips wanted to be called populist, proudly distinguishing themselves from stuffy Burkeans. When the writer Kevin Phillips (no relation to Howard) listed the issues that motivated the New Right, his list had little in common with the old Populists' pantheon of concerns inspired by a reaction against monopolists, concentrated wealth, and economic injustice. Phillips spoke instead of "public anger over busing, welfare spending, environmental extremism, soft criminology, media bias and power, warped education, twisted textbooks, racial quotas, various guidelines, and an ever expanding bureaucracy."

And in 1992, along came a populism of the center defined by a multi-millionaire named Ross Perot. Perot managed to make the nation's budget deficit a populist concern, linking the deficit to unhappiness over free trade and a backlash against the two major parties. In certain respects, Perot's worldview actually *was* a classically American populist mix. He combined a critique of high finance with strong criticism of free trade's costs to blue-collar Americans ("that giant sucking sound" of jobs being drawn south of our border to Mexico) and a classic critique of political parties as representing privileged interests.

In our time, no movement has been more eager to claim the populist mantle as its own than the Tea Party. And both media analysts and pollsters were happy to grant the movement its wish. Conservative pollsters Scott Rasmussen and Doug Schoen argued in *Mad as Hell: How the Tea Party Movement Is Fundamentally Remaking Our Two-Party System* that the Tea Party was primarily a revolt against a "political elite" that had been unaffected by the Great Recession. While the Tea Party's supporters suffered, they argued, this elite continued "to be upwardly mobile, to send their children to expensive and exclusive schools, and to believe that the country is heading in generally the right direction."

"The right-wing populism we are experiencing today is significant," they wrote, "because it represents the conjoining of three separate, distinct, and not easily reconcilable strands of conservatism: economic conservatism, small-government libertarians, and social conservatism." Of course, there was nothing new about what Rasmussen and Schoen were describing. They were simply listing the three wings of garden-variety conservatism— the same coalition that had brought Ronald Reagan to power—and endowing it with a new label. As we've seen, most Tea Party supporters were nothing more (or less) than Republicans who happened to be more upset than most people about Barack Obama's victory in 2008 and the failures of the Bush years. Nonetheless, a conservative movement that can claim to be "populist" carries more public legitimacy than a big-business conservatism offering precisely the same platform. And the Tea Party saw its approval ratings decline as its champions in Congress became more closely associated with the movement's actual policies, including tax cuts for the wealthy.

Larrey Anderson, a conservative philosopher who had been an Idaho Republican politician, offered the intriguing view that the Tea Party represented "Populist constitutionalism." This certainly had a plausible connection with what actually happened at Tea Party rallies. "I have attended several local Tea Party gatherings (and addressed a couple of them)," he wrote. "There is one document that is ubiquitous at these events: the *Constitution for the United States of America*. People hand out copies of the Constitution like *hors d'oeuvres* that are served at . . . a *de rigueur* tea party."

"Love and respect for the Constitution is driving the movement," he concluded. "Sharing the document, and then discussing its meaning, purpose, and ideas—that is the process that is taking place as a result of this love and respect." One might argue that the very content of the book you are now reading, with its focus on the foundational ideas of our republic, is a tribute (if of a rather critical sort) to the success of the effort Anderson described. But was it *populism*?

Chris Cillizza, the *Washington Post*'s popular political blogger, offered a distinctive take on Tea Party populism, centered on one of its principal figures. Writing of Michele Bachmann's disclosure that she had to "weather the sorrow of a miscarriage," Cillizza noted that her revelation meant she was running "as a sort-of personal populist—someone who not only feels your pain but has lived it." Cillizza was certainly right about the natural sympathy that flowed to Bachmann over her loss and the link her story allowed her to forge with "millions of families." Personal populism seemed like a new concept. But it was as old as the 1840 "log cabin and hard cider" campaign in which the Whigs cast William Henry Harrison and their party "as paragons of plain rustic virtue" even though, as Sean Wilentz observed, Harrison was in fact "a native Virginian and scion of a great Tidewater family."

This kaleidoscope of populisms underscored what Leo Ribuffo, with generous understatement, called the "methodological imprecision" of our discussions of the meaning of Populism in both casual political analysis and historical debate. If the Tea Party's rise demanded a reengagement with the meaning of our Constitution and the earliest periods of American history, it also required a new seriousness about what Populism meant for our past, and means for our present.

II

To the extent that Populism refers to something specific in our history, it is to the movement of agrarian rebellion on behalf of notions of a "cooperative commonwealth" that erupted in the 1880s. This uprising created a remarkably successful third-party movement that won a significant share of the popular and electoral vote in 1892 and merged with the Democrats to support the Great Commoner, William Jennings Bryan, in 1896.

The People's Party platform of 1892 is an impressive and radical document. "We meet in the midst of a nation brought to the verge of moral, political, and material ruin. Corruption dominates the ballot-box, the Legislatures, the Congress, and touches even the ermine of the bench." The preamble, written by veteran reformer and celebrated Populist orator Ignatius Donnelly, has many resonances in our day's protests against Wall Street and the financial world:

> The people are demoralized; most of the States have been compelled to isolate the voters at the polling places to prevent universal intimidation and bribery. The newspapers are largely subsidized or muzzled, public opinion silenced, business prostrated, homes covered with mortgages, labor impoverished, and the land concentrating in the hands of capitalists. The urban workmen are denied the right to organize for self-protection, imported pauperized labor beats down their wages, a hireling standing army, unrecognized by our laws, is established to shoot them down, and they are rapidly degenerating into European conditions. The fruits of the toil of millions are badly stolen to build up colossal fortunes for a few, unprecedented in the history of mankind; and the possessors of

these, in turn, despise the Republic and endanger liberty. From the same prolific womb of governmental injustice we breed the two great classes—tramps and millionaires.

"We seek to restore the government of the Republic to the hands of 'the plain people,' with which class it originated," the platform promised. "We believe that the powers of government—in other words of the people—should be expanded (as in the case of the postal service) as rapidly and as far as the good sense of an intelligent people and the teachings of experience should justify, to the end that oppression, injustice and poverty shall eventually cease in the land." The preamble, as the historian Robert Mc-Math observed, succinctly distilled the Populists' philosophy as it had developed over two decades in the halls of the Farmers' Alliance and the struggles of the labor movement.

What followed were specific and far-reaching proposals that proved genuinely prophetic in describing what the Progressive and New Deal reformers would achieve in the not-too-distant future: a graduated income tax, a shorter workday, initiative and referendum, the secret ballot, and the direct election of United States senators. "One by one," wrote Harold U. Faulkner in *Politics, Reform, and Expansion*, "the reforms advocated by the Populists were taken up by the very people who had denounced the Populists as socialists, anarchists and Jacobins." It's a familiar pattern in our history.

The platform also called for government ownership of the railroads and the telephone and telegraph systems. Responding to the interests of indebted farmers, it proposed inflationary monetary policies, including the "free and unlimited coinage of silver," which became Bryan's battle cry four years later. Prophetic in a different way was the platform's call for restrictions on "undesirable immigration." The "present system," the Populists proclaimed, "opens our ports to the pauper and criminal classes of the world and crowds out our wage earners."

For historians who focused on the actual content of the Populists' program and the underlying demands of the organizations that built the People's Party, the 1882 platform was a straightforward expression of what Populism was: a social reform movement rooted in agrarian and labor organizations that sought relief in hard times and the redress of legitimate grievances. For many years, the definitive account of populism was John D. Hicks's *The Populist Revolt*, which viewed Populism largely in these terms. Hicks saw the Populists as engaged in "the last phase of a long and perhaps a losing struggle—the struggle to save agricultural America from the devouring jaws of industrial America." Published in 1931, Hicks's view was clearly influenced by the Great Depression and the economic discontent it let loose. His account, as McMath noted, saw farmers on the Great Plains "locked into an agricultural market over which they had little control" and buffeted by "falling commodity prices, high freight rates, and expensive credit, compounded by capricious acts of nature." At heart, Populism was rational, reformist, egalitarian, and democratic—if also angry and mistrustful of big-city elites and, sometimes, of immigrants.

But a funny thing happened to the Populists in the 1950s. More precisely, a funny thing happened to their image, especially among liberals. An important group of intellectuals, almost all of them urban *and* urbane liberals and anti-Communists, challenged the straightforward view that the populists were primarily about defending the economic interests of those who felt shortchanged by the wealthy and powerful. These writers mistrusted mass movements, feared populism's allegedly anti-intellectual tendencies, and worried about political "extremism." Such feelings arose from their understandable horror over Nazism and Soviet Communism, both murderous mass movements that purported to be bold responses to economic breakdown and deeply felt injustices. The liberal anti-Communists of the 1950s also confronted the rise of McCarthyism and the "pseudo-conservatism" Hofstadter and Viereck described. They borrowed the concept from the social psychologist Theodor Adorno, who defined a pseudo-conservative as someone "who, in the name of upholding traditional American values and institutions and defending them against more or less fictitious dangers, consciously or unconsciously aims at their abolition."

In the introduction to *The Age of Reform*, his enormously influential critical reexamination of Populism and Progressivism, Hofstadter is candid in acknowledging that his interest "has been drawn to that side of Populism and Progressivism—particularly of Populism—which seems very strongly to foreshadow some aspects of the cranky pseudo-conservatism of our time."

Hofstadter criticized intellectuals (he was clearly talking about liberals) who "suffer from a sense of isolation which they usually seek to surmount by finding ways of getting into rapport with the people, and they readily succumb to a tendency to sentimentalize the folk." As a result, "they periodically exaggerate the measure of agreement that exists between movements of popular reform and the considered principles of political liberalism. They remake the image of popular rebellion closer to their heart's desire." No sentimentalist, Hofstadter was determined to expose the less attractive sides of Populism and Progressivism. He was not, he insisted, trying to argue that these great reform movements "were foolish and destructive but only that they had, like so many things in life, an ambiguous character."

Still, in light of the largely positive treatment afforded the Populists by Hicks—and Hicks, in turn, was influenced by the towering historian Charles Beard's emphasis on the importance of economic forces—Hofstadter's was a radical revision, hostile to the Populists in its emphasis on their proclivity for dark schemes and conspiracy theories.

"There was something about the Populist imagination that loved the secret plot and the conspiratorial meeting," Hofstadter wrote. "There was in fact a widespread Populist idea that all American history since the Civil War could be understood as a sustained conspiracy of the international money power." Hofstadter devoted several pages of his book to describing and analyzing Ignatius Donnelly's popular 1891 political novel, *Caesar's Column*, which sketched a dystopia (it was set in 1988) that would engulf America if reformers failed. For Hofstadter, the novel was permeated with a "sadistic and nihilistic spirit" and offered "a frightening glimpse into the ugly potential of frustrated popular revolt."

Hofstadter also accused the Populists of having "activated most of what we have of modern popular anti-Semitism in the United States." Hofstadter emphasized that Populist anti-Semitism was "entirely verbal . . . a mode of expression, a rhetorical style, not a tactic or a program. It did not lead to exclusion laws, much less to riots or pogroms." Nonetheless, in a book published just a decade after the end of World War II and the liberation of the Nazi death camps, it was a loaded charge.

It was not just the Populists' style that Hofstadter found distasteful. He also challenged their very understanding of the interests that they were organized to advance. They failed, he said, to understand that they were "an organic part of the whole order of business enterprise and speculation that flourished in the city." Mistakenly, they embraced an "agrarian myth" and cast themselves as "innocent pastoral victims of a conspiracy hatched in the distance." Populism, in Hofstadter's telling, was explained less by economics than by status anxiety over farming's declining "rank in society." The farmer, Hofstadter said, "was beginning to realize acutely not merely that the best of the world's goods were to be had in the cities and that the urban middle and upper classes had much more of them than he did but also that he was losing in status and respect as compared with them." For the farmer, said Hofstadter, it was "bewildering, and irritating too, to think of the great contrast between the verbal deference paid him by almost everyone and the real status, the real economic position, in which he found himself."

This brief summary does not do full justice to the richness of *The Age of Reform*. Many of its observations have withstood the test of time, and Hofstadter was both brilliant and devastating in describing how so much of the radical and reformist energy of Populism was lost when Bryan's 1896 campaign concentrated its energy on the cause of "free silver." This "was not distinctively a People's Party idea, nor was it considered one of the more 'radical' planks in the People's Party platform." His description of the modernization of the farm lobby into a hugely powerful force in Washington is relevant to our day. And more than half a century before Barack Obama's struggles to get his program through the United States Senate, Hofstadter wrote of the substantial imbalance of representation in Washington in favor of rural areas, and concluded: "The Senate represents this inequity in its most extreme form." It still does.

Nevertheless, Hofstadter's negative judgments on Populism—and, to only a slightly lesser degree, his critique of the Progressives—proved to be the most politically consequential feature of *The Age of Reform*. In a brilliant reconsideration of the book, Alan Brinkley noted that Hofstadter's portrait of Populism "was from the beginning the target of strenuous (and often vituperative) attacks."

It is a measure of the durability of Hofstadter's interpretation that it was the object of a 1996 column by the late Molly Ivins, an enthusiastic fan of populism who mourned the historian's continuing impact:

> The problem with trying to redeem populism—the most small-d democratic movement in American history, a rich strain of native American radicalism—from the political press corps is that reporters were all forced to read Richard Hofstadter in college. And Hofstadter, an otherwise commendable historian, always mistook populism-in-decline for populism itself. In the words of *The Economist*, this led him to mistake populism for "a pathetic but also rather offensive group of economic illiterates and political nostrum-mongers, victims of the Agrarian Myth and propagators of xenophobia and racial prejudice." How sad. In fact, populism spanned classes, races and sections of the nation in a way nothing else ever has. It included black sharecroppers, industrial workers and small-business men all over America at a time when both sectionalism and racism were viciously strong.

At the time of *The Age of Reform*'s publication, Hicks, whose verdicts Hofstadter in many ways overturned, offered a surprisingly gracious response, calling it "a delightfully refreshing book," although he argued that Hofstadter had overemphasized Populist anti-Semitism, a critique of Hofstadter's view other historians have supported. But as David Brown, Hofstadter's biographer, notes, Hicks's student George Mowry zeroed in on an important truth. "One has the feeling," Mowry wrote of Hofstadter, "that the author occasionally fails to understand the agrarian mind and that he is making some of his judgments about Populism and agrarian progressivism not in terms of the conflicts of the past, but rather more fully in terms of the author's urban present." C. Vann Woodward—one of the greatest historians of the South, the biographer of Populist Tom Watson, and a Hofstadter friend—eventually took to the pages of the *American Scholar* to offer a balanced defense of the agrarian rebellion. His title went straight at the distance between Ivy League halls and waves of grain: "The Populist Heritage and the Intellectual." While personally kind to Hofstadter and his book, Woodward insisted that the Populists were not deluded, that theirs was an authentic struggle for power based on real economic grievances. Earlier scholars may have been too uncritical of the Populists, he wrote, but historians now faced a new problem. "The danger," he wrote, "is that under the concentrated impact of the new criticism the risk is incurred not only of blurring a historical image but of swapping an old stereotype for a new one. The old one sometimes approached the formulation that Populism is the root of all good in democracy, while the new one sometimes suggests that Populism is the root of all evil."

"Populism was hardly 'status politics,'" Woodward argued, "and I should hesitate to call it 'class politics.' It was more nearly 'interest politics,' and more specifically 'agricultural interest politics.'" Woodward was polite in his choice of words, but he was insisting that Populism was what it was, not what midcentury New York academics *thought* it was.

And both Woodward and Michael Paul Rogin, a political scientist and the author of *The Intellectuals and McCarthy*, vigorously disputed the easy link that Hofstadter and his allies made between Populism and McCarthyism. Sam Tanenhaus, the editor of the *New York Times Book Review*, nicely captured the implications of Hofstadter's position in a 2006 essay: "[William Jennings] Bryan's authentic heir wasn't Roosevelt, the Dutchess County squire. It was Joe McCarthy, who even delivered—in Wheeling, W. Va., in 1950—his own cross of gold speech, a carnal roar against subversives, real and imagined, recipients of 'all the benefits that the wealthiest nation on earth has to offer—the finest homes, the finest college education and the finest jobs in government.'"

Rogin carefully analyzed election returns and found little connection between those who supported McCarthy and those who had backed progressive reformers or agrarian populism. McCarthyism, Rogin insisted, had far more to do with the agendas of Republican and conservative politics. (It's another case of, it was what it was.) And as Brown reports, Woodward made a similar point in a letter to Hofstadter. "In the McCarthy movement," Woodward wrote, "I believe a close study would reveal a considerable element of college-bred, established-wealth, old family industrial support."

If history sometimes repeats itself, so do historical errors. Seeing Mc-Carthy as the heir to Bryan or Tom Watson was much the same as seeing members of the Tea Party—a largely middle-class group with right-wing views—as successors to the Populists. Both comparisons mistake form for substance and fail to take seriously what movements and their members actually say and believe.

At heart, the debate about Populism is a debate about the nature of our democracy, about political and economic equality, and about the role of average citizens in politics. It is also a debate within liberalism itself. Linking the New Deal closely to Populism, as those who wrote in Hicks's tradition did, had important implications for how contemporary liberalism should be understood. Populism's sympathizers saw the New Deal as part of a broad Populist-Progressive egalitarian tradition. Hofstadter, on the other hand, sought to distance the New Deal from this past. "The difference I hope to establish," he wrote, "is that its indignation was directed far more against callousness and waste, far less against corruption or monopoly, than the indignation of the Progressives." The "inspiration" behind the New Deal "was much more informed by administration, engineering and economics, considerably less by morals and uplift."

As a matter of history, Alan Brinkley observed, Hofstadter "clearly underestimated the degree to which progressive ideology had influenced New Deal policymakers." On the other hand, Hofstadter was right to see that "in the course of more than a decade of political and ideological pulling and tugging, new ideas had slowly and haltingly emerged in response to the failure of old ones to deal with pressing realities." A decade after he wrote these words, Brinkley described how New Deal thinking changed in the course of Roosevelt's tenure in a book whose title, *The End of Reform,* echoed Hofstadter's.

Scholarship about the Populists did not stay still. The Populists enjoyed a historical renaissance with the publication in 1976 of Lawrence Goodwyn's *Democratic Promise: The Populist Moment in America.* The first full-scale study of Populism since Hicks's work more than forty years earlier, it cast Populism (in Brinkley's words) as "coherent, enlightened, and fundamentally democratic." The product of the interest of New Left scholars and civil rights veterans in mass democratic movements, Goodwyn's account portrayed Populism as the creation of a movement culture and its supporters as people transformed by the very experience of organizing against injustice. "To describe the origins of Populism in one sentence," Goodwyn wrote, "the cooperative movement recruited American farmers, and their subsequent experience within the cooperatives radically altered their political consciousness. The agrarian revolt cannot be understood outside the framework of the economic crusade that was not only its source but also created the culture of the movement itself."

For a generation of progressive historians and activists, Goodwyn's account was liberating. In her 1996 column taking Hofstadter to task, Molly Ivins praised Goodwyn for understating populism "as the self-empowering fulfillment of real democracy that it was at its best." Ivins's view of Populism was pure Goodwyn:

> Populism was up-from-the-bottom politics, a system of alliances and sub-alliances and alliance halls where people met and talked over their problems and shared ideas and solutions. They took on the largest institutions of their day: the railroads and the banks. They allied with the Knights of Labor and fought "replacement workers" . . . They used the boycott and the strike and the ballot.

As Goodwyn himself put it: "The thing to remember about the historic connection between 19th century populism and modern politics is that populism can be understood as an attempt to create popular democracy, an attempt to enrich the popular democratic input into the American system of governance."

This view has continued to be influential. Robert C. McMath Jr.'s *American Populism: A Social History*, published in 1993, concluded that "most studies of the last quarter century have depicted American Populism as a movement that advanced a serious critique of monopolism and offered alternative visions of democratic capitalism." Reflecting the continuing relationship between the study of Populist history and the development of democratic aspirations, McMath concluded:

> Neither proto-fascists nor proto–New Dealers, the Populists fashioned a powerful movement out of the cultures of nineteenth-century reform and out of their own shared experiences. In the end,

they failed to bend the forces of capitalism and technology toward humane ends, and many of them shared with other Americans of their time a myopic view of equal rights, one still distorted by racism and sexism. But for all their failures and limitations, the Populists fashioned a space within which Americans could begin to imagine alternative futures shaped by the promise of equal rights. There is a legacy waiting to be fulfilled.

More recent scholarship has forcefully challenged the idea that the Populists were either anti-modern or anti-intellectual. In *The Populist Vision*, published in 2007, the historian Charles Postel argues persuasively that the Populists were not "Don Quixotes tilting at the windmills of modernity and commercial change." Rather, they were forward-looking, much taken by science and education—they were known as a "reading party" and a "writing and talking party"—and much affected by the late nineteenth century's "ethos of modernity and progress." They sought to use government as a "counterbalance" to "corporate and financial power" in their quest for "fair access to the benefits of modernity." Postel is fully alive to the Populists' shortcomings, yet he is right to remind the reformers of our day that Populism gave birth to "one of the most powerful independent political movements in American history."

No wonder so many later political movements have claimed lineage to the Populist tradition. While the negative image of Populism created by the pluralist intellectuals of the 1950s has had real staying power (as Molly Ivins mourned), political activists with views quite distant from those of the 1892 People's Party have been more than happy to take up the name. And this continues to sow confusion. A striking and quite typical example: in a commentary published in the *Huffington Post* in February 2010, the actor Alec Baldwin declared that Sarah Palin's performance at the Tea Party convention a few days earlier marked her as an "incurious, phony populist." But two days later in the *Washington Post*, the late David Broder, his age's premier political reporter, concluded that Palin was offering "a pitch-perfect recital of the populist message that has worked in campaigns past."

Phony or pitch-perfect? With populism, it seems, all things are possible.

III

When Hofstadter, Daniel Bell, Seymour Martin Lipset, and other intellectual critics of Populism linked it to right-wing movements and even "right-wing extremism," they were doing so to cast doubt upon a creed that earlier generations of liberals had viewed with some sympathy. This skeptical view was a consistent subtheme in *The Radical Right*, an important collection of essays published in 1963. (It was an expanded version of a book published eight years earlier as *The New American Right*.)

"Social groups that are dispossessed invariably seek targets on whom they can vent their resentments, targets whose power can serve to explain their dispossession," Bell wrote. "In this respect, the radical right of the early 1960s is no different from the Populists of the 1890s, who for years traded successfully on such simple formulas as 'Wall Street,' 'international bankers,' and 'the Trusts' in order to have not only targets but 'explanations' for politics." Lipset pointed out that the Populists were no friends of intellectual freedom, noting that they "discharged many university professors in state universities in states where they came to power in the 1890s." (Lipset acknowledged that Republicans, in turn, "dismissed teachers who believed in Populist economics.")

The irony here is that while a certain kind of liberal was using Populism's alleged right-wing tendencies to discredit it as a disposition, right-wingers themselves were eager to make the same argument in reverse: that conservatives now had the most legitimate claim on Populism, since liberal "elitists" were denigrating the religious beliefs, ethical commitments, and day-to-day values of ordinary people.

From the late 1940s on, the Populist form, if not the substance, was indeed most popular on the right. Less than a decade after Joe McCarthy came George Wallace, whose rhetoric was about race but whose favorite targets were elite groups—the "so-called experts," the "so-called intellectuals," "the sociologists," "the pointy-headed bureaucrats with thin briefcases full of guidelines." His oratory was addressed to the aggrieved. "Yes, they've looked down their nose at you and me a long time," he said. "They've called us rednecks—the Republicans and the Democrats. Well, we're going to show, there sure are a lot of rednecks in this country."

The great civil rights historian Taylor Branch quotes an "awestruck" Alabama reporter who decoded Wallace's technique. "He gave every hearer a chance to transmute a latent hostility toward the Negro into a hostility toward big government," the reporter said. As Branch observed, "The reporter recognized that Wallace's power began in rhetorical innovation. Without harping on racial epithets, as everyone expected him to do, Wallace talked all around race by touching on the related fears of domination, coining new expressions such as 'forced busing' and 'big government,' which were anything but common clichés" at the time he invented them.

It is insufficiently appreciated that the style largely invented by Wallace still shapes the rhetoric of right-wing populism. Wallace's use of the "law and order" theme became a staple of Richard Nixon's 1968 campaign and had a powerful impact long after, notably in 1988, when George H. W. Bush used the crime issue to defeat Michael Dukakis. Ads showing the face of an African American criminal in attacks on Dukakis's prison furlough program in Massachusetts were a signal event in that contest. The linking of law and order to racism had the unfortunate side effect of discouraging liberals from grappling with legitimate public concerns about rising crime rates, a problem Bill Clinton in the White House and Joe Biden in the Senate tried to remedy with their crime bill in the 1990s.

Wallace's impact continued to be felt even after conservative populism sought to distance itself from all but the most veiled references to race. (Obama's rise, of course, brought forth a troubling resurgence of racial and racist themes.) The politics of the 1960s and after created a large new cast of elitist villains, many of them identified first by Wallace. Viewed as a whole, it was truly an awesome list of malefactors: scruffy, privileged college students protesting the war in Vietnam, a few of whom tarred the rest by burning American flags; dissenting college professors easily painted as "arrogant" and "out of touch"; a larger "new class" of upscale professionals whose social liberalism was said to put them at odds with the values of ordinary Americans; a related group of "secularists" or "secular humanists" accused of trying to drive God and religion out of the public square; feminists, homosexuals, and libertines intent on destroying the two-parent heterosexual family; powerful bureaucrats and politicians in Washington seeking to use federal power to impose such defective values on unwilling states, cities, and towns around the nation; a "liberal media" determined to ignore, distort, or mock the views and arguments of the patriotic, the God-fearing, and the traditional; and a cosmopolitan elite that encompassed many of these groups and was so internationalist (or "globalist" or "multi-lateralist") in its outlook that its members were indifferent or hostile to the very idea of American patriotism. This last sentiment was nicely encapsulated in the 2004 presidential campaign by conservative snickers that "John Kerry looks French."

The historian who best described the migration of the populist approach rightward is Michael Kazin. His 1995 book, *The Populist Persuasion*, saw populism as a deeply rooted American *method*—which is quite different from viewing it as a program or a set of ideas. Populism became a way of communicating, "a language that sees ordinary people as a noble assemblage not bound narrowly by class." Its supporters view "their elite opponents as self-serving and undemocratic, and seek to mobilize the former against the latter."

"I do not contend that my subjects *were* populists, in the way they were unionists or socialists, Protestants or Catholics, liberal Democrats or conservative Republicans," Kazin wrote. "Populism, more an impulse than an ideology, is too elastic and promiscuous to be the basis for such an allegiance. Rather, my premise is that all these people employed populism as a flexible mode of persuasion."

America's populist rhetoric, Kazin argues, blends two traditions, "the pietistic impulse issuing from the Protestant Reformation" and "the secular faith of the Enlightenment, the belief that ordinary people could think and act rationally, more rationally, in fact, than their ancestral overlords."

"It became a convenient label for left, right, center, and anyone simply out to make a profit," Kazin observed, "a handy way to signify that one was on the side of the *real* people—those with more common sense than disposable income—and opposed to their elite enemies, whoever they might be." Kazin made clear how far contemporary right-wing populists are from the 1890s variety. "Activists who blame an immoral, agnostic media for America's problems," he wrote, "have little in common with those who indict corporations for moving jobs overseas."

The "major alteration" in American politics, Kazin argues, began in the 1940s "when populism began its journey from left to right."

> The rhetoric once spoken primarily by reformers and radicals (debt-ridden farmers, craft and industrial unionists, socialists attempting to make their purposes sound American, even prohibitionists eager to wipe out the saloon interests) was creatively altered by conservative groups and politicians (zealous anti-Communists, George Wallace, the Christian Right, and the campaigns and presidential administrations of Richard Nixon and Ronald Reagan).
>
> It was a remarkable shift. The vocabulary of grassroots rebellion now served to thwart and reverse social and cultural change rather than promote it.

What emerged, "gradually and unevenly," was "a conservative populism that pledged to defend pious, middle-class communities against the amoral governing elite." This was a strange development. It turned Populism from a relatively coherent set of egalitarian ideas into a collection of impulses, a strategy rather than a philosophy, a form of rhetoric and not a program.

The diverse and contentious approaches to Populism among historians matched the confusion in the political world over what it took to be "populist." The Tea Party was willing to embrace the label, even if it would see the actual nineteenth-century populist program as "socialistic," which in certain respects it was. Indeed, many in the Tea Party proposed to repeal the very amendments to the Constitution (authorizing the income tax and providing for the direct election of senators) that the Populists had fought for. If the Tea Party regarded itself as "populist," these were small-p populists against Populism. Liberals, in the meantime, were torn. Some, still influenced directly (or perhaps unconsciously) by Hofstadter, assumed that Populism was tinged by anti-intellectualism, narrow-mindedness, and bigotry. Other liberals such as Molly Ivins, Jim Hightower, and a significant pro-labor contingent in Congress were proud to make the cause of Populism their own, continuing to regard it as a democratic and egalitarian call to battle.

The frustration on the left over liberalism's ceding of Populism's power to the right exploded in one of the most important political books of the Bush years, Thomas Frank's *What's the Matter with Kansas?* It carried the subtitle: *How Conservatives Won the Heart of America.* Frank located his story in Kansas for personal reasons and also because the state had been part of the original Populism's heartland. In the past, he noted, the state's "periodic bouts of leftism were what really branded Kansas with the mark of the freak." While "every part of the country in the nineteenth century had labor upheavals and protosocialist reform movements," Kansas was special because in Kansas, "the radicals kept coming out on top." There is intentional irony in Frank's title, which is drawn from an 1896 essay by the famed Republican journalist William Allen White, who hailed from the Kansas town of Emporia. For White, the state's radicalism had been "what was the matter with Kansas." It was a place, White said, that wanted "more men . . . who hate prosperity, and who think, because a man believes in national honor, he is a tool of Wall Street." Frank focused on the opposite problem, which was why Kansas *wasn't* Populist anymore.

Frank used Kansas as the prototype for the rise of right-wing populism. "Today's Republicans are doing what the Whigs did in the 1840s," he wrote, "putting on backwoods accents, telling the world about their log-cabin upbringings, and raging against the over-educated elites . . . Hence the situation in Kansas, where the most prominent conservatives, themselves an assortment of millionaires and lawyers and Harvard grads, lead a proletarian uprising against . . . millionaires, lawyers, and Harvard grads."

But Frank's real scorn was directed against Democrats who "no longer speak to the people on the losing end of a free-market system that is becoming more brutal and more arrogant by the day." The Democrats' problem, he argued, was not that they "are monolithically pro-choice or anti–school prayer; it's that by dropping the class language that once distinguished them sharply from Republicans they have left themselves vulnerable to cultural wedge issues like guns and abortion and the rest whose hallucinatory appeal would ordinarily be far overshadowed by material concerns." The Republicans, he concluded, "talk constantly abut class—in a coded way, to be sure." Democrats, on the other hand, "are afraid to bring it up."

All this represented, in an odd way, the triumph of Hofstadter's argument. It's not surprising that Hofstadter's most enthusiastic moment of personal political activism was on behalf of Adlai Stevenson's 1952 and 1956 presidential campaigns. Stevenson's urbane persona and style led to the popularization of the word "egghead," and his rejection by the electorate came, as Hofstadter saw things in *Anti-Intellectualism in American Life*, after a campaign in which "intellect and philistinism" squared off, and philistinism won. Hofstadter mourned what he saw as a "national distaste for intellect." By the time Frank wrote, Democrats were more likely to be identified with intellectuals than with Populists—they were more Stevenson than Bryan. And this, as Frank argued, often produced disastrous results.

There is much to Frank's insistence that something is badly awry when those who are, in principle, committed to greater economic equality become wary of identifying with the very people their program is designed to benefit. The rejection by some Democrats and liberals of their Populist gene also accounted for how slow the Obama administration was to appreciate the dangers of too close an association with the banks and Wall Street. It should not have taken the Occupy Wall Street movement to awaken the administration to both the problems inherent in its position and the political potential of a more forceful response to financial abuses.

It is also strange that partisans of movements stoutly defending inequalities, strenuously opposing higher taxes on the wealthy, and passionately critical of labor unions become more eager than anyone else in politics to proclaim themselves "populists."

But something else is going on here as well. Contemporary liberalism's problem was not just the reluctance of some in its ranks to speak a populist language of class injustice or its failure to offer a plausible program of economic uplift for those caught in the downdrafts of the global economy, though the latter poses a deep and enduring challenge. Liberalism also suffered because from the end of World War II—and especially since the 1960s—it had "a weaker connection with the idea of community than most of the progressive and reform traditions that preceded it," as Alan Brinkley observed. Conservatives, even highly individualistic conservatives, profited from speaking in unapologetic terms about faith, family, neighborhood, and nation. Partisans of liberalism and the left, who are in principle community builders, gravitated in the postwar years to an individualistic language focusing on rights and entitlements. Yes, there was much honor in the willingness of liberals to take losses among socially conservative voters because they spoke up for racial and religious minorities and for equal rights for women, gays, and lesbians. But they also lost ground among more moderate traditionalists not so much because of what they said about family, faith, and community but because they seemed reluctant to talk about these things at all. For many years, conservatives were able to occupy this ground by default. This is why the communitarian correction among liberals described in Chapter 4 was an urgent necessity, and why communitarian language has appealed so much to politicians such as Clinton and Obama. They understood that there was a hole in liberalism left by the absence of community. Eventually, a similar logic may finally lead conservatives toward second thoughts about shearing off their communitarian wing. Many who think of themselves as conservative revere the unregulated economic market far less than they do the ties of church, neighbors, and kin.

Here again, history is instructive. The original Populism was suffused with the language of community. It did not shrink from class warfare, but it was not about class struggle for its own sake. Populism spoke of building a "cooperative commonwealth" and, as McMath wrote, "developed among people who were deeply rooted in the social and economic networks of rural communities." Many of the activities of the Populists "took place within membership organizations—voluntary associations such as churches, fraternal organizations and agricultural societies." Populists built a political movement. They also nurtured a community.

Similarly, the Progressives who rose after the decline of the original Populist movement are often accused, as we've seen, of being relentless centralizers more interested in the scientific management of public problems than in deepening democracy. There is truth in this critique, especially since Progressives sometimes sought to limit the franchise in the name of cleaning up politics. Yet there was a side of Progressivism linked to the community building of the Settlement House movement and to a Christian left whose great spokesman, Walter Rauschenbusch, looked forward to the "evolution of a cooperative economic organization as wide as society." Progressives made common cause with Rauschenbusch's Social Gospel Christians, who sought to build a "beloved community," later a pivotal phrase for Martin Luther King Jr. and the civil rights movement. Jane Addams echoed the prophet Micah in calling on settlement house workers to "love mercy," "do justly," and "walk humbly with God." She insisted, as the historian Eugene McCarraher notes, "that the Christian spirit lay not in the manger of organized religion but in a recognition of mutuality that sought 'simple and natural expression in the social organism.'"

And while the New Deal did "contribute in significant ways to the creation of the rights-based liberalism that has been so much in evidence in the last half century," as Brinkley observed, it "was also deeply committed to the concept of community—both to the restoration of local communities and to the strengthening of the overarching national community."

"From the beginning of his administration, Franklin Roosevelt's rhetoric was suffused with images of nationhood, of interdependence, of community," Brinkley said. In his first inaugural address, Roosevelt "never once used the words 'liberty,' 'individual,' or 'equality.'" The early New Deal especially "was, above all else, an effort to find concepts of community capable of transcending the bitter struggles dividing groups in the economy and the society from one another." It sought "to temper the brutality of the industrial economy, to insist on national standards of 'community interest' amid the brutal competitive struggle of capitalism."

IV

A year and a half into the Obama administration, Tom Frank was not enamored. He was as frustrated with Obama as he had been a few years before with other upper-middle-class Democrats. He saw Obama not as a transformative leader but as a technocrat obsessed with process. "It should not surprise us," he wrote when he was still the lively house dissident on the *Wall Street Journal* op-ed page, that Obama "values process so highly and that in the health-care and financial regulation debates he has chosen complex solutions over simpler, better, but more ideological ones." After all, "the Democratic Party itself is shifting away from its blue-collar roots toward professionals and well-educated voters. It is an obvious reflection of the way his party is heading."

Despite the seemingly transformative campaign of 2008, Frank did not see the story line as having changed much since *What's the Matter with Kansas*. "The people now flocking to the Democratic Party might eat artisanal foods and zealously sort containers for easy recycling," he wrote in June 2010, "but they also know that regulation causes more problems than it fixes and that sophisticated people don't use Thirties-style phrases like 'economic royalists.'" Again, he highlighted the links between the intellectual assumptions and the class affiliations of the non-Populist liberals, noting that "while it is fun to trash new-style Democrats for their Ivy League ways, let us also remember that, should you happen to study economics at one of those Ivy League colleges, you will likely imbibe a kind of free-market orthodoxy that would not be out of place in a Wall Street boardroom."

Frank wrote more than a year before the rise of the anti–Wall Street demonstrations, but he captured their sensibility quite accurately. Polls showed that while most of the Occupy demonstrators were Democrats or leaned that way, they were frustrated over the ambivalence within the Obama administration about populism. They were troubled that practices within the financial industry that had enriched a small number at the expense of the economy itself had not faced either the scrutiny or the condemnation (or the prosecution) they deserved. The Occupiers did not see nearly as much change in the government's relationship to the financial world as they felt Obama had promised during his campaign.

It's true, as even Obama's critics acknowledged, that the administration's fears of a collapse in the markets during the first months of Obama's term were understandable. These limited his capacity to push the marketplace and challenge the financial industry as much as seemed appropriate in light of its behavior. Nonetheless, the rise of Occupy Wall Street and, more important, the broad support many of its demands and criticisms won in the polls were a lesson to Obama and to liberals generally. American liberalism is far more than a technocratic creed. Its historical roots are firmly planted in a Populism that was not anti-market but did demand more accountability from those who ran the marketplace and a better deal for those who lived and worked outside the country's most privileged circles. Elizabeth Warren, the architect of the Consumer Financial Protection Bureau and later a candidate for the U.S. Senate from Massachusetts, became a hero within more populist and progressive circles because she spoke with both passion and precision for this sensibility. Ironically, in light of Frank's observations, she was also a Harvard professor, though not one who bought into economic orthodoxy.

The anti–Wall Street movement did something else: it reminded Americans of the deeper commitments of the American Populist tradition and, in so doing, challenged the Tea Party's populist claims. At the very least, progressives no less than the Tea Party had found a populist voice—and it was one that Obama himself began to heed.

At this point in our history, there would seem to be little point in arguing too much about who is a true populist and who is operating under a false flag. The word is too much with us, and no one has the authority to impose a set of tests to determine who deserves membership in some populist club. Yet it's still worth the effort to rescue an important and constructive American tradition from promiscuous misappropriation and the distortions this entails.

Alan Brinkley suggests a set of goals for American politics that, while not explicitly populist, define quite well what this tradition hoped to achieve. "We need a vigorous government and a healthy market," Brinkley argued. "We need strong national institutions and strong local ones. We need a healthy public sector and a healthy private one. Above all, perhaps, we need—to paraphrase Webster—liberty and community, for neither is sustainable without the other."

True populism in the American tradition is not the philosophy of the angry, prejudiced mob inspired by envy and parochialism. It is a well-tempered democratic wish for the sense of balance among shared objectives that has always allowed Americans to move forward—together. And it was toward these ends that the United States moved, with some interruptions and detours, over the century that began with the rise of the Progressive movement.

CHAPTER IX

The Long Consensus and Its Achievements

The Quest for Balance from the Progressive Era to the Reagan Era

I F it is judged in the narrowest terms, the Populist rebellion against the Gilded Age failed. Populism's hero, William Jennings Bryan, went down to defeat in 1896 and again in 1900. He lost to William McKinley, whose cause was championed by a business class politically unified to a degree unprecedented in American history. The politics of the Gilded Age, with its emphasis on the centrality of private enterprise and untrammeled individualism, seemed destined to endure indefinitely. The Supreme Court of the time was determined to lock this vision into the nation's law. Continuing to rule in favor of strict separation between public and private endeavor, it blocked or hampered government efforts to protect a growing industrial working class and to write new rules for an economy undergoing a sweeping process of consolidation.

Yet to hold that Populism died without effect or that conservatism triumphed unreservedly misreads the period entirely. For in 1900, the country was on the verge of one of the great reform moments in its history. Decisions made over the next twenty years would come to define much of the next century and inaugurate the rise of American global power. And the Long Consensus that the Progressive Era would establish allowed many of Populism's dreams to come true.

On its own, Populism could never hope to triumph in an increasingly urban and industrial country. Bryan's 1896 campaign was a glorious cry of protest against the power of the urban rich—the financiers who were transforming the economic landscape and the industrialists who seemed intent on monopolizing American industry. But McKinley's triumph was made possible in part by his success in winning support from urban workers. He was not simply the candidate of the well-to-do. McKinley's economic approach was successfully cast as being more connected to the America of the future, while Bryan, forward-looking in so many respects, gave his opponents the ammunition they needed to paint him as a figure of a soon-to-be-lost rural past. This was true even if Charles Postel was right to argue that Populists were at heart modernizers more interested in a just distribution of modernity's benefits than in overturning its achievements. Bryan won the hearts of millions, but McKinley appealed to the pocketbooks of millions of others. McKinley was helped by the shamelessness of employers who secured Republican votes by threatening to lay off workers the day after a Bryan victory. Yet many urban workers did not need this inducement. After prosperity returned, McKinley cruised to reelection in 1900 by campaigning on behalf of "the full dinner pail."

Bryan worried many in the cities by embracing his role as the champion of the countryside so passionately. "Burn down your cities and leave our farms, and your cities will spring up again as if by magic," Bryan had declared in his "Cross of Gold" speech. "But destroy our farms and the grass will grow in the streets of every city in the country." The line brought cheers in the vast open spaces of Kansas and Nebraska. It fell flat among many on the teeming sidewalks of New York or Pittsburgh. And the voters were moving, in droves, to the cities. Many of the urban newcomers were immigrants from southern and eastern Europe who brought with them their own traditions and, in the case of Catholics and Jews, religious faiths quite distant from the evangelical Protestantism that inspired Bryan and many among the Populist rank and file.

Yet the spirit of protest at the heart of Populism spoke to the hopes and discontents of Americans in the cities no less than to those on the farms and prairies. It was a protest against the individualism of the Gilded Age, against courts aggressively foiling democratic efforts to right the injustices of a new capitalism, against the power of the monopolies and the trusts, against the loss of control over their lives that so many people were experiencing. Populism did not give way to nothing. The cause of social reform at the heart of the Bryan movement did not disappear. After the turn of the century, Americans who had embraced the Great Commoner joined with a new and larger Progressive movement that brought middle-class voices and middle-class votes to a much broader coalition for the common good. "After 1900," wrote Richard Hofstadter, "Populism and Progressivism merge."

That the new Progressivism enjoyed successes that the old Populism did not reflected a lesson repeated throughout American history: reform movements based on the dispossessed alone have often ended in failure. Campaigns on behalf of fairness and justice have often succeeded when they joined the aspirations of the left-out with those of the aspiring middle class. To the adage "March without the people, and you march into the night" might be added another: march without the middle class, and you march toward defeat. It's a double-edged lesson: middle-class reform movements that lack populism's edge and its broadly democratic commitments founder; but so do populist movements untempered by the middle class's inclinations toward stability and moderation.

The merger of Populism and Progressivism into a successful movement was possible because McKinley's victories were not unalloyed triumphs of reaction. McKinley was certainly the candidate of big business, but his electoral coalition included many voters of at least a mildly Progressive disposition. And his vice presidential candidate in 1900, Theodore Roosevelt, understood these forces viscerally. After Roosevelt succeeded to the presidency following McKinley's assassination in 1901, TR slowly transformed himself from a reformist conservative into a full-fledged progressive and then, during his 1912 third-party presidential campaign, into something of a radical.

It might be said that TR made the aspirations of Populism safe for the middle class by discussing them in a middle-class idiom. Roosevelt, Hofstadter observed, "persistently blunted Bryan's appeal by appropriating Bryan's issues in modified form." Progressivism thus "became nationwide and bipartisan, encompassing Democrats and Republicans, country and city, East, West, and South." It produced "a working coalition between the old Bryan country and the new reform movement in the cities, without which the broad diffusion and strength of Progressivism would have been impossible." At the time, the philosopher John Dewey used an arresting metaphor to describe their differences: "Roosevelt borrowed much from Bryan, but Bryan came from Nazareth in Galilee, and spoke the cruder language of the exhorter and itinerant revivalist. When Roosevelt uttered like sentiments, his utterances had the color and prestige of a respectable cult and an established Church."

This merger of interests and sentiments did not come out of nowhere. Already a confluence of Populist and nascent Progressive forces had come together to pass the Interstate Commerce Act in 1888, regulating rates and prohibiting discriminatory pricing, and the Sherman Anti-Trust Act of 1890, outlawing monopolies. As the historian Eldon Eisenach has noted, the laws may have been "contradictory in their aims," the first aimed at controlling concentrated economic power, the second at breaking it up. The courts often rendered both laws "ineffectual." Yet both, as Eisenach argued, "symbolized a new national commitment to responsible oversight of the flourishing industrial economy."

This was a central goal for both Populists and Progressives. It was the beginning of the end of the Gilded Age exception to the American rule of a government creatively engaged in the nation's economic life. The goals of this new coalition were in keeping with the objectives of Hamilton, Clay, and Lincoln: to foster a flourishing private sector while also achieving public purposes and common ends. It was a return to the classic American balance between individual freedom and the community interest.

With a brief interruption during the 1920s, the Progressive impulse shaped American thinking about public life for the next eight decades. It both brought about and defined what came to be known as the American Century. Eisenach was not exaggerating when he wrote of Progressivism that

> the movement's leading minds founded the modern American university and created the modern academic disciplines and journals; they created the ligaments of the national administrative and regulatory state and founded and supplied a mass national journalism independent of political parties and churches; and they witnessed and helped legitimate the creation of a national financial and industrial corporate economy that soon became the engine driving

the international economy. In short, they helped transform America into the dominant world power it is today.

Note that Eisenach calls attention to how the Progressives helped "legitimate" the corporate economy. By criticizing, reforming, and rationalizing the workings of capitalism, the Progressives helped the system survive. In this sense, left-of-center revisionist historians such as Gabriel Kolko were on to something important when they pointed to Progressivism's "conservative" achievements. It would not be the last time that capitalism was saved not by its most unapologetic enthusiasts but by critics who understood the system's imperfections and inadequacies and saved it from itself.

Inspired by the Populists, spurred by the rising Socialist and trade union movements, and encouraged by Social Gospel Christians, the Progressives took a step beyond their forebears in linking government's engagement with the economy to the cause of social justice. In doing so, the Progressives brokered an informal settlement in the battles between the Jeffersonians and the Hamiltonians, the Jacksonians and the Whigs. They embraced the Jefferson-Jackson tradition of deepening American democracy and promoting greater social equality (even if many of them retained a Whiggish mistrust of both). But they found their path to these ends through the methods of Hamilton and Clay. They would use federal and state governments on behalf of a new set of "internal improvements" that would lift up the economically downtrodden and ensure fair economic competition. Herbert Croly, the progressive thinker who gave shape to what became modern liberalism, as the historian Edward Stettner rightly argued, put the new movement into precisely this context. Its goal, Croly wrote, was "to use Hamiltonian administrative nationalism in the interest of a democratic social policy"—as we saw earlier, to deploy Hamiltonian means to Jeffersonian ends.

Progressivism was a vast and varied movement, and in the 1912 election it presented itself in two different forms. Theodore Roosevelt's "New Nationalism" battled Woodrow Wilson's "New Freedom." The differences between the two reverberate to this day. Roosevelt, influenced by Croly, argued that economic concentration was inevitable and that efficiency and justice were best served through government regulation of the large new enterprises. Wilson, adopting the views of Louis Brandeis, argued for breaking up the large agglomerations of economic power in the interest of creating a fair and competitive marketplace energized by smaller businesses. Charging Wilson with believing in the "outworn academic doctrine" of laissez-faire economics, Roosevelt pledged to "use the whole power of government" to combat "an unregulated and purely individualistic industrialism." Wilson replied that Roosevelt's policies would leave sprawling, inefficient, and domineering corporations intact. "Have we come to a time," Wilson asked, "when the President of the United States or any man who wishes to be President must doff his cap in the presence of high finance and say, 'You are our inevitable master, but we will see how we can make the best of it?'"

"There is," Wilson insisted, "a point of bigness—as every businessman in this country knows, though some will not admit it . . . where you pass the point of efficiency and get to the point of clumsiness and unwieldiness." And in words that would have been quite at home at an anti–Wall Street occupation, Wilson warned that the country was nearing "the time when the combined power of high finance would be greater than the power of government."

Yet both Roosevelt and Wilson recognized this as a problem, even if they proposed different solutions. Both spoke to widespread anger at the captains of industry and finance, as did the Socialist candidate, Eugene V. Debs. Debs won 6 percent of the vote, the high tide of electoral Socialism in the United States in an era when Socialists ran major cities and won election to state legislatures and to Congress.

By contrast, President William Howard Taft—his background was moderately progressive, but he was moving toward a genial but firm conservatism—outlined the classic laissez-faire response that is also familiar in our day. "A National Government cannot create good times," declared the only Republican nominee in history to run third in a presidential election. "It cannot make the rain to fall, the sun to shine, or the crops to grow, but it can, by pursuing a meddlesome policy, attempting to change economic conditions, and frightening the investment of capital, prevent a prosperity and a revival of business which might otherwise have taken place." John Milton Cooper, Wilson's biographer, observed that Taft's declaration "marked an early step toward the ideological transformation of the Republican Party during the rest of the twentieth century."

In rejecting unregulated markets and unchecked individualism, both Wilson and Roosevelt were arguing within the framework of the old republican tradition familiar to our founders. As Michael Sandel observed, Wilson and Roosevelt—along with their intellectual guides Brandeis and Croly—"agreed despite their differences that economic and political institutions should be assessed for their tendency to promote or erode the moral qualities self-government requires. Like Jefferson before them, they worried about the sort of citizens the economic arrangements of their day were likely to produce. They argued, in different ways, for a political economy of citizenship."

This is not how the conservatives of our day view the Progressives. Contemporary critics highlight the Progressives' support for a strong central government and their fascination with applying scientific expertise to the solution of social problems. Voices on the left have sometimes joined with those on the right in arguing that many Progressives replaced faith in democracy with a confidence in rational, scientific management. This, in turn, led to a preference for government by experts and the centralization of authority. The conservative writer Chester Finn argued in the 1990s that Progressivism created a "cult of governmentalism" that "made us lazy and dependent while taking vast sums out of our pockets." From a different perspective, the historian Michael McGerr saw Croly's "preoccupation with strong government, strong leaders and strong nationalism" as making "explicit what was implicit in middle-class culture at the turn of the century: a subtle but significant loss of faith in traditional democratic notions."

There is something to this criticism. Some Progressives *did* harbor an ambivalence about democracy, and some progressive reforms—aimed in theory at reducing electoral fraud—impeded access to the ballot box. Many southern progressives imbibed their region's reactionary attitudes toward race. TR's approach to race was ambivalent, and Wilson's record in office was shameful and the source of bitter disappointment to W. E. B. Du Bois, the author, intellectual, and cofounder of the NAACP, who had supported Wilson in 1912. It took decades for many progressives to free themselves from a racism that engulfed the country for decades after the end of Reconstruction.

Yet in their advocacy of initiative, referendum, and recall as well as the direct election of United States senators, the Progressives could also be seen as radical democrats. Here the Populist influence was clear. Theodore Roosevelt went further still, supporting democratic ways of overturning conservative judicial rulings. But, again, there was an ambivalence: many of the Progressives were also mistrustful of urban working-class voters, particularly immigrants, who lent their ballots to political machines. The newcomers were in turn skeptical of—or even hostile to—the efforts of largely Protestant social workers who tried to "improve" them by pushing them away from strong drink and toward Protestant conceptions of morality and faith. Cultural barriers between Progressives and significant parts of the working class long predated the culture wars of the 1960s.

Nonetheless, it is misleading to cast the Progressives as pure centralizers indifferent to local government, local community, and the need to strengthen civic and social institutions outside government. Their record belies this. Progressives often achieved their reforms through local and state institutions, partly because they could not always succeed at the federal level, and also because they were mindful that hostile courts would find it easier to undo their work if they relied on federal power alone. Their campaign to outlaw or regulate child labor began in the states—non-southern states, it needs to be said—before taking hold at the national level. Twenty-five states had passed such laws by 1901, Eisenach notes, while twenty-two states acted between 1903 and 1908 to make it illegal for corporations to contribute to political campaigns.

If the Progressives were hyper-centralizers, why did they pay so much attention to the reform of local governments? As Eisenach observed, Progressives (and in some cases the Socialists who did quite well at the local political level in those years) wrote new municipal charters for cities they controlled. They "formed their own municipal corporations to supply transportation, water, gas and electricity," and often created "nonpartisan commissions to regulate these industries." Progressive engagement with the idea of community was not simply national and abstract. It was also local and concrete.

The Progressive spirit pushed against pure individualism in another way, creating a vast array of civil society institutions devoted to building social capital outside (or alongside) both government and the marketplace. Community and institution building was a passion for the overlapping Populist and Progressive moments. Robert Putnam offered a catalogue of the era's organizational achievements:

> If you look at the dates at which they were created, almost all of the major civic institutions of the United States today—the Red Cross, the YWCA, the Boy Scouts, the NAACP, the Urban League, many labor unions, the Sons of Italy, the Sons of Norway, parent-teacher associations, the Rotary Club, the Sierra Club, the Knights of Columbus and many others—almost all of them were formed between 1880 and 1910, an astonishingly concentrated period. We had a social capital deficit as a country created by great technological and economic change, and at that point we could have said, "Whoa, wait a minute, stop! Everybody back to the farm. It was much nicer there. We knew everybody."

For most Americans in the Progressive Era, the farm was becoming less and less of an option, so the men and women of the time built organizations instead, many of them linked to the reform efforts Progressives, Socialists, and Populists were pursuing in the political sphere. In his book about New York City Progressives, *Civic Engagement*, John Louis Recchiuti points to the work of the NAACP, the National Urban League, the American Association for Labor Legislation, the National Consumers League, the National Child Labor Committee, and grassroots efforts social reformers undertook in the settlement houses. These organizational initiatives were as much a part of the Progressive surge as were the campaigns of TR and Wilson. For the Progressives, there was no sharp separation between the local and national, between charitable work and political work. Progressives such as Jane Addams were nudged toward political action when they concluded that one-on-one social work was insufficient to alleviate the dire conditions that existed in the neighborhoods where they worked. The individual, the social, and the political were bound together. Community building at the local level and at the national level went hand in hand; they were not opposed to each other and did not undermine each other.

This was the conclusion the sociologist Theda Skocpol reached in her research, cited in Chapter 5. "Early twentieth-century local, state, and national policies to help mothers and children were championed by the Women's Christian Temperance Union, the National Congress of Mothers (later the PTA), and the General Federation of Women's Clubs—groups that themselves expanded in part because of encouragement by government," she wrote. "State and federal efforts to support farmers and farm families have been championed and administered by associations such as the Grange and the American Farm Bureau Federation, the latter of which grew into a nationwide federation in conjunction with New Deal farm programs."

Indeed, later on, one of the most successful programs of the FDR era was the product of exactly this sort of interaction between the federal government and an organization that was founded in the waning years of the Progressive Era and had built deep local roots. "The GI Bill of 1944 never would have taken the inclusive shape it did, opening up American higher education to hundreds of thousands of less privileged men," Skocpol wrote, "had not the American Legion taken the lead in writing generous legislation and encouraging public and congressional support for it. In turn, the GI Bill aided the postwar expansion of the American Legion."

What these efforts had in common was the reassertion of the idea of community at all levels—federal and state, county and city, small town and neighborhood. Progressives understood that in a nation with both strong local traditions and an increasingly powerful national economic market, local groups could not always thrive on their own in the face of the centralizing (and, one might add, then and now, globalizing) forces of the marketplace. It is not simply that rapid economic change can ravage local communities. Even in flourishing areas, both advocates of the unregulated market and supporters of holding the market to social standards understood the need for national allies.

The courts were inevitably enlisted in these battles. As we saw earlier, there were no courts more "activist" than those of the Gilded Age, and they freely imposed themselves against both state and national measures to regulate the marketplace in goods and labor. In the best recent account of the transformative 1912 election, the political scientist Sidney Milkis stresses the importance of Theodore Roosevelt's crusade against court decisions restricting the ability of state and federal governments to create rules for corporate behavior. Roosevelt accused conservative jurists of using the Fourteenth Amendment's due process clause as if "property rights, to the exclusion of human rights, had a first mortgage on the Constitution." To Taft's consternation, TR sympathized with efforts to allow the democratic will to take precedence over judicial rulings. Roosevelt argued that "when a State court cast aside as unconstitutional a law passed by the legislature for the general welfare," the issue of the law's validity should "be submitted for final determination to a vote of the people, taken after due time for consideration."

Roosevelt's campaign to weaken judicial review failed, but the election of judges was a widespread practice, and voters did have an impact on jurisprudence below the federal level. It is a paradox of our time that as the courts sweep away the very campaign finance rules Roosevelt promoted to limit the power of big businesses and its lobbies, the election of judges has become an increasingly problematic feature of our democracy. But the larger point is that Roosevelt's battle with intrusive conservative courts— the struggle his cousin FDR took up again in the 1930s, with mixed results— should remind us that the confrontation between community-minded reformers and a jurisprudence based on radical forms of individualism has been a staple of our politics for more than a century.

Progressivism, as Milkis insisted, was "not a radical rejection of the American tradition. Rather, it marked an important effort to reconcile the country's celebration of individualism and reformers' recognition of the need to strengthen the national government." It was something else as well. "The most exalted purpose of the insurgency that crested in 1912," Milkis wrote, "was to transform the right-based culture that had long shaped American life into a society awakened by sentiments of duty and obligation."

Progressivism and Populism represented both innovation and restoration. The Progressives' creativity was impressive, as was their willingness to alter long-standing constitutional arrangements. In constitutional terms, the Progressives were certainly more audacious than today's liberals are, speaking critically (as Wilson and Beard did) of the Constitution's shortcomings and amending it to accommodate new circumstances. A short list of Progressive achievements would include the income tax, women's suffrage, the direct election of senators, stepped-up anti-trust enforcement, the creation of the Federal Reserve Bank, the regulation of food and drugs, the creation of the Federal Trade Commission, the establishment of the Department of Labor, the creation of the U.S. Forest Service, and the preservation of more than 170 million acres of land through a vast expansion of the national parks system.

All this entailed substantial growth in the federal government, but far from being interlopers who broke with the nation's "small government" history, the Progressives are more appropriately seen as *restoring* a longer tradition of government interaction with the marketplace. They tempered market values with republican and civic values, protected individual rights against concentrations of private power, and sought to harmonize those rights with the interests of the community. The Gilded Age had departed from this tradition, and the Progressives brought it back, looking, as Croly did, to the models of Hamilton and Lincoln.

It should also be stressed that that the nationalization of the economy *preceded* the Progressives' nationalizing innovations in government. They concluded that in the new circumstances, only national action could be fully effective in enforcing new rules for a radically transformed national marketplace. Their arguments for regulating and containing the monopolies and the trusts often saw property rights as in competition with individual rights. Judge Ben Lindsey of Colorado made this explicit in a speech to the 1912 Progressive Party convention when he declared that "property rights shall not be exalted over human rights." Individualism, properly understood as protecting individual autonomy and choice, was quite different from the Gilded Age's *radical* individualism, which had defined corporations as people and property as the primary human right.

This contrast grew naturally from the Progressives' fascination with the interaction between individuality and the individual's need for community, an issue explored fruitfully by Wilfred McClay in *The Masterless: Self and Society in Modern America*. True individuality in the Progressive view *required* a connection to community, to one's "fellows," as Croly put it. For Croly, McClay argued, "individualism had become particularly disastrous and self-negating." The economic system of the time "compromised a man as much in his success as in his failure" because "the system's emphasis upon 'acquisitive motives' forced all men into a common mold, namely that of cash value." Croly believed that self-expression included social as well as individual aims, and he insisted that "the achievement of the national purpose will contribute positively to the liberation of the individual."' Similarly, John Dewey's call for the creation of "Great Community" did not stem from a reflexive or ideological preference for the national over the local, or for larger over smaller community. It was, Dewey wrote, a logical and necessary response to a nationalized society and economy that had "invaded and partially disintegrated the small communities of former times without generating a Great Community." As McClay noted, Dewey saw the "Great Community" he sought to build as requiring "a perception of common interest, a high degree of conscious moral and intellectual association, and flexible and comprehensive networks of communication." (Dewey might be viewed as a prophet who foresaw the online social networks that are a hallmark of our era.) Progressives, then, were engaged in far more than building effective, "scientific," centralized government. They also sought to strengthen the bonds of community that were fraying as the nation moved from farm to factory, from small town to big city, and from more compact forms of business to sprawling enterprises and corporations. They addressed the new in the old language of republicanism, self-rule, and civic virtue.

The Progressive-Populist fusion created a way of thinking and a passion for balance that defined American attitudes toward public life for the rest of the century. Perhaps the greatest tribute to its achievement was the extent to which conservatives over time accommodated many of its assumptions, and embraced its methods—from the initiative and the referendum to its language of class conflict, directed not against wealth and corporate privilege but at "elitist liberals." And especially after the Great Depression, the New Deal, and American victory in World War II, most conservatives accepted, if sometimes grudgingly, the need for a stronger national government as a response to a more centralized economy and a geographically mobile people whose ties to the nation were weakening their ties to locality and state.

Two of the initiatives undertaken by Dwight D. Eisenhower, the first Republican elected president after the twenty-year New Deal–Fair Deal era, are revealing. The creation of the Interstate Highway System—it might be seen as the fulfillment of Henry Clay's dreams, the ultimate "internal improvement"—not only bound the nation more closely together but quite literally made concrete the idea that the boundaries between states had far less meaning than they once did. In large metropolitan areas that spilled over state lines, the planning of the new transportation system assumed that the new forms of social organization created by housing and retail markets (greater New York, greater Washington, "Chicagoland") mattered far more in the daily lives of citizens than the old political boundaries between states. Eisenhower also championed the National Defense Education Act, whose college loan program not only promoted social and economic mobility but also accelerated geographical mobility as millions of young Americans moved far and wide to pursue the new opportunities their educations afforded them. The Progressives and the Populists did not invent the idea of a far more unified American nation. They simply recognized it and accommodated it. Subsequent generations concluded they had been right to do so.

II

The new balance the Progressives championed did not go unchallenged. Progressivism suffered a grievous blow when Woodrow Wilson, having successfully campaigned for reelection in 1916 as the president who "kept us out of war," decided a year later to intervene in World War I. Most damaging for the Progressive cause, he made his case for our participation not on national interest grounds alone but as a logical extension of the Progressive idea at home. By the end of Wilson's term, the country was tired of grand adventures and sought the safety of a serene, inward-looking conservatism.

It's hard to think of a more profound rise and fall of the impulse toward public action throughout the West than World War I and its aftermath. It is no surprise that this brutal and in many ways inconclusive war unleashed a deep cynicism about public life and grand aspirations among the "Lost Generation" of the 1920s. As the economist Albert Hirschman noted in *Shifting Involvements: Private Interest and Public Action*, the mad slaughter of the war and an outcome that was dissatisfying even to the victors produced a deep disillusionment with public engagement, with the ideas of "heroic action and sacrifice," and with the concept of "glory" itself.

This was certainly true in the United States, even though Americans suffered nothing remotely like the losses Europeans experienced. By turning World War I into a Progressive war rooted in idealism, Wilson made it inevitable that the disappointment arising from a flawed peace would, for a time, discredit Progressive idealism itself. "The world must be made safe for democracy," Woodrow Wilson had declared in bringing the United States into the war. "We have no selfish ends to serve. We desire no conquest, no dominion . . . We shall be satisfied when those rights have been made as secure as the faith and the freedom of nations can make them."

Victory came, but the aftermath did not—and almost certainly could not—live up to Wilson's sweeping hopes. The ensuing public disillusionment was well described by H. L. Mencken, a reactionary with a gift for invective who proclaimed idealism's death in 1920. After two decades of Progressivism, he wrote, Americans were weary "of a steady diet of . . . highfalutin and meaningless words," and sickened by "an idealism that is oblique, confusing, dishonest and ferocious." This, said Mencken, explained why Americans embraced the Republican candidacy of Warren G. Harding, hardly a man of great intellectual or moral distinction. "Tired to death of intellectual charlatanry," Mencken memorably observed, the electorate "turns to honest imbecility."

But when it came to understanding the nation's mood, Harding was no imbecile. The country, he said in the spring of 1920 in his most famous pronouncement, wanted "not heroics, but healing; not nostrums, but normalcy; not revolution, but restoration; not agitation, but adjustment; not surgery, but serenity; not the dramatic, but the dispassionate; not experiment, but equipoise; not submergence in internationality, but sustainment in triumphant nationality." As Arthur Schlesinger Jr. quipped: "He should have added: not action but alliteration."

In the short run, the 1920s seemed to mark a return to the Gilded Age. Conservative ideas predominated, and the country's prosperity seemed to justify the enthusiastic turn back to laissez-faire. President Calvin Coolidge captured the spirit of the decade when he declared: "After all, the chief business of the American people is business." Coolidge's defenders note that in the same speech, the president also insisted: "The chief ideal of the American people is idealism. I cannot repeat too often that America is a nation of idealists. That is the only motive to which they ever give any strong and lasting reaction." Coolidge's idealism, however, seemed inspired primarily by an almost mystical (and perhaps idolatrous) devotion to the American business system. "The man who builds a factory builds a temple," Coolidge wrote. "The man who works there worships there."

Yet the "normalcy" of the Harding-Coolidge years did not destroy Progressivism. As the historian Arthur Link noted, "Large and aggressive components of a potential new progressive coalition remained after 1920." Despite "reversals and failures, important components of the national progressive movement survived in considerable vigor and succeeded to a varying degree, not merely in keeping the movement alive, but even in broadening its horizons."

The 1924 election was a triumph for Coolidge, as he overwhelmed conservative Democrat John W. Davis by a popular vote margin of 54 percent to 29 percent. But the remaining 17 percent went to the Progressive third-party insurgency led by Senator Robert M. La Follette. He managed to carry only one state outright, his home ground of Wisconsin. But La Follette ran second, ahead of the conservative Davis, in ten states, and the La Follette coalition was a partial precursor to the realignment that Franklin Roosevelt would bring about eight years later.

Moreover, a band of urban and rural progressives in Congress—among them Fiorello LaGuardia and Robert Wagner from New York, George Norris from Nebraska, and Bronson Cutting from New Mexico—battled the conservative tide in the 1920s by pushing for a range of reforms that prefigured Roosevelt's New Deal. These included proposals for public power that eventually led to the creation of the Tennessee Valley Authority; for empowering labor unions that culminated in the Wagner Act; and various proposals for social insurance that prefigured Social Security. The progressives were not marginal figures in politics. As Link observed, "Various progressive coalitions controlled Congress for the greater part of the

1920s and were always a serious threat to the conservative administrations that controlled the executive branch." The progressives drew electoral sustenance from millions of Americans left out of the great bonanza of the 1920s. A soaring Wall Street was accompanied by a near depression on the farms, and economic inequality reached a high point in 1929 that it would not hit again until 2007.

Herbert Hoover, who assumed the presidency in 1929, was no reactionary. He had been a Bull Moose Progressive in 1912, and his admirers included Franklin D. Roosevelt. "He is certainly a wonder, and I wish we could make him president of the United States," Roosevelt said of Hoover in 1920. "There could not be a better one." Hoover described himself at the time as an "independent progressive" and declared he was repelled by "reactionaries" and "radicals" alike. If Hoover later became a staunch conservative, his response to the Depression, though ineffectual, could not be described as laissez-faire. Roosevelt freely (and opportunistically) used this against him in the 1932 campaign. FDR condemned Hoover for having presided over "the greatest spending Administration in peace times in all our history." The Roosevelt who would vastly expand the number of government agencies, from the AAA to the CCC to the TVA, had no compunction in 1932 about accusing Hoover of having "piled bureau on bureau, commission on commission."

III

The 1920s proved to be an interruption but not a reversal of the progressive thrust in American politics. The New Deal was many things, but one thing it did *not* represent was a break from history. Roosevelt's program was adventurous in certain respects because the circumstances he confronted were so dire. But Roosevelt, the former Wilson administration official, was acting well within the framework of the progressive tradition and the capitalist system. If his New Deal lacked philosophical tidiness (and Roosevelt had declared plainly that his central purpose in the face of an economic collapse was to "above all, try *something*"), it could not be charged with radicalism.

In retrospect, the critique of the New Deal from the *left*—that its

purposes were fundamentally conservative, aimed at saving capitalism and
the traditional American system—is more persuasive in a descriptive sense
than right-wing claims that Roosevelt inaugurated a new era of American
socialism. "Using the federal government to stabilize the economy and
advance the interests of the groups Franklin D. Roosevelt directed the
campaign to save large-scale corporate capitalism," wrote the New Left
historian Barton Bernstein, "Franklin D. Roosevelt directed the campaign
to save large-scale corporate capitalism . . . Despite the flurry of activity,
his government was more vigorous and flexible about means than goals, and
the goals were more conservative than historians usually acknowledge." In
light of capitalism's enormous success in the years after the New Deal, can
anyone deny that saving the market system was one of FDR's singular accomplishments?

Within all the experimentation and apparent incoherence of the early
New Deal, Alan Brinkley identified four discernable philosophical strains.
The "anti-monopolists . . . envisioned a frontal assault on 'bigness' and concentration in the corporate world and . . . often called as well for policies
that would redistribute wealth and income." The "advocates of centralized
economic planning" sought "to curb the power of corporations by greatly
increasing the managerial power of government" and envisioned a "state
apparatus closely involved in the day-to-day workings of the economy."
Supporters of "the vaguely corporatist concept of business 'associationalism'"
looked toward creating "cartelistic arrangements within major industries
to curb the destabilizing impact of competition." They foresaw government
playing "a modest, largely uncoercive role."

Only "on the edges of liberal thought," Brinkley observed, were "more
radical ideas" that saw the Depression as revealing "the obsolescence of
capitalism and the need for a fundamentally new system."

Each of these tendencies, particularly the first three, found expression
in various early New Deal policies. Yet as Brinkley notes in his seminal
book *The End of Reform*, the boldness of the early New Deal had largely
dissipated as an influence on American liberalism by 1945. When Roosevelt
embarked on deep reductions in federal expenditures in 1937—a choice
chillingly similar to the moves toward fiscal austerity around the world in

2010 and 2011—the economy turned down sharply. It did not recover again until large-scale military spending, first in preparation for World War II and then in its execution, finally created the jobs and the mass consumer spending that full recovery required. The economy soared, and it continued to do so, with relatively brief interruptions, for nearly seventy years.

There was an irony in the success of Keynesian "pump priming" so vilified over the years by conservatives. It resulted, as Brinkley documents, in a more conservative form of progressive liberalism. "When liberals spoke now of government's responsibility to protect the health of the industrial world," Brinkley wrote, "they defined that responsibility less as a commitment to restructure the economy than as an effort to stabilize it and help it to grow." There was less talk about "controlling or punishing 'plutocrats' and 'economic royalists.'" Instead, the new liberal emphasis was on "providing a healthy environment in which the corporate world could flourish and in which the economy could sustain 'full employment'."

The new Keynesian liberalism was remarkably successful. But in light of the deep economic difficulties of the last several years, it is worth pondering Brinkley's conclusions about the new liberalism, which he offered in 1995, long before the Great Recession. "In the end," Brinkley wrote, "it was not as easy as many liberals once expected to create a just and prosperous society without worrying about the problems of production and the structure of the economy." Many of the difficulties that the early New Dealers faced and that later New Dealers thought had been resolved came back to haunt the country in the economic meltdown of 2008 and 2009.

And this led to another irony. In the Obama years, many progressives longed for the president to embrace the aggressively populist FDR of the early New Deal—the man who condemned "economic royalists" while gleefully observing that the "money-changers have fled from their high seats in the temple of our civilization." But the policies Obama pursued were broadly consistent with the New Deal's *later* Keynesian emphasis on seeking economic stability and encouraging private sector investment and growth. The economic argument among progressives in our time can thus be seen as the playing out of the differences between the rival forms of New Deal liberalism described by Brinkley.

The struggles of the early New Deal itself are also enlightening in relation to Obama's political strategy. The robust criticisms of business and the "economic royalists" that today's progressives cite so fondly came late in Roosevelt's first term. (Roosevelt's condemnation of the economic royalists was a rhetorical high point of his June 1936 speech before the Democratic National Convention, more than three years after he took office.) Much of the early New Deal was aimed at stabilizing the business system. Initially, with the National Recovery Administration (later declared unconstitutional by a conservative Supreme Court), Roosevelt actively sought to work *with* business to end the Depression. The more adventurous parts of the New Deal—widely known as the Second New Deal—came later, between 1934 and 1936. This is when Roosevelt pushed for the enactment of the Wagner Act, the empowerment of labor unions, the WPA to put the unemployed to work on government projects, and his most enduring legacy, the Social Security system.

Roosevelt acted out of frustration with the failures of some of his earlier measures and from the need for a new program in light of judicial hostility to some of his old approaches. But he also came under pressure from a variety of mass movements that rose after conditions in the country began to improve. He faced an increasingly militant union movement; politicians such as Huey Long, who was championing his "share the wealth" plan until he was assassinated in September 1935; and a variety of organizers and agitators urging the country to go far beyond New Dealism. One of them was Dr. Francis Townsend, who found himself unemployed and nearly broke at the age of sixty-seven. Townsend electrified the country with his proposal to pay all Americans over sixty a $200-a-month pension—provided they retired and promised to spend the entire sum over the course of the month. The idea was to free up jobs for younger Americans and boost the economy with new spending. Townsend's pressure led to Social Security, a far more modest and conservative program than Townsend had demanded.

The merits of proposals offered by Townsend, Long, and others need not detain us. What mattered is that they pressed Roosevelt toward the left. So did the results of the 1934 elections, which produced a Democratic landslide and a Congress that, as William Leuchtenburg noted, "threatened to push him in a direction far more radical than any he had originally contemplated." Over time, Roosevelt developed a working relationship with the left, particularly within the labor movement, that tried to move Roosevelt beyond his instinctive cautiousness, but also gave him critical support against his foes on the right.

The parallels with Obama are not straightforward. The midterm elections of 2010 went in exactly the *opposite* direction from the Democrats' 1934 triumph. During Obama's first two years, the biggest mass movements, above all the Tea Party, were to the president's right, not to his left. The trade union movement was rising in Roosevelt's time. It had been fading for decades, except in the public sector, before Obama took office. (This makes it all the more puzzling that the Democrats did not make labor law reform a higher priority when they controlled both houses of Congress.) And, of course, assigning responsibility for the economic difficulties to his predecessor was far easier for Roosevelt than for Obama. Hoover had been president for three very long years as unemployment spiraled upward. Obama, by contrast, took office as the impact of the September 2008 market blowup was reaching full force, and unemployment continued to rise after his inauguration.

Nonetheless, the new vigor that the Occupy Wall Street protests injected into the broader progressive movement began to change both the nature of the national conversation—toward jobs, inequality, and the concentration of wealth—and Obama's own approach. The Obama administration, impatient with critics to its left in its early years, seemed to welcome a counterpoint to the Tea Party, and the president sharpened his rhetoric about economic inequality, most visibly in his 2012 State of the Union address. Given the array of political forces in the country (Obama facing a far stronger right than Roosevelt did), it's unlikely that the forty-fourth president will be able to follow the same political path as did the thirty-first. Nonetheless, in moving from the center to a position somewhere to its left in response to both the Occupy movement and the intransigence of Republicans in Congress, Obama's trajectory could prove to be more similar to Roosevelt's than progressives thought possible.

I V

It has been common in American public discourse—among liberals as well as moderates and conservatives—to speak of the obsolescence of the New Deal and its approaches.

It is certainly true that the nature of the American economy is quite different now than it was in the 1930s and 1940s. The "vision of villages and clean small factories" that Leuchtenburg invoked as emblematic of the New Deal imagination seems sweetly quaint at a time when so much of the economy has shifted toward technology and services—and when the word "village" is most commonly used by developers trying to conjure the warmth of a distant past in their suburban and exurban building projects.

The United States should not resign itself to the disappearance of well-paying manufacturing work—we can be "neo-industrial," as Harold Meyerson has argued and President Obama has begun asserting—but the new economy cannot be repealed by statute, and there are many reasons why we would not want to do so. The rise of China, India, and Brazil along with a vast new industrial economy across the rest of Asia is transforming the world in ways that neither progressives nor New Dealers envisioned. The prospect of lifetime employment at a single firm, which underwrote the social contract during much of the Long Consensus, is unlikely to be revived.

Nor can the United States again expect to enjoy the degree of dominance in the global economy it gained during World War II and held for years afterward. Even as the war quite literally destroyed the plants and equipment of so many of our global competitors, it left the United States with vastly enhanced productive capacities. And the sheer speed and comprehensiveness of technological change has made national borders more porous, national planning more difficult, and the redistribution of resources more challenging. The very process through which the book you are holding was written, edited, and produced is vastly different from how my first book was created only two decades ago. Indeed, the odds are good that you are not holding a book at all but reading these words on a device that even ten years ago existed only in the imaginations of innovators.

Labor unions, so successful in organizing large industrial plants, reducing inequalities, and mobilizing support for New Deal policies, are vastly weaker and find themselves under threat from conservative politicians around the nation. The family structure has changed, and so, too, have attitudes toward women, racial and religious minorities, and, more recently, gays and lesbians.

As a result, the limitations of the New Deal itself are also more obvious. Leuchtenburg notes that the New Deal "achieved a more just society by recognizing groups which had been largely unrepresented—staple farmers, industrial workers, particular ethnic groups and the new intellectual-administrative class." But he also pointed to the many Americans left "outside of the new equilibrium," among them "sharecroppers, slum dwellers," and (he was writing in 1962) "most Negroes."

Yet for all the changes in the country and for all the New Deal's shortcomings, ours is still a nation shaped by the New Deal's legacy. If some of its core commitments are under challenge as never before, its moral basis still galvanizes not only progressives and liberals but also many who do not think of politics in ideological terms.

New Dealism accepted and fostered a cooperative connection between government and the private economy. It understood government's role as constructive, and assigned government a moral responsibility. "Governments can err, presidents do make mistakes," Franklin Roosevelt famously declared in 1936, "but the immortal Dante tells us that Divine justice weighs the sins of the cold-blooded and the sins of the warm-hearted on different scales. Better the occasional faults of a government that lives in a spirit of charity than the consistent omissions of a government frozen in the ice of its own indifference."

Roosevelt explicitly broke with the view dominant in the Gilded Age, and still popular among orthodox conservative economists, that the economy operated according to laws as "natural" as those of science. "We must lay hold of the fact that economic laws are not made by nature," Roosevelt said. "They are made by human beings." This view was no less controversial in his day than it is in ours. "Two more glaring misstatements of the truth could hardly have been packed into so little space," the conservative Boston *Transcript* grumbled. Roosevelt, however, was closer to the American tradition of viewing economic questions through a pragmatic lens.

The New Deal wrote the basic rules that allowed the United States to become the most powerful economy in the world while avoiding a major meltdown for more than six decades. The social and labor policies Roosevelt championed laid the groundwork for the growth of the American middle class after World War II, for an increasingly prosperous working class, and for the creation of a nationwide system of social insurance for widows, orphans, the aged, and the unemployed. Large-scale spending on public buildings and public works—undertaken initially to relieve mass unemployment—permanently affirmed the national government's role in investing in the nation, a commitment Eisenhower reaffirmed.

The New Deal's philosophical eclecticism aroused criticism from the left and right alike. But the New Deal shared both John Dewey's goal of building a "Great Community" and a vital interest in constructing (and reconstructing) thriving local community. "Hardheaded, 'anti-utopian,' the New Dealers nonetheless had their Heavenly City," wrote Leuchtenburg, "the greenbelt town, clean, green, and white, with children playing in light, airy, spacious schools." Its most adventurous experiment in community building was the Tennessee Valley Authority "with its model town of Norris, the tall transmission towers, the white dams, the glistening wire strands, the valley where 'a vision of villages and clean small factories has been growing in the minds of thoughtful men.'" When the New Dealers looked abroad for models, they turned primarily to Scandinavia, Leuchtenburg noted, "because it represented the 'middle way' of happy accommodation of public and private institutions the New Deal sought to achieve." The balance and inherent moderation of the New Deal may have stunted the development of a bolder American left, as historians such as Bernstein have argued, but it also prevented the rise of the anti-democratic and fascist movements that swept through Europe in the 1930s.

And if it was war spending that ultimately pulled the United States out of the Depression, the government's domestic policies during World War II advanced many of the New Deal's goals, including—thanks to the rise of unions, progressive taxation, and various wartime regulations—a more equal distribution of income. "The sharp contraction in income inequality during the 1940s," noted the economists Carola Frydman and Raven Molloy, "was the largest and fastest compression of the distribution of income in the US of the twentieth century." This was part of a broader egalitarian surge that led the historian Geoffrey Perret to conclude that the war brought about "the closest thing to a real social revolution the United States has known in this century." Developments on the home front, Perret concluded, swept away "barriers to social and economic equality which had stood for decades," ended the "old pyramidal class structure," and created a "genuine middle class nation." It was during the war that "access to higher education became genuinely democratic for the first time," and it was also the period when "the modern civil rights movement began."

Thus did the interaction among Depression, the New Deal, and World War II create an ethic that endured for decades, shaping conservative as well as liberal presidencies. It was an ethic of community and solidarity that promoted individual mobility and expanded individual rights for African Americans and others that the New Deal had partly or wholly left out. Bound together by the experience of Depression and war, wrote Robert Reich, the country took a far different view of itself than it had in the Gilded Age or the 1920s. Society, he argued, "was not seen as composed of *us* and *them*; it was the realm of *we*."

The widespread embrace of a fundamentally communitarian view grew out of lived experience. "The goals of reviving the economy and winning the war, and the sacrifices implied in achieving them, were well understood and widely endorsed," Reich wrote. "The public was motivated less by altruism than by its direct and palpable stake in the outcome of what were ineluctably *social* endeavors."

It took extraordinary convulsions—the reactions to the civil rights movement and the 1960s counterculture, deep divisions bred by the Vietnam War, the cynicism that was a product of Watergate, the stagflation of the late 1970s that undercut confidence in Keynesian economics and bolstered the anti-tax movement—to disrupt a set of attitudes that were reinforced by the experiences of the 1930s and 1940s but had deep roots in our history and a rhetorical resonance even for politicians who were critical of so much of what the New Deal accomplished.

V

Eight decades after Roosevelt's election, the New Deal's programs—and subsequent initiatives that built on their achievements—remain among the most popular undertakings of government. That's certainly true of

Social Security, and it's also true of Medicare, added to FDR's social insurance system by Lyndon B. Johnson. Republicans paid homage to these programs not only by failing to repeal them but also by making them more generous, as Richard Nixon did with Social Security and George W. Bush did with Medicare. Ronald Reagan, once a New Dealer himself, became an outspoken critic of Roosevelt's program on the conservative speaking circuit in the 1950s and early 1960s. Yet as president, he shied away from taking on the New Deal, and even signed tax increases to make Social Security more secure.

His chosen successor, George H. W. Bush, could boast of two major domestic achievements, both of them consistent with the Long Consensus: the Americans with Disabilities Act, a historic expansion of the rights of the disabled, and amendments that strengthened the Clean Air Act, which allowed Bush to keep his promise to be "an environmental president" in the tradition of Teddy Roosevelt. Bush also bravely faced up to the budget deficit not only by cutting spending but also by raising taxes, even in the face of his campaign pledge not to do so. Bush paid a high political price for this—so high that most members of his party have, ever since, been reluctant to support tax increases under any circumstances.

It's equally notable that the most important legislative defeat George W. Bush suffered came when he proposed a partial privatization of social security that would have transformed part of the program into "personal" accounts. The idea never even came to a vote because so many in Bush's own party were wary of the political costs of trying to enact it. Just as significant, Bush's most daring domestic achievements expanded the federal government and built on New Deal and Great Society initiatives. The prescription drug program under Medicare, though structured in a way friendly to drug and insurance companies, added an essential benefit to the country's most costly social insurance program. And his No Child Left Behind Act aggressively used the influence of federal funding of local schools—an initiative begun under Roosevelt during World War II and expanded by Lyndon Johnson through the Elementary and Secondary Education Act—to promote standards and an assertive testing regime. The No Child Left Behind law was opposed by many conservatives precisely because it expanded

Washington's power, and it was passed with support from leading liberals, including the late Edward M. Kennedy.

The New Deal regulatory state did come under attack in the 1970s and the 1980s, and a wave of deregulation in fields such as airlines and trucking—and, with catastrophic results, banking and securities—won support from some liberals. As noted earlier, the Clinton administration backed financial deregulation that helped destabilize the system a decade later.

Yet many of the core New Deal structures (the Securities and Exchange Commission, the Federal Deposit Insurance Corporation) remained vital. They proved essential to President George H. W. Bush in resolving the savings and loan crisis in the late 1980s and early 1990s. And the financial and securities regulation that FDR championed seemed more relevant than ever after 2008, when scandalously weak oversight led to the abuse of financial instruments and a dangerous adventurism by banks that the brain trusters of the New Deal had once tried to curb. The Dodd-Frank bill passed in 2010 sought to restore and renovate the supervision of the financial sector that the New Deal pioneered.

In theory, Keynesianism was displaced by the reemergence of pre-Keynesian economics in the form of monetarism and supply-side nostrums. Keynesian policies seemed powerless in the face of stagflation in the late 1970s. Yet Ronald Reagan's own approach amounted to Keynesianism in heavy disguise. Reagan made the case for his tax cuts in 1981 on the basis of supply-side theory, which simply codified the economics of Calvin Coolidge. But the *effects* of Reagan's policies were exactly as Keynes might have predicted: they pumped up the economy through deficit spending, much of it passing through the Pentagon. The Reagan Democrats, who never lost their affection for New Dealism, kept voting for Reagan in part because he left untouched many of the pillars of the state Roosevelt built, and because Reagan was not afraid to use some of Roosevelt's ideas on the sly. Reaganism in practice fell well short of Reaganism in theory. The Tea Partiers who claim to be the true heirs of Reagan have paid more attention to his speeches from the 1950s and 1960s than to his choices as president in the 1980s. And, of course, Keynesian policies were essential around the world in keeping the Great Recession from becoming another depression.

Because the terms "New Deal" and "liberalism" are so often heard together, and because the New Deal did indeed accomplish a great deal, what is most easily forgotten is the fundamental moderation of Roosevelt's approach. He did not abolish capitalism; he regulated it. He did not wipe out inequality; he tempered it. He attacked the "economic royalists," but the wealthy survived and prospered in the Roosevelt years. He created many bureaus and agencies, but his largest accomplishment was not building up government as such but rather using government to alter the balance of influence in society and empower new groups: workers, by making it easier for them to organize unions; recent immigrants, by making them a powerful component of a new political coalition; the rural poor, by bringing them the liberation of electric power; famers, by freeing them from tyrannical gyrations in agricultural prices; and southerners, by bringing them into the nation's economic mainstream through large-scale federal investment.

Consider that the main effect of the New Deal was not to create a large class of would-be socialists dependent upon government but rather to build a nation of property owners who could buy homes, save securely, and invest with reasonable confidence that the stocks they purchased were not fraudulent. Such was the impact of the Federal Housing Authority, the Federal Deposit Insurance Corporation, and the Securities and Exchange Commission. Perhaps the best single description of the New Deal's impact came from onetime neoconservative intellectual Mark Lilla, who called it "a great act of civic inclusion." Roosevelt was an effective large-d Democrat because he proved to be a passionate small-r republican.

This, even more than the particulars of New Deal programs, explains the durability of the Long Consensus. New Dealism, like Progressivism and Populism before it, was rooted in America's tradition of balance, and no one understood this better than Roosevelt himself.

In the most philosophical speech of his first campaign, delivered at the Commonwealth Club in San Francisco in September 1932, he brought together the two sides of the American political heart. He argued that true American individualism was of a moderate, not radical, sort, tempered by our obligations to each other:

Every man has a right to his own property; which means a right
to be assured, to the fullest extent attainable, in the safety of his
savings. By no other means can men carry the burdens of those
parts of life which, in the nature of things, afford no chance of labor;
childhood, sickness, old age. In all thought of property, this right is
paramount; all other property rights must yield to it. If, in accord
with this principle, we must restrict the operations of the speculator,
the manipulator, even the financier, I believe we must accept the
restriction as needful, *not to hamper individualism but to protect it.*
[emphasis added]

Long before the Great Recession, when financial institutions received government bailouts to ensure their survival and then complained about government interference in the face of reforms aimed at preventing a repeat of
the abuses just past, Roosevelt was aware of the inconsistency—one might
say hypocrisy—in the uses of anti-government rhetoric. But he made his
case gently:

The same man who tells you that he does not want to see the government interfere in business—and he means it, and has plenty of good
reasons for saying so—is the first to go to Washington and ask the
government for a prohibitory tariff on his product. When things get
just bad enough—as they did two years ago—he will go with equal
speed to the United States government and ask for a loan; and the
Reconstruction Finance Corporation is the outcome of it. Each group
has sought protection from the government for its own special interest, without realizing that the function of government must be to
favor no small group at the expense of its duty to protect the rights of
personal freedom and of private property of all its citizens.

Always, there was Roosevelt's emphasis on balance:

We know that individual liberty and individual happiness mean
nothing unless both are ordered in the sense that one man's meat is

not another man's poison. We know that the old "rights of personal competency"—the right to read, to think, to speak, to choose and live a mode of life—must be respected at all hazards. We know that liberty to do anything which deprives others of those elemental rights is outside the protection of any compact; and *that government in this regard is the maintenance of a balance*, within which every individual may have a place if he will take it; in which every individual may find safety if he wishes it; in which every individual may attain such power as his ability permits, consistent with his assuming the accompanying responsibility. [emphasis added]

Roosevelt's ideas will continue to have resonance because they are consistent with our quest, from the very beginning of the republic, to achieve individual liberty rooted in a thriving sense of community and mutual obligation. That is why the Long Consensus is still relevant and requires an urgent defense in the face of efforts to dismantle its achievements.

The Long Consensus, of course, faced challenges from the beginning. Taft's resistance in 1912 proved ineffectual. The opposition in the 1920s was stronger, and then collapsed in the face of the popular demands for national action that the Great Depression called forth. Many of the ideas the Tea Party and its allies are putting forward now arose first in opposition to the New Deal. They did not begin to gather broad support until *National Review*'s journalistic and intellectual efforts in the 1950s, the Goldwater campaign's political exertions in the 1960s, and the tax revolt in the 1970s. Opponents of the Long Consensus continued to gain strength in the lead-up to Ronald Reagan's election and during the Reagan era itself. And they won an especially powerful foothold in the Supreme Court as conservatives steadily moved the country toward a pre–New Deal jurisprudence.

But only after the turmoil of the Bush presidency, the economic calamity of the Great Recession, and the rise of Barack Obama did the challenge to the Long Consensus reach full force. With nearly complete control of the Republican Party and hegemony within the conservative movement, radical individualism is as close to triumph as it has been at any point since the Gilded Age. Whether it will succeed or fail is now the central question in American politics.

Part Three

Recovering Our Balance, Restoring Our Greatness

CHAPTER X

The New American System
Building a Community of Freedom

W HEN he announced his ill-fated presidential candidacy in August 2011, Rick Perry, in a single sentence, brought to life the stakes in our national argument at this moment in our history. "I'll work every day," he declared, "to make Washington, D.C., as inconsequential in your life as I can."

That same month, Mitt Romney, in theory the Republicans' least ideological contender, delivered a memorable and revealing line at the Iowa State Fair when someone in the crowd shouted out a demand to increase taxes on corporations. Romney smiled and gave a reply more heartfelt than was typical of a candidate whose comments were so proudly disciplined.

His proclamation heard round the political world? "Corporations are people, my friend."

Romney's language echoed the legal point that the Gilded Age Supreme Court had made and on which the *Citizens United* decision was built. But that wasn't his purpose. He was presenting a simple argument that "everything corporations earn ultimately goes to people." Yet his comment went viral because it seemed to go to the heart of the divide in the nation—and perhaps also to Romney's identity as a corporate conservative. For many, endowing corporations with the same standing as actual human beings (and often with additional privileges) was precisely what ailed the country.

A month later, the Occupy Wall Street protests were launched on a sea of homemade signs. Naturally, one of the earliest placards proclaimed,

"Corporations are *not* people." Another declared: "Due to recent budget cuts, the light at the end of the tunnel has been turned off."

Barack Obama's first term in office began with the rise of the Tea Party movement and drew to a close with the protests against the power and influence of America's richest "1 percent." The two movements represented bookends of the American political sensibility, one directed at the power of government, the other at the power of high finance. They highlighted two aspects of the American character, reflected in the Tea Party's focus on liberty, self-reliance, and the unencumbered individual, and Occupy Wall Street's emphasis on equality, interconnection, and social obligation.

The Tea Party was the more conventionally political of the two movements, at home in Republican caucuses and at the ballot box. The Occupy movement was mistrustful of political power, of leaders, of "the system." Yet as the *New Yorker*'s Hendrik Hertzberg insisted, it would have to come to terms with them all. "Ultimately, inevitably, the route to real change has to run through politics," Hertzberg wrote, "the politics of America's broken, god-awful, immutably two-party electoral system, the only one we have." Then he added: "The Tea Partiers know that. Do the Occupiers?" His observation and his question felt like they carried the weight of history.

Barack Obama's presidency, which opened with such hope for national concord, was not expected to call forth two battalions of protest. They were the most dramatic evidence of how far we had traveled from the aspirations of Obama's 2004 address to the Democratic National Convention that made him a political phenomenon. There was a red America and a blue America after all, and they were not coming together.

In better economic times, we might have expected a different outcome. Yet there was a certain inevitability that no matter now hard Obama tried to make it otherwise, his presidency could never avoid becoming the locus of a great national struggle over who we are as a people. The crisis the country faced economically, the crisis of identity created by fears of decline, the crisis of national authority that began taking hold under George W. Bush, and the crisis of contemporary conservatism: all came together to force the country to a decision point. At stake was the Long Consensus that had guided the nation for a century, and it would fall to Obama to refashion it and defend it.

It was not inevitable that conservatives would respond to Bush's failures and their defeat in 2008 by moving to the right. In similar circumstances, other conservative parties and movements had regained power by pursuing moderate paths, proposing to check the excesses of their progressive foes without undoing all their work. This is how the Republican Party had eventually dealt with the New Deal, accepting its achievements as reflecting the popular will. In following this course, the Republicans went with rather than against the grain of American history. The Civil War had decisively settled the question that we were a nation, not a collection of states. The economic developments that followed thoroughly nationalized our commercial life. The federal government grew in tandem with the economy. After the New Deal, Dwight Eisenhower was the quintessential figure in this new settlement.

But many Republicans and conservatives never accepted the path of accommodation. With Barry Goldwater's nomination, they began pulling the party in a new direction. The shift was gradual, and even Ronald Reagan did not try to unravel the New Deal consensus. But Bush's failures opened the way for a decisive break, and Tea Party activists became the agents and symbols of a new conservative revolution.

For all his difficulties as a candidate, Perry captured his movement's new objective with great succinctness in his pledge to make the federal government as "inconsequential" as possible. His statement would have horrified Hamilton, Clay, and Lincoln (and of course Roosevelt, Kennedy, and Johnson). And that, was, in a way, his point. With more candor and radicalism than politicians typically muster, Perry was calling into question not only Obama's decisions, not only the achievements of the Great Society, the New Deal, and the Progressive years, but also a much older American project that envisioned a national government that the country's citizens would see as both consequential and constructive—just what Hamilton promised long ago in Federalist 27. Perry's emphasis on states' rights echoed Calhoun more than Lincoln, his view of the unfettered market the ideas of the Gilded Age, not those of the Long Consensus. Perry's compact sentence got to the essence of the starkly individualistic new conservatism that has replaced the more community-minded conservatism of old.

There are many grounds on which to fault Obama, but he was not the driver of the new polarization, even if he found himself at its center. What needs to be recognized is how far Republicanism and conservatism have strayed from their own history and their own past commitments. They have chosen—on principle, it could be said—to make middle-ground politics impossible. They have done so by jettisoning their communitarian commitments, by adopting a highly restrictive view of the federal government's role, and by advancing (in the Supreme Court no less than on the campaign trail) a view of the Constitution that would prohibit or restrict activities that the federal government has undertaken for a century or more. In the process, they have chosen to rewrite the American story and unsettle the American balance.

I I

There is no shortage of explanations for why Obama encountered so many political problems from almost the moment he took the oath of office. A great deal can be understood simply by looking at what he confronted and how he responded.

When he crossed the threshold of the White House on January 20, 2009, he walked into a nightmare. Assuming power in the aftermath of the financial crisis, he responded, appropriately, with a stimulus program. His stimulus was large enough to make it prey for parody as a big-government escapade (even if a third of it came in tax cuts), but smaller than the staggering economy needed. Obama's opponents tried to compound the political damage by linking the stimulus to the unpopular Wall Street bailout—and politically, it did not seem not to matter that many of his critics had supported the rescue when it was originally proposed by President Bush. In the meantime, Obama never adequately defended the stimulus—and even though it did help create jobs and begin a recovery—or the idea behind it. He got it passed, and moved quickly on to health care.

Passage of the health care law was a substantial victory, an achievement that had eluded every Democratic president from Harry Truman forward. For all the criticism Obama received, he was right to undertake the fight and to carry it to success. Yet the battle for heath care reform took too long and the process through which the measure passed was ugly, given the Republicans' refusal to cooperate and Obama's insistence that bipartisan cooperation be attempted long after it had any chance of succeeding. The process tainted the bill, and the time needed to pass it allowed a great achievement to turn sour for voters who felt they never heard an adequate explanation of what the intricate law accomplished.

All of this made it easy for Obama's enemies to brand him as an advocate of big government—and, given the ongoing sluggishness of the economy into 2011, an ineffectual one at that. His onetime allies on the left, meanwhile, saw him as too compromising, too conciliatory, too reluctant to fight for more progressive options, and too eager to heed the advice of advisors with close Wall Street ties. The combination blew the fuse on what might have been a more gradual cyclical correction toward liberalism, given the country's negative verdict on the Bush era.

These failures spoke to core contradictions in the promises Obama made to the country in 2008. As a candidate, Obama pledged to change the tone in Washington and restore amicable relations between the parties. But he also promised to accomplish large things, including health care reform, major steps to ease global warming, and a reshaped and more responsible financial system. The first pledge put his fate in the hands of his Republican opponents. If they refused to work with him, there could be no bipartisanship. And this was, in many ways, a predictable outcome: at some point, Obama's ambitions were destined to collide with the views of a Republican Party fundamentally opposed to the direction he wanted to take. It turned out that he could try to get big things done or he could work easily with Republicans. He could not do both.

The entire context of the nation's political conversation shifted to the right within months of Obama's inauguration. Conservative funders were quick to realize that the Tea Party movement that took off after Rick Santelli's rant was the most efficient way to organize opposition to Obama's initiatives and rebuild a shattered Republican Party. In the meantime, Obama's victory partially demobilized the left. With Democrats in control of the White House and both houses of Congress, stepped-up organizing didn't seem quite so urgent. Yet the absence of a strong, organized left made it easier for conservatives to label Obama a left-winger because actual left-wing positions were largely out of public view—until the anti–Wall

Street demonstrators took to the parks and the streets in the fall of 2011 and began reminding the country of what a left looked like and believed.

It is precisely because the nation's political agenda had veered so far rightward that the Occupy Wall Street movement had such a large impact so quickly. A significant part of public opinion yearned for a form of populism that directed its rage at the failures and abuses of the financial system, not at government (except to the extent that government had been too influenced by Wall Street and inattentive to its duties to the economy) and not at Obama (except to the extent that he had been too cautious in dealing with the financial sector). The rise of a movement such as Occupy was essential to restoring a sense of balance to the American conversation. This was important, as we've seen, not only for the left, but also for political moderates who don't stand a chance in the absence of a fair fight between the right and the left. The relative silence of the left allowed the entire public conversation to be dominated by the Tea Party and its ideas. And by repeatedly seeking a middle ground with a newly strident conservatism, Obama made himself complicit in this shift. Over many months, he looked for moderation in all the wrong places, trying to find center ground that he already held.

The irony before the rise of Occupy was that so much of what passed for "progressive" or even "left-wing" politics was, by the measure of even the relatively recent past, the politics of moderation. A moderate view could be painted as "left-wing" only because conservatives had been so successful in moving the philosophical boundaries.

Consider that no one on the left denies the importance of American individualism. Today's left does not seek to overturn the private economic market, enact confiscatory taxation, or nationalize industries for the long term (even if there were progressives who argued, for pragmatic and defensible reasons, in favor of nationalizing certain failing banks early in the financial crisis in order to speed recovery). No one on the left seeks a radical centralization of power in the federal government. Indeed, much of Obama's original stimulus package and his 2011 jobs bill involved either tax cuts for individuals or aid of various sorts to state and local governments that resembled nothing so much as Richard Nixon's revenue-sharing program—or Henry Clay's proposals for distribution of assistance to the states. And Obama's health plan faced solid Republican opposition even though it was based on market-oriented ideas that had been pioneered by Republican senators a decade or two earlier—and, once upon a time, by Mitt Romney in Massachusetts. Obama's plan was far more conservative and less government-centered than Nixon's health proposals of the early 1970s. But Nixon was operating within the Long Consensus. His successors in the Republican Party are not.

To say all these things risks accusations of "partisanship," and that, too, is part of the problem. If describing developments in American political life candidly is dismissed as a form of partisanship, then honest speech becomes impossible. The etiquette of political discussion prevents a reckoning with the new stakes in politics. Partisanship is indeed destructive when party advantage or personal ambition prevents two sides from solving problems by reaching agreements that they would otherwise be prepared to make. (And Republican resistance to Obama's moderate proposals to boost the economy did take on this cast as the 2012 elections approached.) But when two sides do not operate within the same framework, identify the same problems, or even share a common understanding of our history, the difficulty of finding accord cannot be ascribed to pettiness, selfishness, or a lack of imagination. It reflects the fact that the country has reached "a time for choosing," to echo the title of Ronald Reagan's memorable 1964 speech on behalf of Barry Goldwater. The time for choosing Reagan had in mind was delayed, partly by the relative moderation of Reagan himself when he was president. But it is upon us now.

America has worked well on the whole because we have faced such times for choosing only rarely. Our divided political heart inclines us to resist such moments. The American experiment from the beginning recognized both sides of our character, and successful American politicians understood with Tocqueville that we are a nation of private striving *and* public engagement, of rights *and* responsibilities. Americans understood that individualism needed to be protected from concentrated power in both the private marketplace and the government. They also understood that individuality seeks expression in communal acts as well as individual deeds and that the self longs for autonomy but also freely embraces the encumbrances and responsibilities of family, friendship, community, and country. These truths have usually been accepted, albeit in different ways, by progressives and conservatives alike. It is this deep American consensus that is now in jeopardy, and its disappearance threatens to block constructive action at the very moment when our position in the world is precarious.

It can fairly be said that I have placed more emphasis in these pages on community than on individualism. I have done so to underscore the extent to which the American conversation has veered away from an understanding of our communal impulses. But nothing here is intended to deny the fierce independence that Americans so value. We have always held up as heroes inventors and adventurers, cowboys and private eyes, entrepreneurs and free spirits. "Telling Americans to improve democracy by sinking comfortably into a community, by losing themselves in a collective life, is calling into the wind," wrote the historian Robert Wiebe. "There has never been an American democracy without its powerful strand of individualism, and nothing suggests there ever will be."

Wiebe is entirely right. But it is also calling into the wind to pretend that Americans have lived by individualism alone. We are the nation of both *High Noon* and *It's a Wonderful Life*. Our current discontent has many roots. But we will not resolve our problems or restore our greatness by fleeing from either of our twin commitments, from either side of our character.

For Obama in the short run, and for moderates and progressives in the long run, there is no point in seeking compromise at the midway point between the Long Consensus and the radical individualists. The Long Consensus *itself* embodies moderation, balance, and compromise, a view Obama himself finally embraced in a series of speeches in the fall of 2011 and early 2012. There is much room for argument within that consensus over when and whether to tilt more toward the public or the private, the individual or the community. What the country neither needs nor wants is an endless series of campaigns and political battles revolving around competing fears—of excessive government on one side and of an end to core programs such as Medicaid and Social Security on the other.

This need not be our future. The rising generation that rallied to Obama in 2008 did not do so simply because of their fascination with an unusual and compelling human being—"the biggest celebrity in the world," as John McCain's campaign correctly called him. They also mobilized because as a generation, they espouse even more than their elders the values and commitments of the Long Consensus. Obama ended his first term by embracing the imperative of defending the Long Consensus—belatedly, perhaps, but also forcefully. But it will be the task of the new generation to make it vital in the unfolding century.

III

Balance and moderation typically are seen as traits of older people—or so older people like to think. But it is the Millennial generation that appreciates what the American balance promises, and demands.

Young Americans are, at once, more passionately individualistic *and* more passionately communitarian than any other age group in the country. The Millennials (generally defined as Americans born in 1981 or later) are the most socially tolerant of the generations. They are also the generation most comfortable with racial and ethnic diversity, most open on matters such as gay marriage, and most welcoming to new immigrants. The fact that they are such a racially and ethnically diverse generation explains and undergirds many of their attitudes. Latinos, who combine a determination to succeed with a strong commitment to community and the idea of a common good, are an important component of the millennial generation. It is a generation whose members have faith in their own capacity, collectively and as individuals, to effect change.

Their sense of communal obligation is made manifest in their exceptional devotion to service—as volunteers in tutoring programs, soup kitchens, homeless shelters, environmental initiatives, and community organizing. They are also the generation that bore the largest burden of fighting the nation's two longest wars. Surveys have consistently found that helping those in need is a high personal priority for members of this generation.

They have more faith than their elders do in government's constructive capacities, even as they also wish for a government that is less bureaucratic and more nimble. They combine the idealism of the sixties generation with the more worldly concerns of the generation that came of age in the 1980s and the 1990s. One might say that they are more practical than the 1960s generation and more idealistic than younger Americans were in the 1980s. They want to do good, but they want the good they do to last. They are willing to take risks, but they are not foolhardy. They have doubts about politics, but they have shown a willingness to give politics a chance. They have few illusions, but they do have hope.

No one harnessed those hopes more effectively than Obama. In the 2008 election, two-thirds of voters twenty-nine and younger supported him; by contrast, Obama won only 45 percent among voters who were sixty-five and older. As the Pew Research Center pointed out, this was "the largest disparity between younger and older voters recorded in four decades of modern Election Day exit polling."

Moreover, Pew observed, "after decades of low voter participation by the young, the turnout gap in 2008 between voters under and over the age of 30 was the smallest it had been since 18- to 20-year-olds were given the right to vote in 1972." The members of this generation are more engaged in politics at this point in the life cycle than any generation in four decades. Their attitudes and their activism are not simply or even primarily the product of an Obama effect. Turnout among the young rose steadily beginning in 2000, as has support for Democrats. In 2008, Obama built on something that was already happening even as he mobilized the young in unprecedented ways.

If the new generation resembles any generation that came before it, it is the Greatest Generation of the Depression, the New Deal, and World War II. Pew, which in 2010 conducted one of the best studies of the Millennials, found that Americans under thirty—like those largely departed New Dealers and World War II vets—were not affected by the allergy to the word "liberal" to which every other American age group is now susceptible. Americans under thirty included the largest proportion of self-described liberals and the smallest proportion of self-described conservatives of any age group in the country. Not only are the younger generation more socially tolerant; they are also far more sympathetic than their elders to activist government. The Pew researchers asked respondents to choose between two statements: "Government should do more to solve problems" and "Government is doing too many things better left to business and individuals." Fifty-three percent of Millennials wanted government to do more. In every other age group, pluralities said that government was doing too much. Skepticism about government was highest among the oldest respondents, who are the political base of the Tea Party—and, ironically, benefit the most from government social insurance programs. Among those over sixty-five, only 39 percent thought government should do more.

Perhaps surprisingly, the Millennials are also far more likely than older cohorts to believe that government can be efficient. Pew asked those surveyed to respond to the statement "When something is run by government, it is usually inefficient and wasteful." In every other age group, significant majorities agreed; only 42 percent of the Millennials did.

Members of the new generation believe in voluntary action *and* in government action. They are more skeptical of traditional norms than older Americans are, yet their goals in life might have found approval from old-line Whigs. When asked by Pew's researchers to list their most important goals in life, "being a good parent" ranked first at 52 percent, followed by "having a successful marriage" at 30 percent and "helping those in need" at 21 percent. Interestingly, this last came in ahead of "having a high-paying career," which came in at 15 percent. This generation is pioneering a blend of progressive politics and back-to-basics values.

With unemployment running stubbornly high through Obama's term, young Americans—particularly blacks and Latinos—started their work lives with constrained opportunities. Their failure to turn out in large numbers in 2010 and some movement away from Obama in the polls afterward suggested the millennials' 2008 passions had cooled.

This posed an important political challenge for Obama. But the larger and long-term challenge for the members of this rising generation is whether they will maintain their level of public engagement and their confidence in their power to transform the nation through political action. In our nation's history, the great reforming generations have successfully married their aspirations to service with the possibilities of politics. They have harnessed the good work done one-on-one in local communities to larger movements for change in the nation and the world. They have always remembered, as Michael Sandel has written, that "when politics goes well, we can know a good in common that we cannot know alone." That is still the Millennial generation's aspiration.

But it is precisely because the fate of the next consensus is in the hands of younger Americans that the Long Consensus of old cannot be restored in exactly the same form it took in the twentieth century. As we've seen, the Progressivism and New Deal liberalism that did so much to shape the Long Consensus took root within a very different economy, even as it shaped the way that economy worked. For the new generation, the model company is Apple, not General Motors. The model entrepreneurs are Bill Gates and the late Steve Jobs, not Andrew Carnegie and John D. Rockefeller. Confidence in both government and collective action was higher in the New Deal and postwar years than it is likely to be for some time.

Yet the citizens of this new economic and technological world have lost neither their desire for social justice nor their inclination to protest conditions that narrow their opportunities. The anti–Wall Street demonstrations and the support they won are evidence of this. Consider that we are a nation that celebrates the liberating possibility of new technologies, and then we quickly form social networks. We disparage the federal government, and then we heap praise and honor on our men and women in uniform, who represent the most self-sacrificing part of that government. More prosaically, we demand that government do less and spend less, even as we demand that it do more: for the elderly, for the unemployed, for the education of our children, for the eradication of disease, for safeguarding our natural environment, for protecting consumers, for preventing financial fraud and abuse. We are libertarians when things go well for us, but we want to socialize the risks that threaten us, notably those arising from old age, natural disasters, unsafe products, and ineffective drugs. "Government is the enemy," former Republican Senator Bill Cohen once said, "until you need a friend."

It was one of the great strengths of the Long Consensus that it was neither static nor backward-looking. It fostered, absorbed, and managed change. Paradoxically, by building a sense of social and economic security, the consensus encouraged risk taking and innovation by making risk less frightening. Government underwrote the infrastructure—social as well as physical—within which innovation could occur. By promoting mass education, research, and scientific breakthroughs, government increased the capacity of individuals to prosper and society's capacity to advance technologically. The GI Bill and subsequent federal college scholarship and student loan programs were classics in the genre: they expanded individual opportunities while increasing the community's economic resources (and its level of knowledge and expertise). Hamilton and Clay might be shocked at the speed with which American society democratized itself; they would not be surprised by government's capacity to foster growth or promote mass education.

At the very beginning of this book, I noted that "government" is not the same thing as "community." That is certainly true. But the fact that many readers no doubt nodded in vigorous assent to this proposition, wanting to disentangle the two, is also a problem for democratic government. This speaks to how distant many Americans feel government is from their own communities.

It is not just that government is so often seen as creaky and backward-looking when its operations are compared to the bold new technological world in which we live. We also typically see government as running behind both the private and not-for-profit sectors in the ways it recruits and hires people, responds to new data, and makes decisions. We imagine it, not without reason, as enveloped in thickets of rules that are designed to promote accountability but often produce the opposite.

Those who propose to use government to achieve large ends cannot ignore these criticisms, particularly in a technological age when citizens and consumers demand responsiveness and a rapid resolution of their problems. Advocates of active government must also be supporters of innovative government.

At the same time, those who devote their lives to public service through government too often find themselves demonized, their significant contributions disparaged, their sometimes heroic efforts to innovate and reform dismissed. This creates a vicious cycle that further erodes government's capacities. Broad assaults on government tarnish its image, which in turn discourages the innovators and the reformers from joining the public sector in the first place. Paul Light, a close student of the bureaucracy, has observed that young people interested in public service have gravitated more to the not-for-profit sector than to government. This is certainly good for the third sector; it is not good for the future of government.

We must thus create a new virtuous cycle in which government's need to attract new talent leads it to create dynamic work environments. Public sector work should again provoke pride. Those who work for government should experience the same sense of efficacy that their peers in the private and nonprofit sectors do. It was, after all, only a half century ago that John F. Kennedy created a genuine excitement over the prospect of government work. "When my brother John and I were growing up," Caroline Kennedy Schlossberg declared in a speech in 2000, "hardly a day went by when someone didn't come up to us and say, 'Your father changed my life. I went into public service because he asked me.'" The devotees of the New Frontier who descended upon Washington in 1960 were not saints, but neither were they mere opportunists. "The mood," wrote the journalist Godfrey Hodgson, "was strangely blended from ambition and idealism, aggressive social climbing and a sense of youthful adventure." We could do, and have done, much worse.

But restoring this enthusiasm for public service will require us to create a government that is much less distant from our aspirations to a sense of community. Government is not just a bureaucracy. It is also a town square. It is not simply a place that issues licenses and permits but also the institution that builds the schools, colleges, libraries, parks, and neighborhood centers that foster community life. In a democracy, government should be seen less as an entity that issues commands than as a forum where citizens debate the future of their community and their nation. Government is not just the FBI and the IRS, as important as those two institutions are to our security and our solvency. It is also the TVA, the Corporation for National and Community Service, and the National Science Foundation.

Liberals and progressives have sometimes forgotten that their purpose is not and never has been to defend government as such. Big government is not an end. Government's most successful ventures have involved empowering individuals and communities, often by increasing the bargaining power of those who previously had been at an unfair disadvantage. The New Deal's most successful venture in redistributing wealth and income to the less affluent was not any particular tax-spend-and-transfer program but the National Labor Relations Act, which enabled employees to form unions and bargain on their own behalf. Requiring manufacturers and lenders to provide consumers with adequate information on the products they buy and the loans they receive costs government little, but it can shift the balance in market transactions decisively in the consumer's direction. Government's massive commitment to education at all levels is not—or certainly should not be—about the employment of educators and administrators. It is (and has been through most of our history) an effort to provide citizens with the capacity for self-government, prosperity, self-reliance, and personal growth. At a moment of skepticism about all institutions, reforms that promote public and private transparency, accountability, and responsiveness will speak to all of the disparate villages and neighborhoods that make up the world of Bill Bishop's Big Sort.

Democratic self-government, if it is functioning properly, is simply the expression of the will of the community. The republican conception of government to which our Founders subscribed stoutly opposed the idea of a government captured by factions or for sale to particular interests. This is why the *Citizens United* decision opening the electoral system to the intrusion of large sums of money is antithetical to the Founders' intentions. Republicanism insisted that citizens should participate in public life not simply to serve their legitimate personal or group interests but also, and primarily, because self-rule is essential to liberty. "Unless citizens have reason to believe that sharing in self-government is intrinsically important," Michael Sandel has written, "their willingness to sacrifice individual interests for the common good may be eroded by instrumental calculations about the costs and benefits of political participation." Paradoxically, restoring republican idealism is the only *practical* remedy for our democratic distemper. All other solutions are likely to fall short. One senses it was this intuition that inspired tens of thousands to knock on doors in 2008 in pursuit of nothing more, or less, than "change we can believe in."

I V

In analyzing our tendency to sort ourselves into communities organized by attitudes, lifestyles, and political inclination, Bill Bishop notes our increasing propensity to refer to political opponents as "those people." In a competitive democratic system, there will always be a certain amount of such talk. In tough political campaigns, being nice is rarely a top priority.

But in a democratic republic, "those people" are also fellow citizens and self-government ultimately requires us to work with them, too.

In the course of these pages, I have been unapologetically critical of the ideas of some of my fellow citizens, who subscribe to the doctrines of what I have referred to in shorthand as radical individualism. In particular, I have been critical of the Tea Party, its approach to both politics and history, and the eagerness of some in its ranks to recycle old extremist ideas. Supporters of such views who have come this far might well feel that I have dealt with them in a way that turns them into "those people."

Yet I am as frustrated as anyone else with a politics organized around battles between a supposedly enlightened (or patriotic, or freedom-loving) "us" and "those people" who are presumed to be less thoughtful (or less tolerant, or less devoted to their country and its traditional freedoms). I have emphasized the two sides of the American character to make it clear that I see even those with whom I passionately disagree as speaking for something that is authentic in the American story. My plea to them is to acknowledge that the American idea is built from materials that include the individualism they so treasure, but also republican and communitarian commitments that have been essential to our country's prosperity, endurance, and, yes, its freedom.

Even those whom I have taken to task for ignoring our communitarian past, after all, have their own yearnings for community. Adele Stan, a thoughtful left-of-center journalist who disagrees with the Tea Party, nonetheless argued that a desire for community was a central element in bringing its partisans together. It is a paradox that the cause of individualism provided a venue for forging common bonds among those who had once been strangers. A large proportion of Tea Party supporters, moreover, are also members of the Christian conservative movement, which has obvious connections to America's biblical communitarian tradition.

On the other side, many liberals are also uneasy with a more communitarian disposition. They are fearful that the demands of community might supersede the individual rights they treasure. Has it not been the American rights tradition that produced such large social gains for African Americans, for women, and for gays and lesbians?

How might the opposing forces in our currently fierce political wars acknowledge both sides of our political heart—and both sides of our nation's history—in ways they now sometimes resist?

To at least some degree, as I argued in Chapter 5, liberals—especially the politicians among them—have embraced the need to temper a creed oriented toward rights with commitments to community and responsibility. But there is still a great deal of liberal ambivalence about community, and about populism. Any time a liberal uses words such as "flyover country" or "Jesusland," he or she is breaking faith with a broad democratic tradition that included Bryan no less than Roosevelt. This tradition acknowledges the wisdom that exists in small towns and the countryside no less than the genius of our sophisticated metropolitan areas. It honors the rights and dignity of religious believers and secular people alike. It respects the loyalties of old tightly knit working-class neighborhoods no less than the cosmopolitanism on the more affluent side of town.

Franklin Roosevelt added an urbane gloss to the Populist-Progressive tradition, as Hofstadter observed, and the bifurcation between expert opinion and popular instincts still presents problems for liberals. Yet Roosevelt never lost sight of the Populist roots of his coalition, or of the moral underpinnings of Progressive policies in the republicanism of the past. The most powerful criticisms of the Wall Street behaviors that led to the calamities of 1929 and 2008 arose from moral concerns. They focused not simply on greed but also on the failures of the privileged to live up to their obligations of stewardship toward the economic system. The absence of such stewardship was disastrous for the financial system and the larger economy. Populist anger against Wall Street, whether in 1935 or 2011, arose not from envy or jealousy but from a belief in the public obligations imposed by a republican conception of citizenship. Sometimes in inchoate ways and sometimes explicitly, the Occupy Wall Street protesters were speaking from this great republican tradition. As we saw earlier, the Jeffersonian, Jacksonian, and Populist arguments for greater economic equality rest, finally, on republican ideas: that citizens in a free republic need a degree of economic security, independence, and self-sufficiency to carry out their civic duties and to participate fully in self-government. Plutocracy is antithetical to both democracy and republicanism. Our Founders were sensitive to this in a way that recent Supreme Court decisions were not.

Liberals would also do well to acknowledge that recent advances in individual rights were secured not simply by an appeal to our tradition of individual freedom but also by powerful demands for remaking and perfecting the American community—and for extending the obligations (and not just the rights) of democratic citizenship. The preaching of Martin Luther King Jr. made sense to millions of Americans because King rooted what he said in the nation's Founding documents and also in Scripture. The civil rights movement was always more than just a quest for individual rights. It was also a demand for civic inclusion. The movement did not simply defend Americans who had been deprived of justice for more than three centuries; it made a case for transforming the entire nation. "The end is redemption and reconciliation," King declared at the beginning of his ministry in 1957. "The aftermath of nonviolence is the creation of the beloved community, while the aftermath of violence is tragic bitterness." King painted a picture of African Americans enjoying the rights they deserved, but also of a country that had decided to live differently, a republic that would fulfill its destiny of full equality. His goal, he declared most famously in 1963, was "to speed up that day when all of God's children, black men and white men, Jews and Gentiles, Protestants and Catholics, will be able to join hands and sing in the words of the old Negro spiritual, 'Free at last! Free at last! Thank God Almighty, we are free at last!'" For King, freedom and community were inseparable.

And so it has been in the movement for gay and lesbian rights. Consider its core demands of recent years: for equal treatment within the United States military, and for equal rights to marriage. Could there be anything more civic, more republican in the oldest sense of the term, and more communally minded than a demand for equal opportunity to *sacrifice* for the nation? This was a demand not for equal employment opportunities on Wall Street or in corporate management but for an equal opportunity to serve and to defend the liberty of the whole country. There was a wise intuition here: if gays and lesbians were willing to risk their lives for the nation, how could the nation then deny them equal treatment? It was exactly what African Americans said after World War II, after so many in their communities had sacrificed and died. But more than shrewdness was involved. Gays and lesbians understood that full civic equality, an equal opportunity to serve the common good, was an essential component of equality in all other respects.

Similarly, the demand for marriage equality was neither an obvious next step for the gay rights movement nor universally popular among supporters of homosexual equality when it first arose, as Andrew Sullivan, one of the earliest advocates of gay marriage, learned in the sometimes bitter polemics among gays and lesbians. Jonathan Rauch, another early supporter, observed that "Egalitarians of a more radical stripe initially took a dim view of gay marriage, regarding it as capitulating to bourgeois norms, which gay people were supposed to be challenging." Same-sex marriage, he added, "is particularly hard to pin down. You can see it as incremental or radical, as communitarian or egalitarian; you have four permutations to choose from. I see it as incremental and communitarian."

As Rauch argued, demands for gay marriage arose from a 1960s-inspired "liberationist" ethic of equality. But the cause drew strength from another tributary within the gay rights movement. "The new century brought to the fore a generation of younger gay people who, like their straight peers, had all too often learned the importance of marriage from the mistakes of their parents," he wrote. "The result was an intense grassroots demand for the institutional protections and tools that go with marital *responsibilities*." Rauch then offered this telling observation:

> Note how different these two streams are: one is fundamentally egalitarian and liberation-minded; the other fundamentally communitarian and family-minded. One emphasizes civil rights; the other civic responsibilities. They are not at war with each other, by any stretch, but they also are not entirely at ease with one another. Many of the liberationist activists who cut their teeth in the 1970s disdained the domesticating implications of marriage, and many of the younger gay people who came of age in the 1990s disdained the libertine ethos of gay-liberation. Gay marriage thus came on the scene with two constituencies, one more socially conservative than the other, allied, but with somewhat different destinations in mind.

In light of the broader argument I am offering here, the campaign for gay marriage might be seen as a classically American reform movement. It harnesses libertarian individualism to a communitarian emphasis on responsibility. Like the effort to allow gays and lesbians to serve equally and without harassment in the armed forces, the gay marriage movement links rights with duties, self-fulfillment with social obligation. For liberals who value equal rights, it is an instructive story.

Recovering their communal bearings is even more vital for conservatives, if only because the communitarian side of conservatism has been in full retreat from the beginning of the Obama administration—and arguably from early in the Bush years, when the war on terror replaced compassionate conservatism as the administration's driving idea. And as I argued in Chapter 5, the Tea Party has only driven compassionate conservatism further to the margins.

But a conservatism without a strong communal and compassionate side will be untrue to its intellectual roots, unfaithful to the Christian allegiances of so many of its supporters, and disconnected from some of the most vital streams of conservative thought and feeling in American history. Similarly, a Republican Party that cuts itself off from the tradition of republican nationalism embodied by Hamilton, Clay, Lincoln, and Theodore Roosevelt will not only be abandoning the ideas that gave it life and purpose. It will also squander the opportunity to help infuse the next American consensus with the particular blend of entrepreneurialism and public purpose that the past's best Republican leaders always advanced. My concern is that instead of seeking a consensual balance between our libertarian and communal sides, Republicans will continue to push for a one-sided settlement in which government recedes, the nurturing of community is relegated to a purely private endeavor, and the market is allowed to operate with little oversight or public accountability. Such an approach may command occasional majorities. But it will never produce the larger consensus required to save us from many years of polarization and angry discontent.

It would be tragic if conservatives and Republicans sacrificed their great traditions on the altar of an individualism that disdains government, downplays communal obligations, and sees the economic market not simply as an efficient mechanism for the production of goods but also as the ultimate arbiter of what should be valued.

Although the 2012 Republican primaries seemed to push the party ever farther to the right, I would like to think that these fears are misplaced. If nothing else, pure pragmatism and electoral calculation may eventually militate against the dangers I see now. There have been signs in the polls of rising opposition to the Tea Party, and this may nudge the realists among our conservative politicians toward a new appreciation for moderation and balance. They might begin to soften the edges of their individualism and to remember their communal impulses. Perhaps they will decide that the American social insurance system is too popular to be overturned and that modern capitalism is too complicated to be allowed to run with minimal supervision and few safeguards.

What I do know is that we will not restore our greatness as a nation or heal our political wounds unless we acknowledge both sides of our national character. Our history is compelling, after all, because we are neither a simple nor a single-minded people.

At the end of a book insisting that no single trait can be seen as defining us, some readers might be tempted to write off Americans as philosophically contradictory and hopelessly opportunistic in our values and commitments. But to do so would be to misread both America and human nature. Most Americans are aware of their contradictions. The dualities of the American creed and the balances we seek to strike reflect an underlying realism about our conflicting desires and hopes—and about the difficulty of arriving at any settlement that can permanently resolve these tensions. We refer to the "American experiment" for a reason: we are an experimental people constantly searching for provisional answers. The British philosopher Isaiah Berlin has argued that "the very idea of the perfect world in which all good things are realized" is both "incomprehensible" and "conceptually incoherent." Americans have largely been saved from the idea that we could create a perfect world. But we have also been saved *by* the idea that we can create a better one.

V

It was my interest in the Tea Party that led me on a recent July 4 to sit down and read our Declaration of Independence in its entirety. What became abundantly clear from Jefferson's words is that our forebears were not revolting *against* taxes or government as such. On the contrary, they were making a revolution *for* self-government.

In the long list of "abuses and usurpations" the Declaration documents, taxes don't come up until the seventeenth item, which is neither a complaint about tax rates nor an objection to the idea of taxation. Our Founders remonstrated against the British crown "for imposing taxes on us without our consent." They were concerned about "consent"—that is, popular rule—not taxes.

The very *first* item on their list condemned the king because he "refused his assent to laws, the most wholesome and necessary for the public good." Note that the signers wanted to *pass* laws, not repeal them, and they began by speaking of "the public good," not about individuals. They knew that it took public action—including effective and responsive government—to secure "life, liberty, and the pursuit of happiness."

Their second grievance reinforced the first, accusing the king of having "forbidden his governors to pass laws of immediate and pressing importance." Again, our forebears wanted to enact laws; they were not anti-government zealots.

Abuses three through nine also referred in some way to how laws were put in place or justice was administered. When the document finally does get around to anything that looks like big-government oppression, its language against the king is delightful (and far above the norm for the typical anti-government screed in American politics these days): "He has erected a multitude of new offices, and sent hither swarms of officers to harass our people, and eat out their substance." Note that the Founders don't even get to this until grievance number ten.

All of us—from the Tea Party's most resolute supporters to its most ardent foes—praise our Founders annually for revolting against royal rule and for creating an exceptionally durable system of self-government. We can lose this inheritance if we forget our Founders insisted upon a representative form of national authority robust enough to secure the public good. Our institutions are still perfectly capable of doing that if we turn our attention to making them work again.

If we do not accept responsibility for our own democracy, if we pretend instead that we are living in Boston in 1773 and facing an obdurate king who rules far from our shores, we will draw all the wrong conclusions and make some remarkably foolish choices. If we wish to end our fears of decline and honor our character, our history, and, yes, the Founders themselves, we will learn to love and appreciate both yearnings of our political heart.

To suggest at a time of crisis that Americans need to return to their history might seem strange to those who would define our problems in terms of the global military balance of power, the necessity for new departures in domestic policy, the need for innovation in the marketplace, or the imperative of balancing the federal government's books. Of course, all these things are important. But it is precisely at moments when so much is at stake that we need both inspiration and instruction from those who came before us.

As I said at the outset, the Tea Party is right in having an intimation about the importance of the past. If my reading of our history differs from theirs, our disagreement rests not on the question of whether our story is a noble one, but on why the United States has, to this point, been successful. We did not succeed because our institutions were perfect from the outset. They were not perfect, and in truth never will be. Our Founders were gifted, but they were not free from the interests and the passions that affect us all.

They were, however, bold and visionary, prepared to think and act anew at a time when much of the world was skeptical about the possibility of republican government and self-rule. Our task is to follow their example, not to engage in an inevitably futile effort to parse every word they wrote and spoke to discover how we must act now. Their approach was daring, but also balanced, moderate, and temperate. They had confidence that government could be made to work and that it could accomplish great things, but they were always wary of deifying the state and those who ran it. They hugely valued individual freedom, but they were steeped in principles that saw the preservation of freedom as a common enterprise. They were influenced by the Bible and the Enlightenment, by liberalism and republicanism.

Those who came after always understood the imperative of keeping competing goods in balance—and also the need to guide the American system in a steadily more democratic and egalitarian direction. Our history is one in which populists of various stripes have always challenged elites, in which private wealth has always been seen as carrying a social mortgage, and in which public action has always been subject to accountability and searching criticism. We cannot learn all we need to know from our history. But we can learn how to keep faith with a promise that we still have an obligation to keep.

"We Take Care of Our Own"
The 2012 Election and the Triumph
of the Long Consensus

A few weeks before this book was first published, a friend who had read an early draft had some news for me from a Bruce Springsteen concert. She insisted that I listen to a new Springsteen song that she saw as offering a moving musical summary of the core themes laid out here. She also thought it could serve as the perfect anthem for Barack Obama's reelection campaign.

I immediately went out and purchased Springsteen's *Wrecking Ball* album and found myself listening over and over as the Boss, strong and maybe just a bit plaintive, instructed us. "Wherever this flag is flown, we take care of our own."

My friend was a prophet and, for me, an inspiration. I incorporated Springsteen's song in talks describing our political heart as torn by a tension between individualism and community—and urging that we stop ignoring our community-embracing side. I would draw a direct line between our Puritan past and our Springsteen present, pointing to the remarkable similarity between Springsteen's message and the core theme of John Winthrop's 1630 sermon, cited in Chapter 3: "We must delight in each other, make others' conditions our own . . . always having before our eyes our community as members of the same body." I could think of few better examples of the depth and endurance of the powerfully American emphasis on mutuality. Across nearly four centuries, Winthrop and Springsteen stood together in vindication of our most generous inclinations.

And President Obama's campaign eventually caught on to my friend's political insight. "We Take Care of Our Own" punctuated Obama rallies all over the country. If you stayed up late enough to watch Obama's election night victory speech, the first words you heard after he finished were Springsteen's.

The 2012 election was the "We Take Care of Our Own" election. The campaign ended with Americans reaffirming the Long Consensus, the century-long balance we have maintained between individualism and community, private and public endeavor, the market's achievements and government's essential role in cleaning up the problems the market leaves behind. To a degree that surprised even a self-interested author, 2012 reflected the argument outlined in these pages down to the details and the critical moments.

On the Republican side, Mitt Romney's comments about 47 percent of us being hopelessly dependent and his running mate Paul Ryan's past interest in Ayn Rand's philosophy (and his continuing fears of a nation divided between "makers" and "takers") brought into sharp relief the return of a Gilded Age conservatism rooted—only a bit more subtly than before—in ideas that smacked of Social Darwinism.

For his part, Obama ran explicitly in defense of government's role in tempering market outcomes. It turned out that his most controversial and interventionist policy decision (perhaps even the one that came closest to the "socialism" his opponents wrongly accused him of espousing) was also the most politically beneficial choice he made. Absent the rescue of the auto industry, it is likely that Obama would have lost Ohio, and highly probable that he would have lost Michigan as well. The Midwest heartland responded to an approach aimed at preserving the economic vitality of communities throughout their region.

But it was also the election in which economic ideas and judgments were not simply about unemployment and growth rates, but also about values. It was widely said that the Tea Party had transformed the economic debate into a new culture war, and so it had. The "makers and takers" rhetoric pointed not to a society defined by mutuality in which the better-off helped the worse-off to escape dependency, but to a nation stuck in a zero-sum game: what was "taken" from the affluent, in this view, was seized by those intent on preserving their own dependent status.

To be sure, Romney and Ryan tried to sand the rough edges off this rather stark view. As Election Day neared, they sought their own language of mutuality. Ryan even gave a speech on poverty that, for a brief campaign moment, revived some compassionate conservative rhetoric. But beneath it all were the ideas that animated Romney's earlier 47 percent speech to a group of wealthy donors. The release of what he had thought was a private speech was one of 2012's most consequential moments. It froze in place the Romney who had run far to the right during the primaries to win his party's nomination, the Romney who said what was necessary to appease the Tea Party's legions. After the votes were in, Romney reinforced this image of himself by claiming that Obama won because of "gifts" he had conferred on particular voter groups through the public sector.

Obama, for his part, did not shrink from the larger, philosophical argument. It became essential to his effort to ensure that the election did not hinge on unemployment rates alone. And he enlisted as his ally another Democrat who had understood as well as he had the rhythms of a politics rooted in appeals to the common good and the idea of community. Bill Clinton's speech at the Democratic National Convention in Charlotte was one of the campaign's turning points, a moment when Obama's argument jelled for voters who were still holding out. And it was the Clinton of the old "Opportunity, Responsibility, Community" slogan who sent delegates into swoons worthy of—well, a Springsteen concert.

"We Democrats," Clinton told them, "we think the country works better with a strong middle class, with real opportunities for poor folks to work their way into it, with a relentless focus on the future, with business and government actually working together to promote growth and broadly share prosperity."

And then his clincher: "You see, we believe that 'we're all in this together' is a far better philosophy than 'you're on your own.'" As the crowd cheered and applauded, Clinton smiled and quietly underscored his point: "It is," he said.

In his election night speech, Obama reprised and summarized the argument he had made over the previous fifteen months.

"This country has more wealth than any nation, but that's not what makes us rich," Obama declared. "We have the most powerful military in history, but that's not what makes us strong. Our universit[ies], our culture are the envy of the world, but that's not what keeps the world coming to our shores.

"What makes America exceptional," he went on, "are the bonds that hold together the most diverse nation on earth—the belief that our destiny is shared; that this country only works when we accept certain obligations to one another, and to future generations; that the freedom which so many Americans have fought for and died for comes with responsibilities as well as rights, and among those are love and charity and duty and patriotism. That's what makes America great."

Yes, it does.

II

The 2012 campaign began on August 2, 2011, when Obama signed the deal ending the debt-ceiling fiasco. At that moment, the president relinquished his last illusions that the current, radical version of the Republican Party could be dealt with as a governing partner. From then on, Obama was determined to fight—and to win.

It was the right choice, the only alternative to capitulation. A Republican majority both inspired and intimidated by the Tea Party was demanding that Obama renounce every principle dear to him about the role of government in twenty-first-century America. And so he set out to defeat those who threatened to bring back the economic policies of the 1890s. If the 2010 election was the Tea Party's triumph, 2012 was its comeuppance. The GOP establishment rode the Tea Party tiger to power in 2010, and then ended up inside.

Republicans who dared to deal or compromise risked humiliation in primaries at the hands of a far right certain that the president of the United States was a subversive figure. Thus did Indiana Republicans turn away from Senator Richard Lugar and his long service as a solid, if moderate, conservative. Instead, they nominated state treasurer Richard Mourdock, who defined "compromise" as involving the other side coming to agree with him. He later sealed his fate by proclaiming that he understood God's will at work in cases of rape. Todd Akin, another ardent conservative, won a Senate primary in Missouri. He later got himself into trouble by theorizing about the nature of "legitimate" rape.

For his part, Obama sought to work with Republicans in Congress right through the debt ceiling battle. But Obama's aides are unanimous in saying that that this struggle was the breaking point. Republicans, filled with Tea Party zeal, were willing to endanger the nation's financial standing to achieve steep budget cuts. When House Speaker John Boehner walked away from a deal that conservatives of another era would have hailed as a great victory, Obama realized that any "grand bargain" would be a chimera until he could win the battle about first principles.

Everything you needed to know about Obama's argument was laid out in that December 2011 speech in Osawatomie, Kansas, mentioned in Chapter 7. Obama consciously chose as his venue the place where Theodore Roosevelt had laid out the core themes of American progressivism 101 years earlier. "Just as there was in Teddy Roosevelt's time," Obama declared, "there is a certain crowd in Washington who, for the last few decades, have said, 'Let's respond to this economic challenge with the same old tune. The market will take care of everything,' they tell us. 'If we just cut more regulations and cut more taxes—especially for the wealthy—our economy will grow stronger . . . even if prosperity doesn't trickle down, well, that's the price of liberty.' Now, it's a simple theory . . . But here's the problem: It doesn't work. It has never worked." This is when Obama put the Long Consensus on the November ballot.

In Romney, Obama was blessed with an opponent who embraced the "simple theory" Obama denounced, not only in his moves rightward in the primaries but also in his own career as a private equity capitalist. Romney may have flipped and flopped on issues he didn't care about, but his view of American capitalism and American government never wavered.

And so, beneath the attacks, the counterattacks, and the billions invested by small numbers of the very rich to sway the undecided, the country got a choice worthy of a great democracy. Obama's one-word slogan was the very embodiment of the progressive tradition: "Forward." For most of the campaign, the word on the posters that dominated every rally ended with a period. Toward the end, the signs were revised to read, "Forward!" The addition of that exclamation point suggested that Obama's argument became more emphatic and—except for his lapse in his first debate with Romney—more confident as the campaign moved forward.

III

That first debate was Romney's finest hour in the campaign. It was also deeply revealing. It marked the beginning of Romney's hard scramble toward the political middle in the campaign's final month. This was as important a signal about where opinion in the country lay as was Obama's victory. Romney's moves meant that the right and the Tea Party had lost the 2012 election even before the votes were counted.

Romney would not have tried to throw so many of his past positions overboard if he had thought that the nation was ready to endorse the full-throated conservatism he embraced to win the Republican nomination. Yet unlike Ronald Reagan and Barry Goldwater, Romney offered more an echo than a choice. His strategy at the end was to reach the White House on a chorus of me-too's.

The right largely went along because its partisans knew Romney had no other option. This, too, was an acknowledgment of defeat, a recognition that the grand ideological experiment heralded by the rise of the Tea Party had lost traction.

Almost all of the analysis of Romney's highly public burning of the right's catechism focused on such issues as whether his ideological remake would help him win over middle-of-the-road women and carry Ohio. That didn't work out. What mattered for the longer run is that a party that won the 2010 elections with an ideological bang sought victory just two years later on the basis of a tactical whimper.

It turned out that there was no profound ideological conversion of the country. We remained the same moderate and practical country we have been for decades. In 2010, voters were upset about the economy, Democrats were demobilized, and President Obama wasn't yet ready to fight. All the conservatives had left in October of 2012 was economic unease, and that was ebbing as Election Day approached.

The rout of the right's ideology, particularly its neoconservative brand, was visible throughout the debates. In the third one, Romney praised one

Obama foreign policy initiative after another. He calmly abandoned much of what he had said during the previous eighteen months. Gone were the hawkish assaults on Obama's approach to Iraq, Iran, Afghanistan, Israel, China, and nearly everywhere else. Romney was all about "peace." Romney's most revealing line: "We don't want another Iraq." Thus did he bury without ceremony the great Bush-Cheney project. He renounced a war he had, with vehemence and enthusiasm, once supported.

Then there was budget policy. If the Romney/Ryan budget and tax ideas were so popular, why did Romney work so hard to avoid giving details? For that matter, why did Ryan feel obligated to forsake his love for Rand, the proud philosopher of "the virtue of selfishness" and the thinker he once said had inspired his public service?

Romney knew that, by substantial margins, the country favored raising taxes on the rich and opposed slashing many government programs, including Medicare and Social Security. Since Romney's actual plan called for cutting taxes on the rich, he had to disguise the fact.

The clearest sign of the demise of Tea Party thinking was Romney's effort to cloud or even deny his past position on the rescue of the auto industry. In late 2008, Romney had claimed that if the bailout the Detroit-based automakers sought went through, you could "kiss the American automotive industry good-bye." The car companies, he said, would "seal their fate with a bailout check." This would be the same Mitt Romney who later tried to imply that he never said what he said or thought what he thought. The bailout had become good politics. Free-market fundamentalism had collapsed in a heap.

"Ideas have consequences" is one of the conservative movement's most honored slogans. That the conservatives' standard-bearers had to escape the consequences of their ideas tells us all we need to know about the outcome of the philosophical battle.

And therein lies reason for hope. Throughout *Our Divided Political Heart*, I have expressed frustration over what conservatism has become, but also hope that conservatism might rediscover its moderate and communitarian side.

True, some on the right—particularly those in what David Frum, the thoughtful conservative dissenter, called the "conservative entertainment complex" on talk radio and Fox News—sought refuge in denial by blaming it all on Romney or concocting other theories that required no rethinking.

But most conservatives knew that much had gone badly wrong. Against all expectations at the beginning of the year, the Democrats not only held the Senate but actually gained seats, their majority padded by the own-goals scored by Mourdock and Akin. The Republicans held the House of Representatives, but Democrats gained seats and led the GOP in the popular votes cast in all the House races taken together. Republicans held on largely because of gerrymandered districts and the fact that Democrats won urban House seats by very wide margins. And then there was the size of Obama's triumph, involving as it did victory in every swing state but North Carolina and a popular vote majority of some four million.

Many Republicans quickly concluded that Obama's overwhelming margins among Latinos required the GOP to abandon nativist rhetoric and wholesale opposition to immigration reform. This was progress. But it wouldn't be that simple for the right. A more moderate stand on immigration is, indeed, essential, but it would also create new divisions in the party. And the GOP's weaknesses among both Latinos and women owed not simply to immigration or social issues, respectively, but also to the reality that both groups are more sympathetic to government's role in the economy and in promoting upward mobility than current conservative doctrine allows. A party that wants to govern has to do more than run against government. For the right, this was 2012's inconvenient truth.

Among conservative thinkers, conservative columnists Ross Douthat of the *New York Times* and Michael Gerson of the *Washington Post* were especially forceful on this point. "What the party really needs, much more than a better identity-politics pitch," Douthat wrote, "is an economic message that would appeal across demographic lines—reaching both downscale white voters turned off by Romney's Bain Capital background and upwardly mobile Latino voters who don't relate to the current G.O.P. fixation on upper-bracket tax cuts." Douthat cited another New Look Conservative, Henry Olsen of the American Enterprise Institute, who argued that Republicans could find a way of opposing "an overweening and intrusive state" while still recognizing, as Olsen put it, that "government can give average people a hand up to achieve the American Dream."

Similarly, Gerson continued to insist that a compassionate conservatism was the only plausible approach for the right:

> Some of the most important intellectual groundwork is needed on the role of government. Mitt Romney had a five-part plan to encourage job creation. He lacked a public philosophy that explained government's valid role in meeting human needs. Suburban women heard little about improved public education. Single women, particularly single mothers, heard little about their struggles, apart from an off-putting Republican critique of food stamps. Blue-collar workers in, say, Ohio heard little about the unique challenges that face declining industrial communities. Latinos heard little from Republicans about promoting equal opportunity and economic mobility.
>
> Neither a vague, pro-business orientation nor tea party ideology speaks to these Americans—except perhaps to alienate them. Conservatives will need to define a role for government that addresses human needs in effective, market-oriented ways. Americans fear public debt, and they resent intrusive bureaucracies, but they do not hate government.

Those of us who are progressive harbor a certain skepticism about whether conservatives can come up with a plausible program without backing away from some of their fundamental beliefs about the relationship between markets and government. Nonetheless, the fact that the 2012 results pushed many thoughtful conservatives toward a new appreciation of the Long Consensus could be counted as a victory for a more balanced and less divisive approach to both politics and governing. The willingness of many conservative Republicans to abandon their near-theological commitment to the idea that taxes could never ever be raised was also a sign that, as Frum put it, "the ice is breaking" around conservative doctrine.

Obama's reelection was thus at once a deeply personal triumph and a victory for the younger, highly diverse, and broadly progressive America that rallied to him. It was a result that ought to settle the bitter argument that ground the nation's government to a near-standstill. Repeatedly, Obama asked voters to settle Washington's squabbles in his favor. They did. And so a president who took office on a wave of emotion won something more valuable and durable: a majority that thought hard about his stewardship and decided to let him finish the job he had begun.

Yet this should be seen as the beginning of the story, not the end. Having won vindication for the Long Consensus, Obama and the next generation of progressives need to prove that its ideas and approaches are capable of renovation, and can restore the living standards of Americans, particularly those who rallied to the president in the nation's industrial heartland and the inner cities, but also voters in suburban and rural areas who had opposed him. What both sides shared was a desire to put an end to fears of American decline and to inaugurate a New Prosperity that would prove to be durable, and widely shared.

Obama, like Clinton before him, understands the importance of the nation's communitarian tradition, and so does the movement Obama gathered behind him. Progressives remember that the first word of our Constitution is We. They know that ours is a country that truly believes we should "take care of our own"—and that doing so requires attention to the world beyond our borders and a global economy that is transforming the way all economies work. Community is a noble ideal. Building and strengthening it requires practical work and the bold and persistent experimentation that Franklin Roosevelt commended to us. This is still the calling of all who would call themselves progressive.

A Personal Note
My Debts to Historians, and to Many Others

THIS book is built on two forms of indebtedness: personal debts I have accumulated thanks to advice, guidance, and help from a long list of friends, and intellectual debts to the many historians whose work has shaped this account. Some people fall into both categories, but a large number of historians whom I have never met were essential to this work. You might say that I have come to *feel* as if I know some of them, simply because their books and essays were so important to me. I have tried in both the text and the endnotes to honor all my sources. But I'd like to offer a brief bibliographic essay to call attention to particular works and writers who were especially important to me as I wrote this book.

I fell in love with American history when I was young, and I begin by thanking two exceptional high school American history teachers, Jim Garman and Norm Hess, who nurtured that affection. They taught me early on that there are competing accounts of the American story, that we can view ourselves through many prisms, and that there is ample room for argument about core events in our past, including the choices our forebears made, both individually and collectively. Books that Jim and Norm encouraged me to read had a lasting influence, perhaps none more so than William E. Leuchtenburg's *Franklin D. Roosevelt and the New Deal*. Leuchtenburg taught me how a graceful writer could bring politics to life, and his account of FDR and the Depression helped set me on a path toward a practical kind of liberalism that still largely defines my view of politics.

Encountering Richard Hofstadter's work for the first time was thrilling. His wry and tough-minded view of American public life and his skill at getting behind the masks of publicly proclaimed ideologies were liberating for historical writing. He inspired in me a lifelong affection for the ironies of politics. It's hard to forget those paradoxical chapter titles in *The American Political Tradition*: "John C. Calhoun: The Marx of the Master Class," "William Jennings Bryan: The Democrat as Revivalist," "Theodore Roosevelt: The Conservative as Progressive," and "Franklin D. Roosevelt: The Patrician as Opportunist." I have often wondered what subtitle Hofstadter, who died in 1970 at the age of fifty-four, might give to an essay on Barack Obama: "Technocrat as Preacher"? "Progressive as Centrist"? "Professor as Movement Builder"? "Unifier as Polarizer"? Once Hofstadter's paradoxes take hold of you, they don't let go.

As is clear from what I've written, I have come to disagree with Hofstadter on a number of questions. Yet anyone who writes about political or historical subjects can only hope to emulate the elegance and energy of his prose, the clarity of his thought, and the ratio of insights per page in every one of his books. Arguing that Hofstadter's *The Age of Reform* "is the most influential book ever published on the history of twentieth-century America," Alan Brinkley concluded that it is "a book whose central interpretations few historians now accept, but one whose influence few historians can escape." I certainly have not escaped its magic, and I remain inspired by Hofstadter's ennobling view of history's role. "In an age when so much of our literature is infused with nihilism and other disciplines are driven toward narrow and positivistic inquiry," Hofstadter wrote in *The Progressive Historians*, "history may remain the most humanizing among the arts." So it should be, and so it was in his hands. In light of these contributions, lovers of American history should be grateful to David S. Brown for his excellent 2006 intellectual biography of Hofstadter.

I was excited in the late 1960s by the historians of the New Left, and I still treasure my battered paperback copy of *Towards a New Past*, the 1967 collection of essays by dissenting left-wing historians edited by Barton Bernstein. I remember pondering what the exotic idea of a "new past" really meant. It was intriguing to see Harry Truman and Franklin Roosevelt treated as conservatives (which in important ways they were), and bracing to see abolitionists and African Americans rescued from an earlier historical approach that was tinged with racism—a saga in American historiography that plays an important role in these pages. On the whole, my views are less radical than those of many of the dissenting historians, yet our collective understanding of who we are is more honest because of them.

Of course, historians of many different philosophical hues—conservatives and liberals no less than radicals—have been vitally concerned with the politics of their own moments, and the histories they offered were shaped and informed by their own political commitments. Arthur Schlesinger Jr.'s magnificent work on Jackson (and, of course, on FDR himself) cannot be understood apart from his unabashed and unapologetic sympathies for New Deal liberalism. Forrest McDonald's writing about the Founders, particularly Alexander Hamilton, was enlivened by his own conservative disposition. In the preface to his Hamilton biography, McDonald quotes fellow historian Carl Becker, who nicely captured the tendency of all of us to seek reinforcement for our own views from our reading as well as from history itself. "Generally speaking," Becker wrote, "men are influenced by books which clarify their own thought, which express their own notions well, or which suggest ideas which their minds are already predisposed to accept." I don't pretend to be immune to this temptation, though I try to fight it.

I should also declare my gratitude to Sean Wilentz, one of our era's premier historians. His essential book *The Rise of American Democracy* was an inspiration to me as I wrote this one. It conclusively demonstrates the importance of politics: the United States did not start out as fully democratic, and it became more so over time only after difficult arguments, great exertions of organizing, and sometimes bloody struggles. Although my own contemporary political views tend to run Sean's way, I also found enlightenment in Daniel Walker Howe's treatment of an overlapping period, *What Hath God Wrought*, and in his indispensable *The Political Culture of the American Whigs*. Howe's work highlights the inventiveness and entrepreneurial energy of a religiously inflected American spirit and focuses on the "communications revolution" between 1815 and 1848. If Wilentz writes with considerable sympathy for Jacksonian democracy, Howe offers a helpfully sympathetic view of the Whigs. One might say that Wilentz and Howe help us understand the whole story by telling rather different stories. Reading Wilentz and Howe reminded me of my own overlapping allegiances—to Jeffersonian democracy, Jacksonian equality, and Hamiltonian-Whiggish nation building. Abraham Lincoln, it might be said, sought to bring these together and build on them, and so did Franklin D. Roosevelt. (So might Barack Obama, if he finds success.)

The influence of Gordon Wood's monumental work on the American Revolution, the Constitution, and the early republic is plain throughout these pages, and I have also learned a great deal about the historian's craft from his superb essays, notably those collected in *The Purpose of the Past: Reflections on the Uses of History* and *The Idea of America: Reflections on the Birth of the United States*. Wood should in no way be held to account for the use to which I put his work—which, of course, applies as well to the work of the many other historians whose accounts I cite. But since Wood's writing about the origins of our republic has become close to canonical—a word with which he might be uncomfortable—he is probably accustomed to seeing his work used for many purposes by those holding a variety of views. I can only say that I have tried to be true to what he has written, and that his work on our nation's Founding is inspiring.

During a visit I made to the University of Virginia, Brian Balogh told me about his book *A Government Out of Sight*, thought it might be of interest in light of what I was working on, and then sent it to me. He could not have been more right, and I can't thank him enough. It is an enormously insightful book whose importance to my telling of the American story is clear. I have been similarly influenced by my friend and Georgetown University colleague Michael Kazin's work on Populism and American radicalism. His recent history of the American left, *American Dreamers*, is vital to explaining how those outside the political consensus of their time often change popular understandings, alter the prevailing narrative, and transform the country—even if they never take power themselves. Alan Brinkley's work has also played an important role here, particularly his fine book on the development of the New Deal, *The End of Reform*, and his brilliant essays in *Liberalism and Its Discontents* and *New Federalist*

Papers. The influence of Eric Foner's breakthrough work on Reconstruction is also obvious, and his observations in *Who Owns History?* were exceedingly helpful.

Leo Ribuffo, another distinguished historian, has rightly argued that we are rarely mindful enough of the sheer complexity of American history, a lesson I have tried to take to heart, and he has taught me much over the years, through his wit as well as his scholarship. Doris Kearns Goodwin, who was a welcoming young professor when I was in college, has shown that it's possible to combine deep intellectual seriousness with the vivid historical writing that has made her books so popular. My friend Robert Dallek is gifted in the same way. The late Christopher Lasch grabbed my attention when I was young and held it through the many turns of his brilliant, independent mind. Meeting him late in his life is one of the joys of mine.

A few other works deserve special mention for their influence on this one: Daniel Rodgers's *Age of Fracture*, Sidney Milkis's *Theodore Roosevelt, the Progressive Party, and the Transformation of American Democracy*, James Kloppenberg's *The Virtues of Liberalism*, Michael Sandel's *Democracy's Discontent*, George H. Nash's *The Conservative Intellectual Movement in America Since 1945*, Robert G. McCloskey's *American Conservatism in the Age of Enterprise*, Bill Bishop's *The Big Sort*, Jill Lepore's *The Whites of Their Eyes: The Tea Party's Revolution and the Battle over American History* (along with her excellent *New Yorker* articles), James Morone's *The Democratic Wish*, Harold Holzer's *Lincoln at Cooper Union*, Theda Skocpol's *Protecting Soldiers and Mothers*, Thomas Frank's *What's the Matter with Kansas?*, John Milton Cooper's *Woodrow Wilson: A Biography*, Robert Bellah and colleagues' *Habits of the Heart*, and Amitai Etzioni's *The Spirit of Community*. I find it heartening that in recent years a group of younger historians has restored political history to the center of their profession. I'd encourage readers to sample their work in *The Democratic Experiment: New Directions in American Political History*, edited by Meg Jacobs, William J. Novak, and Julian E. Zelizer.

This is not a book of political theory, yet one of the pleasures of writing it was the sojourn it required me to take into the world of philosophers. I have been helped and instructed along the way by conversations with two exceptional philosophers who are also wise and generous friends, William Galston and Michael Sandel. My own views stand somewhere at the intersection of their respective approaches, though the usual disclaimer—that the ideas here are mine, not theirs—may be especially important to emphasize in the case of these two brilliant thinkers. Michael Walzer, as fine a teacher as he is a philosopher, has influenced my views on almost everything.

I have also received enormous help and guidance from James Kloppenberg, an intellectual historian whose work I discovered in the course of writing this book, before I had ever met him, and who has since become a warm friend. Jim read an early partial draft of this book, and he did the two things you would hope a friend might do: first he expressed genuine excitement about and support for what I was up to, and then he offered a slew of valuable suggestions and friendly criticisms.

Thanks, as well, to two insightful British politicians and thinkers: the Rt. Hon. Michael Gove, M.P., for a brilliant conservative communitarian take on the movie *High Noon*, and Lord Stewart Wood, for his wisdom on Labour Party communitarianism.

I have been very fortunate to be connected to three extraordinary institutions, and all of them were very supportive as I was writing, thinking, and rewriting: the *Washington Post*, where I write a twice-weekly column; the Brookings Institution; and Georgetown University, where I make my home at its Public Policy Institute.

As I was working on this book, a few of the ideas I was grappling with snuck into my *Washington Post* column; I'm grateful I was able to give them a first airing there. Even more, I am lucky to have a chance through the column and blogging to be in the middle of our country's political debate at what I really do believe is a moment of decision. My thanks to Fred Hiatt, Jackson Diehl, Autumn Brewington, Vince Rinehart, Lisa Bonos, Marisa Katz, Steve Stromberg, Helen Jones, Crystal Davis, Trey Johnson, and Jim Downie on the *Post*'s editorial and op-ed pages. Particular thanks to Alan Shearer, James Hill, Richard Aldacushion, and Karen Greene at the *Washington Post* Writers Group. I am indebted to so many other people at the *Post*, and I have thanked many of them in earlier books. (In fact, I ask all the friends and colleagues thanked in earlier books to consider themselves thanked again.) Here I will confine myself here to thanking Steve Luxenberg, a brilliant writer and editor. He knows the many reasons for my gratitude. It's hard to imagine a truer friend.

At Brookings, special thanks to Tom Mann for encouraging me to join its ranks; to Darrell West, the vice president of the Governance Studies program; to Strobe Talbott, our president; and to so many wonderful colleagues too numerous to list here.

I feel similar gratitude to all of my Georgetown colleagues. Here I will mention the university's president, Jack DeGioia; Ed Montgomery, dean of the Georgetown Public Policy Institute; Judy Feder, the former dean who brought me to GPPI; and the spectacular (and overworked) GPPI staff, including Kerry Pace, Jennifer Blanck, and Joe Ferrara, now President DeGioia's chief of staff. Thanks also to my teaching assistants at Georgetown, all of whom are destined to become important public intellectuals: Sam Potolicchio, Conor Williams, David Buckley, and Elliot Fulmer.

This book might never have been written without my agent, Gail Ross, who is as devoted to her authors, to book publishing, and to American politics as anyone I've met. She also has a particular affection for journalists, which may be hard for others to understand but which we journalists appreciate. I thank her for all she's done. It was Gail who introduced me to Anton Mueller of Bloomsbury, and there hangs the tale of this book.

Anton is a force of nature. He is always thinking, always coming up with ideas, which he then examines from many different angles. He rejects some, embraces others—and then looks around for new ones. I got to know him because he came to me with a suggestion for a book. About a week after we discussed it, he called to talk about some passionate thoughts I had offered about community and individualism. *That*, he said, was the book I should write, and this is the result. Working with Anton has been a magnificent adventure. He bore with me through several drafts, always trying to sharpen my arguments and expand my view, always mindful of how the news (such as the rise of Occupy Wall Street) related to the case I was making. A highly practical editor, he's also a searcher along for the journey, and it is a joy to share it with him. My thanks also to Rachel Mannheimer, Anton's thoughtful assistant, who made sure everything happened as it should, and on time.

Sue Warga was a magnificent copy editor. The copy-editing process isn't typically seen as fun, but it was with Sue. I have what might be called a communitarian approach to copy editing, which is a glorified way of saying that I love to talk things through, going back and forth with copy editors over particular problems, whether grammatical or conceptual. Sue operated with both great efficiency and a warm spirit (often working between her daughter's lacrosse games). I offer her my gratitude. I also want to thank Laura Phillips, an excellent production editor who sped this book to print with efficiency and understanding.

It's impossible to give adequate thanks to Emily Luken. Em is generally referred to as my "assistant," but she is really many things at once: a brilliant editor, a shrewd political analyst, a subtle diplomat, a gifted organizer, a tough-minded thinker, a savvy publicist, a warm friend, and a deeply moral and ethical citizen. She sees around corners, anticipating problems before they arise, and keeps our show on the road. And she did all this over the last year while planning her wedding to the delightful Edward Yardley, my candidate as a future prime minister of New Zealand.

Both this book and my life were enriched by spectacular interns who were happy to research matters as diverse as the thinking of the Whigs and the subtleties of the individual mandate in the health care law. They also helped clarify my thinking on many issues. So thanks to Sally Bronston, Emma Ellman-Golan, Kristen Gendron, Adam Mandelsberg, Max Nacheman, Amanda Nover, Joshua Pollack, Amanda Ravich, Jacob Silverman, Elizabeth Valentini, Matthew Waring, and Ross Tilchin. Particular thanks to Victoria Glock-Molloy, who was with me during the final months as I was finishing; she did heroic work on many fronts, notably by tracking down those elusive endnotes.

Thanks also to my sister, Lucie-Anne Dionne Thomas, her husband, Drew, and her daughter, Kim. Lu and I learned about community, its joys, and its obligations from our very loving parents, and also from the people of our hometown, Fall River, Massachusetts, a place my heart still honors.

Finally, in a book that speaks a great deal about community, I can't find adequate words to thank the most important community in my life: Mary Boyle and our children, James, Julia, and Margot. One of my most treasured memories will always be of the great snowstorm in February

2010. Everyday work life stopped, and most people in our region were shut in by snow drifts and slick roads. It was during that storm that I began writing this book, and I did so amidst the merry sounds of the many friends our kids brought to our home. One night we counted nineteen of them who stayed for a spaghetti dinner. James, Julia, and Margot have brought a joy to our life that passes all understanding—and I am absolutely persuaded that they and their friends will keep America's promise as part of a great reforming generation.

Mary is the original communitarian. Her approach to life—learned in a Brooklyn neighborhood from a warm, welcoming, thoughtful, and boisterous family—is outlandishly generous, loving, loyal and grounded. On top of that, she's both smart and wise. We met twenty-five years ago on Patriots' Day. That may explain some of the patriotic sentiments in this book. It certainly explains why I celebrate April nineteenth every year—in honor of the heroes of Lexington and Concord, of course, but primarily, I'll admit, in gratitude for Mary.

Bethesda, Maryland
February 2012

Notes

INTRODUCTION

5   **"all one thing":** Abraham Lincoln, "A House Divided" speech at Illinois Republican Convention, 16 June 1858, http://www.ushistory.org/documents/house divided.htm.

7   **"literally out of any old nation that comes along":** G. K. Chesterton, "What Is America?" from *What I Saw in America,* http://libertynet.org/edcivic/chestame.html.

8   **"I bailed out a bank":** Ezra Klein, "The Wonkiest Signs from Occupy Wall Street," Ezra Klein's Wonkblog, *Washington Post,* 17 October 2011.

8   **"the United States has gone from being":** Alexander Stille, "The Paradox of the New Elite," *New York Times,* 22 October 2011.

9   **"there is surging sentiment among voters":** Richard McGregor, "Obama Takes Risky Stance Against the Rich," *Financial Times,* October 28, 2011.

9   ***Citizens United:*** *Citizens United v. Federal Election Commission,* 21 January 2010.

11 **"that the only thing we can do":** Barack Obama, "Address by the President to a Joint Session of Congress," 8 September 2011, http://www.whitehouse.gov/the-press-office/2011/09/08/address-president-joint-session-congress.

13 **"brutal and hurried lives":** John Crow Ransom et al., *I'll Take my Stand: The South and Agrarian Tradition* (Baton Rouge: Louisiana State University Press, 1977), xlii.

13 **"the poverty of the contemporary spirit":** Ibid., xliii.

13 **"family, work, neighborhood":** Ronald Reagan, "Address Before a Joint Session of the Congress on the State of the Union," 25 January 1984, http://www.presidency.ucsb.edu/ws/index.php?pid=40205#axzz1biIUuld7.

13 **"a thousand points of light":** George H. W. Bush, "Inaugural Address of George H. W. Bush," 20 January 1989, http://avalon.law.yale.edu/20th_century/bush.asp.

13 **"rally the armies of compassion":** George W. Bush, "Message to the Congress Transmitting the Blueprint for the Program to Rally the Armies of Compassion," 30 January 2011.

13 **"family, work, neighborhood":** Ronald Reagan to the Republican National Convention, August 15, 1988, as transcribed in "The Republicans in New Orleans; Reagan's Address: Hailing Fruits of the Party's Dream of 1980," *New York Times*, August 16, 1988.

13 **"chronic loneliness":** Barack Obama, "Politics of Conscience," Hartford, CT, 23 June 2007, http://www.ucc.org/news/significant-speeches/a-politics-of-conscience .html?print=t.

14 **"rugged individualism":** Herbert Hoover, "Rugged Individualism," 22 October 1928, http://coursesa.matrix.msu.edu/~hst203/documents/HOOVER.html.

14 **"there is a profound ambivalence":** Robert Neelly Bellah, Richard Madsen, and William M. Sullivan, *Habits of the Heart: Individualism and Commitment in American Life* (Berkeley: University of California Press, 2008), 144.

15 **James Kloppenberg:** James T. Kloppenberg, *Uncertain Victory: Social Democracy and Progressivism in European and American Thought, 1870–1920* (New York: Oxford University Press, 1986).

15 **Daniel Rodgers:** Daniel T. Rodgers, *Age of Fracture* (Cambridge, MA: Belknap Press, 2011).

16 **"that fraternity is a need because":** Wilson Carey McWilliams, *The Idea of Fraternity in America* (Berkeley: University of California Press, 1973), 624.

16 **"communitarian liberal":** Joseph Sobran, "Faith Healing—*Why Americans Hate Politics* by E. J. Dionne," *National Review*, July 29, 1991.

17 ***The Quest for Community:*** Robert Nisbet, *The Quest for Community: A Study in the Ethics of Order and Freedom* (Richmond, CA: ICS Press, 2009).

17 **"force and terror":** Ibid., 73.

17 **"Freedom cannot be maintained in a monolithic society":** Robert A. Nisbet, *Tradition and Revolt: Historical and Sociological Essays* (New York: Vintage, 1970), 136, 141.

18 **"little platoons":** Edmund Burke, *Reflections on the French Revolution*, ed. Charles W. Eliot (New York: P. F. Collier and Son, 1909–14), http://www.bartleby .com/24/3/4.html.

18 **"The United States shall guarantee to every State":** The Constitution of the United States of America, Article IV, Section 4, http://avalon.law.yale.edu/ 18th_century/art4.asp.

19 **"The terrain of history has disaggregated":** Rodgers, *Age of Fracture*, 229.

19 **"Every group its own historian":** Peter Novick, quoted in Rodgers, *Age of Fracture*, 229.

20 **"forming tribes":** Bill Bishop and Robert G. Cushing, *The Big Sort: Why the Clustering of Like-Minded America Is Tearing Us Apart* (Boston: Houghton Mifflin Harcourt, 2009), 6.

20 **"A friend asked the other evening":** Ibid., 301.

21 **"a shift from left to right":** Alan Wolfe, "The Big Shrink," *New Republic*, 10 March 2011, http://www.tnr.com/book/review/age-fracture-daniel-rodgers.

23 **"March without the people":** Ralph Waldo Emerson, quoted in Michael Kazin, *The Populist Persuasion: An American History* (New York: Basic Books, 1995), 7.

24 **"high finance":** Theodore Roosevelt, quoted in John Milton Cooper, *Woodrow Wilson: A Biography* (New York: Alfred A. Knopf, 2009), 165.

24 **"the time when the combined":** Woodrow Wilson, quoted in Cooper, *Woodrow Wilson*, 167.

25 **"America's problem is not that it does":** Richard McGregor, "Why Can't America Be More Like, Well, America?" *Financial Times*, 30 September 2011.

CHAPTER I: TWO CUPS OF TEA

29 **"The government is promoting bad behavior!":** Rick Santelli at the Chicago Board of Trade, 19 February 2009, http://www.youtube.com/watch?v=zp-Jw-5Kx8k.

29 **"they moved from the individual":** Ibid.

30 **"We're thinking of having a Chicago Tea Party":** Ibid.

30 **"Some people say I'm extreme":** John M. Broder, "Climate Change Doubt Is Tea Party Article of Faith," *New York Times*, 20 October 2010.

30 **"little more than a hundred people":** Kate Zernike, *Boiling Mad: Inside Tea Party America* (New York: Times Books, 2010).

31 **"Republican, white, male, married and older than 45":** Kate Zernike and Megan Thee-Brenan, "Poll Finds Tea Partiers Wealthier and More Educated," *New York Times*, 14 April 2010.

31 **"a community committed to standing":** Tea Party Patriots of San Benito County, "About Us," http://www.teapartypatriots.org/GroupNew/770aa503-a165-48dd-ba9d-f16c47093711/Tea_Party_Patriots_of_San_Benito_County.

32 **"a user-driven group of like-minded":** Tea Party Nation, "A Home for Conservatives!!!" http://www.teapartynation.com/?view=rss.

32 **"compulsory participation in social security":** Seymour Martin Lipset and Earl Raab, *The Politics of Unreason: Right-Wing Extremism in America, 1790–1977*, 2nd ed. (Chicago: University of Chicago Press, 1978).

32 **"You attempt to be Professorial":** Paul, "Obama the Arrogant Elitist Marxist—An Open Letter to Obama from a Regular Citizen of the United States," Conservative Tea Party California Style, 19 September 2010, http://www.conservativeteapartycaliforniastyle.com/2010/09/obama-arrogant-elitist-marxist-open.html.

32 **"I can find you a lot more Harvard accents":** Robert Welch, quoted in Seymour Martin Lipset and Earl Raab, eds., *The Politics of Unreason: Right Wing Extremism in America 1790–1970* (New York: Harper Torchbooks, 1973), 257–58.

32 **"From Woodrow Wilson":** Ibid.

32 **"conspiracy conceived":** Ibid.

33 **"In recent years, do you think":** Survey discussed in E. J. Dionne, "Populism of Privilege," *Washington Post*, 10 April 2010.

33 **A survey in the summer of 2011:** "Polling the Tea Party," *New York Times*, 14 April 2010, http://www.nytimes.com/interactive/2010/04/14/us/politics/20100414-tea-party-poll-graphic.html#tab=5.

33 **"something really odd happened":** Tom Tancredo, opening speech to National Tea Party Convention, Nashville, Tennessee, February 4, 2010.

34 **"Some say simplistically":** Randy Golden, "Causes of the Civil War," About North Georgia, http://ngeorgia.com/history/why.html.

34 **"doesn't amount to diddly":** Haley Barbour, quoted in Michael D. Shear, "Discussing Civil Rights Era, a Governor Is Criticized," *New York Times*, December 20, 2010.

34 **"becomes the continuation":** C. Vann Woodward, quoted in Drew Gilpin Faust, "Telling War Stories," *New Republic*, 30 June 2011, 19–25.

34 **"The powers of the centralized":** Ibid.

35 **"significant segments of the American":** Ibid.

35 **"insisted that the nation's":** Robert Sutton, quoted in Faust, "Telling War Stories."

35 **"A century and a half after the civil war":** Eric Foner, "The American Civil War Still Being Fought," *Guardian*, 20 December 2010.

35 **the "cornerstone" of the Confederacy "rests upon":** Alexander H. Stephens, "Cornerstone Address, March 21, 1861," in Frank Moore, ed., *The Rebellion Record: A Diary of American Events with Documents, Narratives, Illustrative Incidents, Poetry, Etc.* (New York: G. P. Putnam, 1862), 1:44–46; also http://www.fordham.edu/halsall/mod/1861stephens.asp.

35 **"Beyond the circumscribed world":** Elbert Ventura, "Making History," *Democracy* 20 (Spring 2011).

36 **"Like the experience of foreign travel":** James W. Ceaser, "The Visionary Generation," *Wall Street Journal*, 14 May 2011.

37 **"belonged to the community":** Rush Limbaugh, "The Story of Thanksgiving," *The Rush Limbaugh Show*, 24 November 2010.

37 **"They were collectivists!":** Rush Limbaugh, "The Real Story of Thanksgiving," *The Rush Limbaugh Show*, 21 November 2007.

37 **"Long before Karl Marx":** Ibid.

37 **Limbaugh's persistence in promoting this view:** Kate Zernike, "The Pilgrims Were . . . Socialists?" *New York Times*, 20 November 2010; Rush Limbaugh, "We're Politicizing Thanksgiving?" *The Rush Limbaugh Show*, 24 November 2010.

37 **For this, she was rebuked by Limbaugh** Rush Limbaugh, "We're Politicizing Thanksgiving?" *The Rush Limbaugh Show*, 24 November 2010.

38 **"The political universe is, of course, very different":** Sean Wilentz, "Confounding Fathers: The Tea Party's Cold War Roots," *New Yorker*, 18 October 2010.

38 **"transplanted Canadian who served as a Mormon missionary":** Ibid.

38 **"much of that time as a special agent":** Ibid.

38 **"Hoover informed inquirers":** Ibid.

38 **"His time in office was contentious":** Bracken Lee, quoted in Wilentz, "Confounding Fathers."

39 **"a lengthy primer published in 1958":** Wilentz, "Confounding Fathers."

39 **"he enlivened a survey":** Ibid.

39 **"decried the Ivy League Establishment":** W. Cleon Skousen, quoted in Wilentz, "Confounding Fathers."

39 **"a treatise that assembles selective quotations":** Wilentz, "Confounding Fathers."

39 **"would have astounded James Madison":** Ibid.

39 **"the motto that came out of the Constitutional Convention":** Ibid.

39 **"essential to understanding why our Founders built this Republic":** Glenn Beck, quoted in Wilentz, "Confounding Fathers."

40 **"put the book in the first spot":** Wilentz, "Confounding Fathers."

40 **"The underlying problem":** William F. Buckley, "The Question of Robert Welch," *National Review*, 13 February 1962, 84.

40 **"paranoid and unpatriotic drivel":** William F. Buckley, "On the Right: The Birch Society," *National Review*, 19 October 1965, 917.

41 **"He insists viewers read books by dead men":** Amity Shlaes, "The University Guild vs. Glenn Beck," RealClearPolitics, 4 June 2010, http://www.realclearpolitics.com/articles/2010/06/04/the_university_guild_vs_glenn_beck.html.

41 **"Every author is glad to sell books":** Ibid.

42 **"The typical procedure of the higher paranoid scholarship":** Richard Hofstadter, *The Paranoid Style in American Politics and Other Essays* (Cambridge, MA: Harvard University Press, 1952), 37.

42 **"We are all sufferers from history":** Ibid.

43 **"religiously inflected multiculturalism":** Gary Gerstle, "Minorities, Multiculturalism, and the Presidency of George W. Bush," in Julian Zelizer, ed., *The Presidency of George W. Bush: A First Historical Assessment* (Princeton: Princeton University Press, 2010).

44 **"multiculturalist project . . . . as a way of building winning electoral coalitions":** Ibid.

44 **"His 'faith-based initiatives' were not a harbinger":** Christopher Caldwell, "Bush's Weak Tea for the Right," *Financial Times*, November 13, 2010.

44 **"has come to grief through his failure":** Ibid.

45 **A poll conducted by the Public Religion Research Institute:** E. J. Dionne Jr. and William A. Galston, "The Old and New Politics of Faith: Religion and the 2010 Election," Brookings Institution, Washington, D.C., 17 November 2010.

46 **A *Washington Post*/Pew Research Center Poll in late October 2011:** Jon Cohen, "A Movement of One's Own—Tea Party Is Red, and OWS Is Blue," *Washington Post*, 24 October 2011.

48 **"Each day, it seems, thousands of Americans are going about their daily rounds"**: Barack Obama, keynote address at Call to Renewal Conference, 28 June 2006, http://www.barackobama.com/2006/06/28/call_to_renewal_keynote_address.php.

49 **"a parent's willingness to nurture a child"**: Barack Obama, "President Barack Obama's Inaugural Address," 20 January 2009.

49 **"the pleasures of riches and fame"**: Ibid.

50 **"lower taxes, less government and more economic freedom for all Americans"**: Freedom Works, "About Freedom Works: Our Mission," http://www.freedomworks.org/about/our-mission.

51 **"Mr. Professor: Do you believe this country was founded on divine providence"**: Glenn Beck, *The Glenn Beck Program*, 5 May 2009.

CHAPTER II: THE POLITICS OF HISTORY

53 **"You're the state where the shot was heard 'round the world"**: Michele Bachmann, speech in Manchester, New Hampshire, 12 March 2011.

53 **"warned the British that they weren't going to be taking away"**: Sarah Palin, remarks in Boston, Massachusetts, 2 June 2011.

54 **"twentieth century Americanism"**: Edward Countryman, "Communism," in Michael Kazin, Rebecca Edwards, and Adam Rothman, eds., *The Princeton Encyclopedia of American Political History* (Princeton: Princeton University Press, 2010).

54 **"our fathers," Lincoln called them**: Abraham Lincoln, Cooper Union address, 27 February 1860.

54 **"the guardian of a threatened Republican tradition"**: Jackson was described this way by Marvin Meyers in *The Jacksonian Persuasion: Politics and Belief* (New York: Vintage Books, 1957), 17.

54 **"tyranny and despotism"**: Andrew Jackson quoted in Meyers, *The Jacksonian Persuasion*, 21.

54 **"A government must so order its functions"**: Franklin Delano Roosevelt, Commonwealth Club address, 23 September 1932.

55 **"Five score years ago, a great American, in whose symbolic shadow we stand today"**: Martin Luther King Jr., "I Have a Dream" speech, 28 August 1963.

55 **"When the architects of our republic wrote the magnificent words of the Constitution"**: Ibid.

55 **"It is obvious today that America has defaulted on this promissory note"**: Ibid.

56 **"the principle of participatory self-government"**: Stephen Breyer, *Active Liberty: Interpreting our Democratic Constitution* (New York: Vintage Books, 2005), 21.

57 **"in explanation and in selection"**: Morton White, *Foundations of Historical Knowledge* (New York: Harper and Row, 1965), 3.

57 **"depends upon generalizations"**: Ibid.

57 **"present the Federalist-Whig-Republican point of view"**: Samuel Eliot Morison, *By Land and By Sea: Essays and Addresses* (New York: Knopf, 1953), 356.

57 **"that did not follow the Jefferson-Jackson-Franklin D. Roosevelt line"**: White, *Foundations of Historical Knowledge*, 11.

57 **"Memory is the thread of personal identity, history of public identity"**: Richard Hofstadter, *The Progressive Historians: Turner, Beard, Parrington* (New York: Knopf, 1968), 3.

57 **"Historians . . . view the constant search for new perspectives"**: Eric Foner, *Who Owns History? Rethinking the Past in a Changing World* (New York: Hill and Wang, 2002), xvi.

57 **" 'Professor,' she asked, 'when did historians stop relating facts' "**: Ibid.

57 **"does not refer mainly, or even principally, to the past"**: James Baldwin, "White Man's Guilt," *Ebony*, August 1965.

57 **"the first great American historian of America"**: Hofstadter, *The Progressive Historians*, 15.

57 **"the progress of the democratic principle"**: Ibid.

58 **"history taught a lesson, the inevitable movement of human affairs"**: Ibid.

58 **"The popular voice is all powerful with us"**: Ibid.

58 **"History can contribute nothing in the way of panaceas"**: Arthur Schlesinger Jr., *The Age of Jackson* (Boston: Little, Brown, 1945), x.

58 **The Conservative Intellectual Movement in America**: George H. Nash, *The Conservative Intellectual Movement in America* (New York: Basic Books, 1976).

59 **"some of our logical statements turn out to be moral and relative in character"**: White, *Foundations of Historical Knowledge*, 291.

59 **" is not simply a collection of facts, not a politically sanctioned listing"**: Foner, *Who Owns History*, 188.

59 **As the *New Yorker* recognized in calling attention to their debate:** Jill Lepore, "People Power: Revisiting the Origins of American Democracy," *New Yorker*, 24 October 2005; Jill Lepore, "Vast Designs: How America Came of Age," *New Yorker*, 29 October 2007.

59 **"in the United States at this time, liberalism is not only the dominant"**: Lionel Trilling, *The Liberal Imagination* (New York: New York Review of Books, 1950), xv.

60 **"status anxieties"**: Richard Hofstadter, "A Paranoid Style in American Politics," *Harper's Magazine*, November 1964.

60 **Before the Storm**: Rick Perlstein, *Before the Storm: Barry Goldwater and the Unmaking of the American Consensus* (New York: Hill and Wang, 2001).

60 **Suburban Warriors**: Lisa McGirr, *Suburban Warriors: The Origins of the New American Right* (Princeton: Princeton University Press, 2002).

60 Turning Right in the Sixties: Mary Brennan, *Turning Right in the Sixties: The Conservative Capture of the G.O.P.* (Chapel Hill: University of North Carolina Press, 1995).

60 Patrick Allitt's *The Conservatives*: Patrick Allitt, *The Conservatives: Ideas and Personalities Throughout American History* (New Haven: Yale University Press, 2009).

60 "a segment of the Right appealed to traditional ideas": McGirr, *Suburban Warriors*, 8.

60 "took hold among a highly educated and thoroughly modern group": Ibid.

60 "not a rural 'remnant' of the displaced and maladapted": Ibid.

60 *Towards a New Past*: Barton J. Bernstein, ed., *Toward a New Past: Dissenting Essays in American History* (New York: Pantheon, 1968).

61 "important business leaders" Gabriel Kolko, *The Triumph of Conservatism* (Glencoe, IL: Free Press, 1977), 4.

61 "preserve the basic social and economic relations": Ibid.

61 William Appleman Williams: See William Appleman Williams, *The Tragedy of American Diplomacy* (New York: W. W. Norton, 1988).

61 Gar Alperovitz offered important books debunking aspects: See Gar Alperovitz, *Atomic Diplomacy* (New York: Random House, 1995).

61 new approaches to the history of both slavery and the American working class: See, e.g., Herbert Gutman, *The Black Family in Slavery and Freedom, 1750–1925* (New York: Vintage Books, 1977); Herbert Gutman, *Work, Culture and Society* (New York: Vintage Books, 1977).

61 long lifetime captivating students with his bottom-up approach: Howard Zinn, *A People's History of the United States: 1492–Present* (New York: HarperCollins, 2010).

61 "introduced a whole lot of people who hadn't thought about it": Jill Lepore, "Zinn's History," *New Yorker*, 3 February 2010.

61 "New Left academics . . . would write about the American past": John Patrick Diggins, *The Rise and Fall of the American Left* (New York: W. W. Norton, 1992), 29.

61 "I am less interested in eighteenth-century radicalism than in twentieth-century radicalism": Staughton Lynd, *Intellectual Origins of American Radicalism* (New York: Vintage Books, 1969), vii.

62 "That is to say, I have always begun with a concern with some present reality": Eric Foner, *Who Owns History*, 41.

63 "The answer to the all-important question of what kinds of lives black people might live ": Nicholas Lemann, *Redemption: The Last Battle of the Civil War* (New York: Farrar, Straus, and Giroux, 2006), xi.

63 "an organized, if unofficial, military effort": Ibid.

63 "the most soul-sickening spectacle that Americans": John W. Burgess, *Reconstruction and the Constitution, 1866–1876* (New York: Charles Scribner's Sons, 1902), 263.

64 **"In due time . . . those who repeated these stereotypes":** Kenneth M. Stampp, *The Era of Reconstruction* (New York: Vintage, 1967), 19.

64 **"the old middle classes of the North":** Ibid.

64 **"vogue of Social Darwinism":** Ibid., 20.

64 **"great numbers of the best breeding stock on both sides":** Madison Grant, quoted in Stampp, *The Era of Reconstruction*, 22.

65 **"racial nondescripts . . . No large policy in our country":** James Ford Rhodes quoted in Stampp, *The Era of Reconstruction*, 22.

65 **A powerful dissent:** W. E. B. Du Bois, *Black Reconstruction in America, 1860–1880* (New York: Free Press, 1999).

65 **"make the blunders of that era, tragic though they were, dwindle into insignificance":** Stampp, *The Era of Reconstruction*, 215.

65 **"Suffrage was not something thrust upon an indifferent mass":** Ibid., 165.

65 **"combine the Dunning School's aspiration":** Eric Foner, *Reconstruction: America's Unfinished Revolution, 1863–1877* (New York: Harper & Row, 1988), xxii.

66 **"Rather than passive victims of the actions of others":** Ibid.

66 **"how the status of white planters, merchants, and yeomen, and their relations":** Ibid., xxiii.

66 **"willing to link their fortunes with those of blacks" ":** Ibid.

66 **"a national state possessing vastly expanded authority and a new set of purposes":** Ibid., xxiv.

66 **"There is a certain irony in the fact that a Columbia historian":** Foner, *Who Owns History*, 17.

CHAPTER III: LESSONS FROM THE HUMBLE PENNY

70 **"When an American needs the assistance of his fellows":** Alexis de Tocqueville, *Democracy in America*, trans. George Lawrence, ed. J. P. Mayer (New York: Harper and Row, 1966), 571.

70 **"The great privilege of the Americans"** Alexis de Tocqueville, *Democracy in America*, trans. Henry Reeve (New York: Colonial Press, 1900), 234.

70 **"In no other country in the world is the love of property keener":** Ibid., 639.

70 **"I have already shown, in several parts of this work, by what means the inhabitants":** Ibid., 525.

70 **"Take a penny from your pocket,":** William Clinton, *Between Hope and History: Meeting America's Challenges for the 21st Century* (New York: Times Books, 1996), 117.

71 **"That humble penny":** Ibid.

72 **"I guess a small-town mayor is sort of like a 'community organizer' ":** Sarah Palin, speech at the Republican National Convention, 3 September 2008.

72 **"the political philosophy by which we live":** Michael Sandel, *Democracy's Discontent: America in Search of a Public Philosophy* (Cambridge: Harvard University Press, 1996), 4.

72 **"a moral unanimity"**: Louis Hartz, *The Liberal Tradition in America* (Boston: Houghton Mifflin Harcourt, 1955), 46.

72 **"fixed, dogmatic liberalism"**: Ibid.

72 **"the reality of atomistic social freedom"**: Ibid.

72 **"as a shorthand for the self-interested, profit maximizing behaviors of liberal capitalism"**: James T. Kloppenberg, "From Hartz to Tocqueville: Shifting the Focus from Liberalism to Democracy in America," in Meg Jacobs, William J. Novak and Julian E. Zelizer, eds., *The Democratic Experiment: New Directions in American Political History* (Princeton, Princeton University Press, 2003), 352.

72 **"elegant and dazzling"**: Ibid.

73 **Daniel Bell's *The End of Ideology*:** Daniel Bell, *The End of Ideology: On the Exhaustion of Political Ideas in the Fifties* (Cambridge, MA: Harvard University Press, 2000).

73 **"seems suddenly to shrink our domestic struggles to insignificance"**: Kloppenberg, "From Hartz to Tocqueville," 354.

73 **"sharing in self-government"**: Sandel, *Democracy's Discontent*, 5.

73 **"a knowledge of public affairs and also a sense of belonging"**: Ibid.

73 **"one of the largest accomplishments of modern historical scholarship"**: Cass Sunstein, "Beyond the Republican Revival," *Yale Law Journal* 97, no. 8 (July 1988): 1540.

74 **"is no longer possible to see a Lockean consensus"**: Ibid.

74 **"it incorporates central features of the liberal tradition"**: Ibid.

74 **"a balanced view that sees the continuous presence of rights talk and the continuous presence"**: James T. Kloppenberg, *The Virtues of Liberalism* (New York: Oxford University Press, 1998), 200.

74 **"arguments for freedom and arguments for community"**: Sunstein, "Beyond the Republican Revival," 1540.

74 **"providing a language of restrained and chastened communitarianism"**: Robert Booth Fowler, *The Dance with Community* (Lawrence: University of Kansas Press, 1991), 78.

74 **"The preservation of liberty, which is the preservation of individualism"**: William M. Sullivan, *Reconstructing Public Philosophy* (Berkeley: University of California Press, 1982), 215.

75 **"more destructive potentialities"**: Robert Neelly Bellah, Richard Madsen, and William M. Sullivan, *Habits of the Heart: Individualism and Commitment in American Life* (Berkeley: University of California Press, 2008), xlviii.

75 **"the archetypal poor boy who made good"**: Ibid., 33.

75 **"what many felt in the eighteenth century—and many have felt ever since"**: Ibid.

76 **"If they are poor, they begin first as Servants or Journeymen"**: Benjamin Franklin, "Information to Those Who Would Remove to America," in Franklin, *The Autobiography and Other Writings*, ed. Kenneth Silverman (New York: Penguin, 2003), 218.

76 **"utilitarian individualism"**: Bellah et al., *Habits of the Heart*, 33.

76 **"expressive . . . success had little to do with material acquisition"**: Ibid., 34. On Walt Whitman's politics, see Edward L. Widmer, *Young America: The Flowering of Democracy in New York City* (New York: Oxford University Press, 1999), 81–85.

76 **"self-sufficient farmer or artisan capable of participation"**: Ibid., 35.

76 **"the ultimate use of the American's independence was to cultivate"**: Ibid.

77 **"a city set upon a hill"**: John Winthrop, "A Model of Christian Charity" (*Arbella* sermon), 1630, excerpted in Timothy Hill, *Religion in America* (New York: Infobase, 2007), 41.

77 **"archetypal . . . understanding of what life in America was to be"**: Bellah et al., *Habits of the Heart*, 32.

77 **"We must delight in each other"**: Winthrop, "A Model of Christian Charity," 41.

77 **"every man might have need of other, and from hence they might all be knit more nearly"**: Ibid.

77 **"A quarterback who begins to act as though he is better than the linemen"**: Wilson Carey McWilliams, *The Democratic Soul: A Wilson Carey McWilliams Reader*, ed. Patrick J. Deneen and Susan J. McWilliams (Lexington: University Press of Kentucky, 2011), 27.

77 **"can be seen as the first of many efforts to create utopian communities"**: Bellah et al., *Habits of the Heart*, 29.

78 **"moral freedom . . . to that only which is good, just and honest"**: Ibid.

78 **"I suppose the most flagrant examples of present-mindedness"**: Gordon S. Wood, *The Purpose of the Past: Reflections on the Uses of History* (New York: Penguin, 2008), 308.

79 **"I am reminded of Rebecca West's wise observation"**: Ibid.

79 **"liberty had been misunderstood and falsely equated"**: Gordon S. Wood, *The Creation of the American Republic: 1776–1787* (Chapel Hill: University of North Carolina Press, 1969), 60.

79 **"True liberty was 'natural liberty restrained in such a manner'"**: Ibid., 60–61.

79 **"ideally, republicanism obliterates the individual"**: Ibid., 61.

79 **"republicanism was essentially anti-capitalistic"**: Ibid., 418.

80 **"as radical and as revolutionary as any in history"**: Gordon S. Wood, *Radicalism of the American Revolution* (New York: Vintage Books, 1991), 5.

80 **"explosion of entrepreneurial power"**: Gordon S. Wood, "The Significance of the Early Republic," *Journal of the Early Republic* 8, no. 1 (Spring 1988): 14.

80 **"America's conception of its national character"**: Gordon S. Wood, *Empire of Liberty: A History of the Early Republic, 1789–1815* (Oxford: Oxford University Press, 2009), 732.

80 **"a new character ideal . . . . . . the man who developed inner resources"**: Joyce Appleby, quoted in Wood, *Empire of Liberty*, 732.

81 **"In France . . . usually carried, and still carries, a pejorative connotation"**: Steven Lukes, *Individualism* (Essex: ECPR Press, 2006), 23.

81 **"realization of the final stage of human progress"**: Ibid., 37.

81 **"a calm and considered feeling which disposes each":** Tocqueville, *Democracy in America*, 477.

81 **"supplied the nation with a rationalization of its characteristic attitudes":** Yehoshua Arieli, *Individualism and Nationalism in American Ideology* (Cambridge, MA: Harvard University Press, 1966), 341–42.

81 **"Individualism, the love of enterprise, and the pride in personal freedom":** James Bryce, *The American Commonwealth* (London: Macmillan, 1889), 2:406–7.

82 **"we mutually pledge to each other our Lives, our Fortunes, and our sacred Honor":** Declaration of Independence, http://www.law.indiana.edu/uslawdocs/declaration.html.

CHAPTER IV: REINVENTING AMERICAN LIBERALISM

84 **"the quest for a public philosophy that could take account":** Philip Selznick, *The Communitarian Persuasion* (Washington, DC: Woodrow Wilson Center Press, 2002), 5.

84 **"created an overly regulated, overly bureaucratic and overly professionalized welfare state":** Rudolph Scharping, quoted in Selznick, *The Communitarian Persuasion*, 5.

84 **"We did not believe in people's capacity for spontaneously helping":** Ibid.

84 **Amitai Etzioni:** Amitai Etzioni, *The Spirit of Community* (New York: Touchstone, 1993).

84 **"the critical arena in which independence and a host of other virtues":** William Galston, "Liberal Virtues," *American Political Science Review* 82, no. 4 (December 1988): 1282.

84 **"The weakening of families is thus fraught with danger":** Ibid.

85 **"Communitarians do not seek to found a new school of thought on the ruins of liberalism":** Bruce Frohnen, *The New Communitarians and the Crisis of Modern Liberalism* (Lawrence: University Press of Kansas, 1996), 10.

86 **"master of the universe":** Tom Wolfe, *The Bonfire of the Vanities* (New York: Bantam, 1988).

86 **"comic sociology":** David Brooks, *Bobos in Paradise: The New Upper Class and How They Got There* (New York: Simon and Schuster, 2001), 12.

87 **"community and common good seriously without abnegating":** Avital Simhony and David Weinstein, *The New Liberalism: Reconciling Liberty and Community* (Cambridge: Cambridge University Press, 2001), 2.

88 **"We Decade":** Paul Taylor, "The Coming of the 'We' Decade," *Washington Post*, 20 July 1985.

88 **"We are all part of one another":** William J. Clinton, remarks at Metropolitan Baptist Church, Washington, D.C., 7 December 1997.

88 **"little platoons":** Edmund Burke, *Reflections on the Revolution in France* (London: J. Dodsley, 1790), 68.

88 **"There is no such thing as society"**: Margaret Thatcher, quoted in Douglas Keay, "Aids, Education, and the Year 2000," *Women's Own*, 23 September 1987.

89 **"There *is* such a thing as society"**: David Cameron, speech after winning the Conservative Party leadership contest, 6 December 2005.

89 **"compassionate conservatism"**: George W. Bush, "Rallying the Armies of Compassion," January 2001, http://archives.hud.gov/reports/rally.pdf.

89 **"common ownership of the means of production"**: Clause IV, Labour Party Constitution, 1918.

89 **"To secure for the workers by hand or by brain"**: Ibid.

90 **"The Labour Party is a democratic socialist party"**: Clause IV, Labour Party Constitution, 1995.

90 **"It allows us to unite old and new"**: Tony Blair, "Values and the Power of Community," First Global Ethics Lecture at Tübingen University, Germany, 30 June 2000.

90 **"They need to be matched by responsibility and duty"**: Ibid.

91 **"opportunity, responsibility, community"**: William Clinton, keynote address to the Democratic Leadership Council, Cleveland, Ohio, 6 May 1991.

92 **"used as a slogan to advance the cause of community"**: Adam Seligman, *The Idea of Civil Society* (New York: Free Press, 1992), 203.

92 **In *Whose Keeper?***: Alan Wolfe, *Whose Keeper? Social Science and Moral Obligation* (Berkeley: University of California Press, 1989).

92 **"where everybody knows your name"**: "Where Everybody Knows Your Name," written by Gary Portnoy and Judy Hart Angelo and performed by Portnoy.

93 **his Harvard colleague Robert Nozick**: Robert Nozick, *Anarchy, State, and Utopia* (New York: Basic Books, 1974).

93 **"the closest thing to a book that people"**: Alexander Nehamas, "Trends in Recent American Philosophy," *Daedalus* 126, no. 1 (Winter 1997): 222.

93 **"veil of ignorance"**: John Rawls, *A Theory of Justice* (Cambridge, MA: Harvard University Press, 1971).

93 **"ideally rational men and women"**: Michael Walzer, *Spheres of Justice: A Defense of Pluralism and Equality* (New York: Basic Books, 1983), 5.

93 **"the particularism of history, culture and membership"**: Ibid.

93 **"Even if they are committed to impartiality"**: Ibid.

94 **"every substantive account of justice is a local account"**: Ibid., 314.

94 **"barren of essential aims and attachments"**: Michael Sandel, *Liberalism and the Limits of Justice* (Cambridge: Cambridge University Press, 1982), 176.

94 **"we cannot regard ourselves as independent in this way"**: Ibid., 179.

94 **"members of this family or community or nation or people"**: Ibid.

94 **Sandel himself has been wary of being labeled "communitarian"**: Michael Sandel, *Democracy's Discontent: America in Search of a Public Philosophy* (Cambridge: Harvard University Press, 1996).

94 **"a sense of belonging, a concern for the whole"**: Ibid., 10.

95 **"The public philosophy by which we live"**: Ibid., 10.

95 **"Community demands a place where people can see"**: Robert F. Kennedy, cited in Sandel, *Democracy's Discontent*, 301.

95 **"no place for people to walk, for women and their children"**: Ibid., 301–2.

96 **"terminal wistfulness"**: Richard Rorty, *Objectivity, Relativism, and Truth* (Cambridge: Cambridge University Press, 1991), 194.

96 **"want us to live in Salem but not believe in witches"**: Amy Gutmann, "Communitarian Critics of Liberalism," *Philosophy and Public Affairs* 14, no. 3 (Summer 1985): 319.

96 **"the first claim is unconvincing while the second claim is unexciting"**: Stephen Holmes, *The Anatomy of Antiliberalism* (Cambridge, MA: Harvard University Press, 1993), 180.

96 **"Liberalism is dissatisfying, these critics contend"**: Ibid.

96 **"an implicitly utopian character"**: Jeffrey Stout, *Ethics After Babel: The Languages of Morals and Their Discontents* (Boston: Beacon Press, 1988), 229.

97 **"the sense of community and civic engagement that liberty requires"**: Sandel, *Democracy's Discontents*, 6.

97 **"social capital"**: Robert Putnam, *Bowling Alone: The Collapse and Revival of American Community* (New York: Simon and Schuster, 2000).

98 **"Our failure as progressives to tap into the moral underpinnings"**: Barack Obama, keynote address at the conference "Call to Renewal's Building a Covenant for a New America," Washington, D.C., 28 June 2006.

98 **"a trillion dollars being taken out of social programs"**: Ibid.

98 **"faith and guidance"**: Ibid.

CHAPTER V: FROM TRADITION TO REVOLT

128 **"Conservatism, as a distinguishable social philosophy"**: Robert A. Nisbet, "Conservatism and Sociology," *American Journal of Sociology* 58, no. 2 (September 1952): 168.

128 **"in reaction to the individualistic Enlightenment"**: Ibid.

128 **"a mechanical aggregate of individual particles"**: Ibid.

128 **"delicate interrelation of belief, habit, membership and institution"**: Ibid.

128 **the best one-volume collection of Nisbet's work**: Robert A. Nisbet, *Tradition and Revolt* (New Brunswick: Transaction Publishers, 1999).

129 **"thin gruel . . . caught in the web"**: George F. Will, *Statecraft as Soulcraft* (New York: Simon and Schuster, 1983), 152.

129 **"Just as all education is moral education"**: Ibid., 276.

129 **"sentiments, manners and moral opinions"**: Ibid., 19.

129 **"It is generally considered obvious that government"**: Ibid., 120.

129 **"Conservatism is something more than mere solicitude for tidy incomes"**: Russell Kirk, quoted in George H. Nash, *The Conservative Intellectual Movement in America* (New York: Basic Books, 1979), 81.

103 **"a fundamental challenge to their power and their place in American society":** Kim Phillips-Fein, *Invisible Hands* (New York: W. W. Norton), xi.

103 **"to resist liberal institutions and ideas, and to persuade others":** Ibid.

103 **"the rise of fascism and Nazism was not a reaction":** Friedrich A. Hayek, *The Road to Serfdom* (Chicago: University of Chicago Press, 1944) 59.

103 **"it is the control of the means for all our ends":** Ibid.

104 **"Unless this complex society is to be destroyed":** Ibid.

104 **"faith in the spontaneous forces of adjustment":** Friedrich A. Hayek, *The Constitution of Liberty* (Chicago: University of Chicago Press, 1960), 400.

104 **"a thorough sweeping away of the obstacles to free growth":** Ibid.

104 **"Frank Meyer, Buckley's chief ideologist":** Frank Meyer, *Principles and Heresies* (Wilmington, DE: ISI Books, 2002).

105 **"objective moral order":** For a superb summary of Meyer's thinking, see George H. Nash, *The Conservative Intellectual Movement in America Since 1945* (New York: Basic Books, 1979), 171–81.

105 **"utilizing libertarian means in a conservative society for traditionalist ends":** Donald Devine, quoted in Dionne, *Why Americans Hate Politics*, 161.

105 **"the primacy of society to the individual":** Nisbet, "Conservatism and Sociology," 169.

106 **"family, work, neighborhood":** Ronald Reagan, acceptance speech at the 1980 Republican National Convention, Detroit, 17 July 1980.

106 ***"those institutions standing between the individual":*** Peter Berger and Richard John Neuhaus, *To Empower People: From State to Civil Society* (Washington, DC: AEI Press, 1996).

106 **"the modern state itself . . . the large economic conglomerates":** Ibid.

106 **"double crisis . . . who must carry on a balancing act":** Ibid.

106 **"Such institutions have a private face":** Ibid.

107 **"argued persuasively that the loss of community":** Ibid.

107 **"The concrete particularities of mediating structures":** Ibid.

107 **"little that is helpful . . . what is now called conservatism":** Ibid.

107 **"We believe it is proper and humane":** Ibid.

108 **"liberalism has a hard time coming to terms":** Ibid.

108 **"a great American *national* community":** William Schambra, "Conservatism and the Quest for Community," *National Affairs*, Summer 2010, http://www.nationalaffairs.com/publications/detail/conservatism-and-the-quest-for-community.

108 **"the sense of community, belonging, and purpose":** Ibid.

109 **"If conservatism's only idea of a civil-rights program":** Ibid.

109 **"drained the strength and moral authority":** William Schambra, "Local Groups Are the Key to America's Civic Renewal," Brookings Institution, Fall 1997, http://www.brookings.edu/articles/1997/fall_communitydevelopment_schambra.aspx.

109 **"popularly rooted voluntary organizations":** Theda Skocpol, "Don't Blame Big Government: America's Voluntary Groups Thrive in a National Network," in

E. J. Dionne, ed., *Community Works: The Revival of Civil Society in America* (Washington, DC: Brookings Institution, 1998).

110 **"Talk of a social citizenship as extensive as the nation":** Daniel Rodgers, *The Age of Fracture* (Cambridge: Harvard University Press, 2011), 198.

110 **"For those working within the tradition of civic republicanism":** Ibid., 196.

110 **"Most novel about the new market metaphors":** Ibid., 76, 5.

111 **"For God so loved the world that he gave his only begotten Son":** John 3:16.

112 **"the sort of faith with which most traditionalists are comfortable":** Schambra, "Conservatism and the Quest for Community."

112 **"would have been a bit lukewarm":** Ibid.

113 **"wonder-working power":** George W. Bush, State of the Union address, 28 January 2003.

113 **"the human heart":** George W. Bush, "The Duty of Hope," speech in Indianapolis, Indiana, 22 July 1999.

113 **"narrow mindsets":** Ibid.

113 **"is that government provides the only real compassion":** Ibid.

113 **"The idea that if government would only get out of our way":** Ibid.

114 **"This will not be the failed compassion of towering, distant bureaucracies":** Ibid.

114 **"The invisible hand works many miracles":** Ibid.

114 **"We are a nation of rugged individuals":** George W. Bush, First Inaugural Address, 20 January 2001.

114 **"In the quiet of American conscience":** Ibid.

116 **" 'Compassionate conservatism' and fiscal conservatism":** Michelle Malkin, "Bush the Pre-Socializer: I Readily Concede I Chucked Aside My Free Market Principles," 12 January 2009, http://michellemalkin.com/2009/01/12/bush-the-pre-socializer-i-readily-concede-i-chucked-aside-my-free-market-principles.

116 **"Traditional conservatism has a piece missing":** Michael J. Gerson, *Heroic Conservatism* (New York: HarperCollins, 2007), 272.

116 **"any idea of the common good":** Ibid., 63.

116 **"Where does someone belong who is pro-life *and* pro-poor?":** Ibid., 288–89.

117 **"If Republicans run in future elections":** Ibid., 16.

117 **"can appeal to the conscience":** Ibid., 289.

117 **"If heroic conservatism really can rally the nation":** David Frum, "Writing Checks," *National Review*, 3 December 2007.

118 **"Americans are deeply compassionate people":** Ibid.

118 **"It's a stirring vision in its way":** Ross Douthat, "The Future of the GOP," *Slate*, 26 November 2007.

119 **"From the 1970s onward, the Republican Party built its majority":** Ibid.

119 **"Why the Tea Party Is Toxic for the GOP":** Michael J. Gerson, "Why the Tea Party Is Toxic for the GOP," *Washington Post*, 25 August 2010.

120 **"The Constitution," Gerson insisted, "in contrast to":** Ibid.

120 **"Most Americans who identify with the Tea Party movement":** Ibid.

121 **"custom and convention"**: Russell Kirk, *The Conservative Mind: From Burke to Eliot* (Washington, DC: Regnery, 2001), 9.

121 **"are checks both upon man's anarchic impulse"**: Ibid.

122 **"pseudo-conservative"**: Peter Viereck, *Conservatism Revisited: The Revolt Against Ideology* (New York: Charles Scribner's Sons, 1949), 60.

122 **"two cheers for capitalism"**: Irving Kristol, *Two Cheers for Capitalism* (New York: Basic Books, 1978).

CHAPTER VI: ONE NATION, CONCEIVED IN ARGUMENT

127 **"The federal government was created by the states"**: Rick Perry, quoted in Jim Rutenberg, "Perry Speaks, but Avoids Big Question," *New York Times*, 14 June 2011.

127 **"The Union is older than any of the States"**: Abraham Lincoln, Message to Congress in Special Session, 4 July 1861.

128 **"The powers not delegated to the United States by the Constitution"**: The Constitution of the United States of America, 1789, http://www.archives .gov/exhibits/charters/constitution_transcript.html.

128 **"If we remove the foundations for our principles and our policies"**: Jim DeMint, speech to the Conservative Political Action Conference, 18 February 2010.

129 **"recommitting themselves and their organizations"**: Tim Pawlenty, speech to the Conservative Political Action Conference, 19 February 2010.

129 **"There's nothing that ails this country"**: Mike Pence, speech to the Conservative Political Action Conference, 19 February 2010.

130 **"fundamental scripture"**: Gordon Wood, "The Fundamentalists and the Constitution," *New York Review of Books*, 18 February 1988.

130 **historians such as Rosemarie Zagarri**: Rosemarie Zagarri, *Revolutionary Backlash: Women and Politics in the Early American Republic* (Philadelphia: University of Pennsylvania Press, 2007).

130 **"Historians today can recognize the extraordinary character"**: Wood, "The Fundamentalists and the Constitution."

130 **"they did their creative thinking on their feet"**: Ibid.

131 **"as Wood argued in *The Radicalism of the American Revolution*"**: Gordon Wood, *The Radicalism of the American Revolution* (New York: Vintage Books, 1991).

131 **"In our eyes the American revolutionaries appear"**: Ibid., 6–7.

131 **"made possible the anti-slavery and women's rights movements"**: Ibid., 7.

132 **"The genius of the Constitution"**: William J. Brennan Jr., speech to the Text and Teaching Symposium at Georgetown University, Washington, D.C., 12 October 1985.

132 **"a set of implicit assumptions about the framers"**: Joseph Ellis, "Immaculate Misconception and the Supreme Court," *Washington Post*, 7 May 2010.

132 **"debates in the state ratifying conventions"**: Ibid.

133 **"unnecessarily degrade ourselves if we think of the Founding Fathers"**: Gordon S. Wood, *The Purpose of the Past: Reflections on the Uses of History* (New York: Penguin Press, 2008), 28.

133 **"deciding constitutional cases should be a straightforward exercise"**: David Souter, Harvard commencement address, 27 May 2010.

133 **"a pantheon of values"**: Ibid.

133 **"Not even its most uncompromising and unconditional language"**: Ibid.

134 **"fair reading model"**: Ibid.

134 **"naïve providential interpretations"**: Richard Hofstadter, *The Progressive Historians: Turner, Beard, Parrington* (New York: Knopf, 1968), 208.

134 **"a house divided against itself cannot stand"**: Harold Holzer, *Lincoln at Cooper Union: The Speech that Made Abraham Lincoln President* (New York: Simon and Schuster, 2004), 123.

135 **"an undiscriminating and almost blind worship"**: Woodrow Wilson, *Congressional Government: A Study in American Politics* (Boston: Houghton Mifflin Company, 1885), 332.

135 **"open-eyed . . . to its defects"**: Ibid., 332–33.

135 **"the constitution is a living thing"**: Albert J. Beveridge, "The Invisible Government," keynote address at the Progressive Party Convention, 5 August 1912.

135 **Charles Beard published *An Economic Interpretation of the Constitution*:** Charles Beard, *An Economic Interpretation of the Constitution of the United States* (New York: Macmillan, 1921).

135 **"Different degrees and kinds of property"**: Ibid., 15.

136 **"essentially an economic document based upon the concept that fundamental rights of property"**: Ibid., 324.

136 **"whole people"**: Ibid., 324–25.

136 **"has been torn to shreds and no one pays attention to it anymore"**: Wood, "The Fundamentalists and the Constitution."

136 **"An economic interpretation"**: Charles A. Beard, "That Noble Dream," *American Historical Review* 41, no. 1 (October 1935).

136 **"the reality of interests and commerce"**: Wood, "The Fundamentalists and the Constitution."

136 **"that the Constitution ought to be seen as the consequence of historical circumstances"**: Ibid.

137 **"a layman's document, not a lawyer's contract"**: Franklin D. Roosevelt, address on Constitution Day, 17 September 1937.

137 **"The millions who are in want will not stand by silently forever"**: Franklin D. Roosevelt, address at Oglethorpe University, 22 May 1932.

137 **"whether or not judges' interpretation of the Constitution is to be sustained"**: Theodore Roosevelt, quoted in Sidney M. Milkis, *Theodore Roosevelt, the Progressive Party, and the Transformation of American Democracy* (Lawrence: University Press of Kansas, 2009), 55–56.

137 **"a lively sense of the importance of the social problems"**: Jeff Shesol, *Su-*

preme Power: Franklin Roosevelt vs. the Supreme Court (New York: W. W. Norton, 2010), 206.

137 **"the catalyst that helped fracture the New Deal coalition":** Ibid.

138 **"To recall the great cases of the Warren and Burger Courts today":** Cass R. Sunstein, "Constitutional Politics and the Conservative Court," *American Prospect*, 21 March 1990.

138 **"Beginning with *Brown v. Board of Education*":** Ibid.

139 **"Many of the rights affirmed by the Court":** Ibid.

139 **"played a major role during the New Deal":** Ibid.

139 **"would have seemed peculiar":** Ibid.

140 **"the current position of the Supreme Court":** Ibid.

140 **"Conservatives spoiling for a fight should watch their language":** George Will, "No (Political) Experience Required," *Washington Post*, 15 April 2010.

141 **"social reform on behalf of the disadvantaged should come from the courts":** Cass R. Sunstein, "What Judge Bork Should Have Said," *Connecticut Law Review* 23, no. 2 (Winter 1991): 225–26.

142 **"no 'irreparable harm'":** Supreme Court of the United States, *George W. Bush, et. al., Petitioners v. Albert Gore, Jr., et. al.*, 12 December 2000.

142 **"comports with minimal constitutional standards":** Ibid.

142 **"Our consideration is limited to the present circumstances":** Ibid.

142 **Authority is "based ultimately upon the consent of those under it":** Robert A. Nisbet, *Community and Power* (New York: Oxford University Press, 1967), xii.

143 **"The Florida Legislature has to be ready to assert its own constitutional prerogative":** William Kristol, "Crowning the Imperial Judiciary," *New York Times*, 28 November 2000.

144 **"There's a right of suffrage in voting for the legislature":** Antonin Scalia, arguments before the Supreme Court, 1 December 1999, : http://abcnews.go.com/Politics/story?id=122350&page=1.

144 **"Contrary to Democratic rhetoric":** John Yoo, "A Legislature's Duty," *The Wall Street Journal* (4 December 2000).

144 **"The individual citizen has no federal constitutional right":** Supreme Court of the United States, *George W. Bush, et. al., Petitioners v. Albert Gore, Jr., et. al.*, 12 December 2000.

145 **"Today, conservatives like Scalia and Yoo cheerfully defend":** Harold Meyerson, "W. Stands for Wrongful," *LA Weekly*, 6 December 2000.

145 **"Never before in the history of democratic government":** Peter M. Shane, "Disappearing Democracy: How *Bush v. Gore* Undermined the Federal Right to Vote for Presidential Electors," *Florida State University Law Review* 29 (2001).

147 **"Essentially, five justices were unhappy with the limited nature":** Supreme Court of the United States, opinion of Stevens, J., in *Citizens United, Appellant V. Federal Election Commission*, 21 January 2010.

147 **"I do think that it is a jolt to the legal system":** John G. Roberts Jr., "Confirmation Hearing on the Nomination of John G. Roberts, Jr. to be Chief Justice of

the United States," *Hearing before the Committee on the Judiciary, United States Senate, One Hundred and Ninth Congress*, 12–15 September 2005.

148   **"To avoid an arbitrary discretion in the judges":** Ibid.

148   **"has been firmly embedded in our law":** Supreme Court of the United States, opinion of the Court in. *McConnell v. Federal Election Commission.*

148   **"to undermine the integrity of elected institutions across the Nation":** Supreme Court of the United States, opinion of Stevens, J., in *Citizens United, Appellant v. Federal Election Commission*, 21 January 2010.

148   **"enlists the Framers in its defense without seriously grappling":** Ibid.

149   **"to encompass the dependency of public officeholders":** Ibid.

149   **"The Framers didn't like corporations":** Supreme Court of the United States, Scalia, J., concurring in *Citizens United, Appellant v. Federal Election Commission*, 21 January 2010.

150   **"Although they make enormous contributions to our society":** Supreme Court of the United States, opinion of Stevens, J., in *Citizens United, Appellant v. Federal Election Commission,* 21 January 2010.

150   **"A democracy cannot function effectively":** Ibid.

150   **"Setting aside the question of whether it makes good law":** Jill Lepore, *The Whites of Their Eyes: The Tea Party's Revolution and the Battle over American History* (Princeton: Princeton University Press, 2010), 122–24.

150   **"In eighteenth-century America, I wouldn't have been able to vote":** Ibid.

151   **"claim that the Constitution was set up to restrain":** Garrett Epps, "Stealing the Constitution," *Nation*, 7 February 2011.

152   **"didn't want to set up a government that could throw people in jail":** Ibid.

152   **"the document as a whole is much more concerned":** Ibid.

152   **"Trust me, I knew the framers":** Ibid.

152   **"Progressives are losing the fight over the courts":** Doug Kendall and Jim Ryan, "The Case for New Textualism," *Democracy* 21 (Summer 2011).

152   **"the original Constitution . . . the whole Constitution as amended":** Ibid.

153   **cite the distinguished legal scholar Akhil Amar:** Akhil Reed Amar, *America's Constitution: A Biography* (New York: Random House, 2005).

153   **"liberals should not pretend that honest answers":** Geoffrey Stone and William Marshall, "The Framers' Constitution," *Democracy* 21 (Summer 2011).

153   **"aroused citizens, lawmakers and judges":** William E. Forbath, "The Distributive Constitution," *Democracy: A Journal of Ideas* 22 (Fall 2011).

153   **"you can't have what the Framers called a 'republican form of government'":** Ibid.

153   **"the material independence and security that citizens must have":** Ibid.

153   **"The Founders believed that personal liberty and political equality":** Ibid.

154   **"Although we may never know with complete certainty":** Supreme Court of the United States, opinion of Stevens, J. in *Citizens United, Appellant v. Federal Election Commission*, 21 January 2010.

CHAPTER VII: THE AMERICAN SYSTEM

155 **at St. Anselm's College in New Hampshire in June 2011:** Jim Rutenberg, "Perry Speaks, but Avoids Big Question," *New York Times*, 14 June 2011.

155 **"This economy is stalled":** Herman Cain, CNN Republican Presidential Debate, St. Anselm's College, 13 June 2011.

155 **"What we need . . . is an economy that's unshackled":** Rick Santorum, CNN Republican Presidential Debate, St. Anselm's College, 13 June 2011.

156 **"cuts taxes . . . also dramatically cuts spending":** Tim Pawlenty, CNN Republican Presidential Debate, St. Anselm's College, 13 June 2011.

156 **"Every time the liberals get into office":** Michele Bachmann, CNN Republican Presidential Debate, St. Anselm's College, 13 June 2011.

156 **"There shouldn't be any government assistance":** Ron Paul, CNN Republican Presidential Debate, St. Anselm's College, 13 June 2011.

156 **"If you explore the mandate":** Newt Gingrich, CNN Republican Presidential Debate, St. Anselm's College, 13 June 2011.

157 **"There is a perception in this country":** Mitt Romney, CNN Republican Presidential Debate, St. Anselm's College, 13 June 2011.

157 **"Did you know":** Mitt Romney, campaign announcement speech, Stratham, New Hampshire, 2 June 2011.

157 **"inches away from ceasing to be a free economy":** Ibid.

158 **"I think the appropriate role for the federal government":** Jon Huntsman, quoted in Daniel Henninger, "A Conservative Problem-Solver," *Wall Street Journal*, 25 June 2011.

158 **"failure" and an "illegal Ponzi scheme":** Rick Perry, *Fed Up! Our Fight to Save America from Washington* (New York: Little, Brown), 171.

158 **"by far the best example":** Ibid., 48.

158 **"federal laws regulating the environment":** Ibid., 51.

159 **"We've got a great union":** "Some Colorful Perry Comments," ABCNews, 17 August 2011, http://abcnews.go.com/Politics/wireStory?id=14321355.

159 **"revitalized the federalist strain in the one-party politics":** Jacob K. Javits, *Order of Battle: A Republican's Call to Reason* (New York: Atheneum, 1964), 56.

160 **"the loose and barren rule under the Articles of Confederation":** Ibid., 62.

160 **"free of the incubus of states' rights":** Ibid., 64.

160 **"Hamilton's experience with the semianarchic states' rights":** Ibid., 62.

160 **"If published today":** Ibid., 66.

160 **"had a coherent public-land policy":** Ibid., 73.

160 **"The legitimate object of government":** Ibid., 93.

161 **"agricultural and mechanical colleges":** Ibid., 91.

161 **"are authorized by the Constitution":** Ibid., 88.

161 **"immediate and efficient aid":** Ibid.

161 **"artificial individuals called corporations":** Theodore Roosevelt, quoted in Javits, *Order of Battle*, 103.

161 **"The citizens of the United States must effectively control":** Ibid., 116.

162 **"tends to disconnect himself from":** Javits, *Order of Battle*, 302.

162 **"It is the rancorous enemy of the politics of civility":** Ibid., 305.

162 **"Anyone who joins us in all sincerity, we welcome":** Barry Goldwater, speech accepting the Republican presidential nomination, Republican National Convention, San Francisco, California, 16 July 1964.

162 **"And let our Republicanism, so focused and so dedicated":** Ibid.

163 **"This reporter went to sleep in the darkness":** Theodore H. White, *The Making of the President 1964* (New York: Harper Perennial, 1965), 231.

163 **"Isn't it illogical for you to be a Republican?":** Javits, *Order of Battle*, 3.

165 **"So familiar is the historical narrative that pits":** Brian Balogh, *A Government Out of Sight: The Mystery of National Authority in Nineteenth-Century America* (Cambridge: Cambridge University Press, 2009), 5.

165 **"funded hospitals located throughout the nation":** Ibid., 145.

166 **"a precedent for national intervention":** Ibid.

166 **"who supposedly feared distant government":** Ibid., 13.

166 **"No other branch of the central government":** Richard R. John, *Spreading the News: The American Postal System from Franklin to Morse* (Cambridge: Harvard University Press, 1995), 4.

166 **in her 1992 book *Protecting Soldiers and Mothers*:** Theda Skocpol, *Protecting Soldiers and Mothers: The Political Origins of Social Policy in the United States* (Cambridge, MA: Harvard University Press, 1992).

166 **"were also on the pension rolls at that point":** Larry DeWitt, "Review: *Protecting Soldiers and Mothers: The Political Origins of Social Policy in the United States* by Theda Skocpol," December 2003, http://www.larrydewitt.net/SSin-GAPE/skocpolreview.htm.

166 **"was very little debate about the constitutionality of Jefferson's actions":** Balogh, *A Government Out of Sight*, 15.

167 **"more amendable to using the latent authority":** Ibid.

167 **"publicly crafted organizations granted special privileges":** Ibid., 14–15.

167 **"Although most historical accounts extrapolate America's modern history":** Ibid., 14.

167 **"In different ways, both parties shared Jefferson's conviction":** Michael Sandel, *Democracy's Discontent: America In Search of a Public Philosophy* (Cambridge: Harvard University Press, 1996), 157.

167 **"few assumed, as Jefferson once did, that the agrarian life":** Ibid.

168 **"curing the mischiefs of faction":** Alexander Hamilton, "Federalist No. 27: Idea of Restraining the Legislative Authority in Regard to the Common Defense Considered (Continued)," 25 December 1787.

168 **"the more the operations of the national authority":** Ibid.

168 **"Man is very much a creature of habit":** Ibid.

169 **"an agent for the states":** Rick Perry, quoted in "Perry Talks Border Security in Edinburgh," 25 May 2011, http://www.governorperry.com/media-articles/perry-talks-border-security-edinburg-trip.

169 **"leave us alone"**: Grover Norquist, *Leave Us Alone: Getting the Government's Hands Off Our Money, Our Guns, Our Lives* (New York: HarperCollins, 2008).

169 **"intermingled in the ordinary exercise"**: Alexander Hamilton, "Federalist No. 27."

169 **"bold and novel"**: Gordon Wood, *Empire of Liberty: A History of the Early Republic, 1789–1815* (Oxford: Oxford University Press, 2009), 98.

169 **"pay for up to three fourths of the shares with government securities"**: Ibid.

170 **"the principal circulating medium of money"**: Ibid., 99.

170 **"a fraction of their worth was available in gold"**: Ibid.

170 **"every dollar of a bank bill"**: Ibid.

170 **"would make money available only to large merchants"**: Ibid.

170 **"launched a passionate attack"**: Ibid., 144.

170 **"carefully refuted the arguments of Randolph and Jefferson"**: Ibid.

171 **"began urging friends to support"**: Ibid.

171 **"but it is nevertheless a maxim"**: Alexander Hamilton, *Report on Manufactures*, communicated to the House of Representatives, 5 December 1791.

171 **"When all the different kinds of industry"**: Ibid.

172 **"The regulations of several countries"**: Ibid.

172 **"Certain nations grant bounties on the exportation"**: Ibid.

172 **"calculated to stir the blood"**: John C. Miller, *The Federalist Era: 1789–1801* (New York: Harper and Row, 1963), 65.

173 **"protective tariffs; bounties for the establishment"**: Hamilton, *Report on Manufactures*.

173 **"In countries where there is great private wealth"**: Ibid.

174 **"the Judas of the West"**: Andrew Jackson, quoted in Robert V. Remini, *Henry Clay: Statesman for the Union* (New York: W. W. Norton, 1991), 1.

174 **"profligate demagogue"**: Ibid.

174 **"essentially a gamester"**: John Quincy Adams, quoted in Remini, *Henry Clay*, 1.

174 **"teaches that in this country, one can scarcely be so poor"**: Abraham Lincoln, "Eulogy of Henry Clay," Springfield, Illinois, 6 July 1852.

174 **"The telegraph made the news of Clay's death instant"**: David S. Heidler and Jeanne T. Heidler, *Henry Clay: The Essential American* (New York: Random House, 2010), xi.

174 **"modern, scholarly biography"**: Remini, *Henry Clay*, xiv.

174 **in Merrill D. Peterson's *The Great Triumvirate***: Merrill D. Peterson, *The Great Triumvirate: Webster, Clay, and Calhoun* (Oxford: Oxford University Press, 1987).

175 **"a vision of progress"**: Remini, *Henry Clay*, 199, 193.

175 **"was not so much a philosophy seeking embodiment"**: Peterson, *The Great Triumvirate*, 69.

175 **"Yet, the ideas, whatever their sources"**: Ibid.

175 **"the commonwealth tradition of using the state actively"**: Michael F. Holt, *The Rise and Fall of the American Whig Party: Jacksonian Politics and the Onset of the Civil War* (New York: Oxford University Press, 2003), xiii.

175 **"Of all the major figures in American political history"**: Daniel Walker Howe, *The Political Culture of the American Whigs* (Chicago: University of Chicago Press, 1979), 137.

176 **"much more precedent for government intervention"**: Ibid.

176 **"Clay's economic nationalism from the 'British system'"**: Ibid.

176 **"Mails imply roads; roads imply their preservation"**: Remini, *Henry Clay*, 226.

176 **"Before long . . . Clay figured out how to circumvent the scruples"**: Howe, *The Political Culture of the American Whigs*, 137.

177 **"not simply the protection of specific items"**: Remini, *Henry Clay*, 228.

177 **"a planned national economy responsive"**: Ibid.

177 **"The policy of Europe refuses to receive from us"**: Henry Clay, quoted in Remini, *Henry Clay*, 229.

177 **"Is there no remedy within the reach of the government?"**: Ibid.

177 **"The truth is, and it is vain to disguise it"**: Henry Clay, quoted in Paul Calore, *The Causes of the Civil War* (Jefferson, NC: McFarland, 2008), 43.

177 **"This Constitution must be a singular instrument!"**: Henry Clay, quoted in Remini, *Henry Clay*, 231.

178 **"commercially oriented Republicans"**: Sean Wilentz, *The Rise of American Democracy: Jefferson to Lincoln* (New York: W. W. Norton, 2005), 203.

178 **"Should Jackson veto it"**: Henry Clay, quoted in Arthur M. Schlesinger Jr., *The Age of Jackson* (New York: Little, Brown, 1945), 87.

178 **"was a blatant act of political self-interest"**: Remini, *Henry Clay*, 379.

178 **"The common characterization of this period"**: Daniel Walker Howe, *What Hath God Wrought* (Oxford: Oxford University Press, 2007), 612.

179 **"The responsibility of the historian"**: Gordon S. Wood, *The Idea of America: Reflections on the Birth of the United States* (New York: Penguin Press, 2011), 21.

179 **"popular and democratic rhetoric"**: Ibid., 18.

179 **"If the Church of England was the Tory Party at prayer"**: Howe, *The Political Culture of the American Whigs*, 18.

179 **"Equality of talents, of education, or of wealth"**: Andrew Jackson, 10 July 1832, quoted in John M. Murrin et al., *Liberty, Equality, Power: A History of the American People* (Boston: Cengage, 2007), 329.

180 **"to enlist the laboring classes against a 'monster bank'"**: Thurlow Weed, quoted in Wilentz, *The Rise of American Democracy*, 86.

180 **"*They* set us the example of organization"**: Lincoln, quoted in David Herbert Donald, *Lincoln* (New York: Simon and Schuster, 1995), 78.

180 **"paradoxically . . . the Whigs fought to establish their vision"**: Harry L. Watson, *Liberty and Power: The Politics of Jacksonian America* (New York: Hill and Wang, 2006), 221.

180 **"the largest vehicle for expanding democracy"**: Ibid., 791.

180 **"created a new kind of political party"**: Ibid.

181 **"Throughout the South, the Whigs showed considerably less enthusiasm"**: Howe, *What Hath God Wrought*, 586.

181 **"the burgeoning cult of domesticity"**: Watson, *Liberty and Power*, 221.

181 **"by the time of the 1844 election"**: Wilentz, *The Rise of American Democracy*, 902.

181 **"If the internal improvement of the country should be left to the management"**: Adams, quoted in Howe, *What Hath God Wrought*, 585.

182 **"If Congress can make canals"**: Macon, quoted in Howe, *What Hath God Wrought*, 221.

182 **"the positive liberal state"**: Lee Benson, *The Concept of Jacksonian Democracy* (Princeton: Princeton University Press, 1961), 102–5.

182 **"lent active government support to a wide range"**: Watson, *Liberty and Power*, 245.

182 **"too much like twentieth century liberals"**: Howe, *The Political Culture of the American Whigs*, 20.

182 **"moral absolutism, their paternalism and their concern"**: Ibid.

183 **"Though they championed the opportunities of the marketplace"**: Watson, *Liberty and Power*, 221.

185 **"Although Jacksonians and Whigs did invoke arguments about economic growth"**: Sandel, *Democracy's Discontent*, 157.

185 **"The Whig case for promoting economic development"**: Ibid.

185 **"the threat to self-government posed by large concentrations"**: Ibid.

185 **"republican ideology served perhaps longer"**: Michael H. Frisch and Daniel J. Walkowitz, "Foreword," in Michael H. Frisch and Daniel J. Walkowitz, eds., *Working-Class America: Essays on Labor, Community, and American Society* (Urbana: University of Illinois Press, 1983), xiv.

185 **"a republican vision that stressed the centrality of labor"**: Harry Watson, *Liberty and Power: The Politics of Jacksonian America* (New York: Hill and Wang, 1990), 188.

185 **"cleared the path for the triumph of laissez-faire capitalism"**: Marvin Meyers, *The Jacksonian Persuasion* (New York: Vintage, 1960), 12.

186 **"laissez-faire was championed in America as it never was before"**: Sidney Fine, *Laissez Faire and the General-Welfare State: A Study of Conflict in American Thought 1865–1901* (Ann Arbor: University of Michigan Press, 1956), 29.

186 **Brian Balogh is persuasive in seeing the Gilded Age period**: Balogh, *A Government Out of Sight*.

186 **"insisted that restraining government action"**: Ibid., 315.

186 **"corporations are persons within the meaning of the Fourteenth Amendment"**: Ibid., 331.

187 **"a distinctly subordinate position"**: Ibid., 329.

187 **"rejected the argument that unequal bargaining strength justified interference"**: Ibid., 328.

187   **"a robust new defense ":** George Will, "Why Liberals Fear the *Lochner* Decision," *Washington Post*, 7 September 2011.

187   **"the liberals' least favorite decision because its premises pose a threat":**
Ibid.

187   **"the eventual replacement of ethics by economics in liberalism":** James T.
Kloppenberg, *Uncertain Victory: Social Democracy and Progressivism in European and American Thought 1870–1920* (New York: Oxford University Press,
1988), 173.

187   **"Although vestiges of civic humanism continued to surface":** Ibid.

CHAPTER VIII: WHAT'S THE MATTER WITH POPULISM?

189   **identification with "the people":** See Richard Hofstadter, *The Progressive
Historians: Turner, Beard, Parrington* (New York: Knopf, 1968), 16.

189   **"March without the people, and you march into the night":** Ralph Waldo
Emerson, quoted in Michael Kazin, *The Populist Persuasion: An American History* (Ithaca: Cornell University Press, 1995), 7.

189   **"a profound outrage with elites":** Kazin, *The Populist Persuasion: An American
History* (Ithaca: Cornell University Press, 1995), 2.

189   **"common welfare . . . talked in populist ways":** Ibid., 6.

189   **"Beneath the sane economic demands of the populists":** Robert McMath,
American Populism: A Social History, 1877–1898 (New York: Hill and Wang,
1993), 12.

190   **"from [William Jennings] Bryan to Stalin":** Leo Ribuffo, *The Old Christian
Right: The Protestant Right from the Great Depression to the Cold War* (Philadelphia: Temple University Press, 1983), 242.

190   **"Tradition lies in the eye of the beholder":** Ibid.

191   **"public anger over busing, welfare spending, environmental extremism":** Kevin Phillips, quoted in John Judis, *William F. Buckley, Jr: Patron Saint
of the Conservatives* (New York: Simon and Schuster, 1988), 367–83.

191   **"that giant sucking sound":** Ross Perot, second presidential debate, University of Richmond, Richmond, Virginia, 15 October 1992.

191   **"to be upwardly mobile, to send their children":** Scott Rasmussen and
Doug Schoen, *Mad as Hell: How the Tea Party Movement Is Fundamentally
Remaking Our Two-Party System* (New York: HarperCollins, 2010), 51.

191   **"The right-wing populism we are experiencing today is significant":** Ibid.

192   **"Populist constitutionalism":** Larrey Anderson, "Populist Constitutionalism
and the Tea Parties," RealClearPolitics.com, 7 February 2010, http://www.real
clearpolitics.com/articles/2010/02/07/populist_constitutionalism__the_tea_
parties_100208.html.

192   **"I have attended several local Tea Party gatherings":** Ibid.

192   **"Love and respect for the Constitution":** Ibid.

192   **"weather the sorrow of a miscarriage":** Chris Cillizza, "Analysis: Michele

Bachmann's Reveal of Miscarriage Puts Unique Appeal on Display," *Washington Post*, 30 June 2011.

192 **"millions of families":** Ibid.

192 **"a native Virginian and scion of a great Tidewater family":** Sean Wilentz, *The Rise of American Democracy: Jefferson to Lincoln* (New York: W. W. Norton, 2005), 497–98.

192 **"methodological imprecision":** Ribuffo, *The Old Christian Right*, 242.

193 **"We meet in the midst of a nation":** Populist Party platform, 1892.

193 **"The people are demoralized":** Ibid.

194 **"We seek to restore the government":** Ibid.

194 **"The Preamble, as the historian Robert McMath observed":** McMath, *American Populism*, 161.

194 **"One by one . . . the reforms advocated by the Populists":** Harold U. Faulkner, *Politics, Reform, and Expansion, 1890–1900* (New York: Harper and Row, 1963), 276.

194 **"free and unlimited coinage of silver":** Populist Party platform, 1892.

194 **"undesirable immigration":** Ibid.

194 **"present system . . . opens our ports":** Ibid.

195 **"the last phase of a long and perhaps a losing struggle":** John D. Hicks, *Populist Revolt: A History of the Farmers' Alliance and the People's Party* (Minneapolis: University of Minnesota Press, 1931), 237.

195 **"falling commodity prices, high freight rates":** McMath, *American Populism*, 10.

195 **"extremism" . . . "pseudo-conservatism":** See, for example, Richard Hofstadter, "The Pseudo-Conservative Revolt," in Daniel Bell, ed., *The Radical Right* (New York: Doubleday, 1963).

195 **"who, in the name of upholding traditional American values":** Theodor Adorno, Else Frankel-Brunswick, Daniel Levinson, et al., *The Authoritarian Personality* (New York: Harper and Row, 1950), 676.

195 **"has been drawn to that side of Populism and Progressivism":** Richard Hofstadter, *The Age of Reform* (New York: Vintage Books, 1955), 20.

196 **"suffer from a sense of isolation":** Ibid., 19.

196 **"they periodically exaggerate the measure of agreement":** Ibid.

196 **"were foolish and destructive but only that they had, like so many things in life":** Ibid., 18.

196 **"There was something about the Populist imagination":** Ibid., 70.

196 **"sadistic and nihilistic spirit":** Ibid.

196 **"activated most of what we have of popular anti-Semitism":** Ibid., 80.

196 **"entirely verbal . . . a mode of expression":** Ibid.

197 **"an organic part of the whole order of business enterprise that flourished in the city":** Ibid., 35.

197 **"was beginning to realize acutely not merely that the best":** Ibid.

197 **"bewildering, and irritating too":** Ibid.

197 **"free silver . . . was not distinctly a People's Party idea":** Ibid., 104.

197　**"The Senate represents this inequity in its most extreme form":** Ibid., 116.

197　**"was from the beginning the target of strenuous":** Alan Brinkley, *Liberalism and Its Discontents* (Cambridge, MA: Harvard University Press, 1998), 137.

198　**"The problem with trying to redeem populism":** Molly Ivins, " 'Populist' a Label Easily Thrown," *Fort Worth Star-Telegram*, 6 February 1996.

198　**"a delightfully refreshing book":** David Brown, *Richard Hofstadter: An Intellectual Biography* (Chicago: University of Chicago Press, 2006), 111.

198　**"One has the feeling":** Ibid.

198　**"The Populist Heritage and the Intellectual":** C. Vann Woodward, "The Populist Heritage and the Intellectual," *American Scholar* 29 (Winter 1959–60), 55–72.

199　**"The danger . . . is that under the concentrated impact":** Brown, *Richard Hofstadter*, 114.

199　**"Populism was hardly 'status politics' ":** C. Vann Woodward, *The Burden of Southern History*, 3rd ed. (Baton Rouge: Louisiana State University Press, 1960),153.

199　**"[William Jennings] Bryan's authentic heir wasn't Roosevelt":** Sam Tenenhaus, "The Education of Richard Hofstadter," *New York Times*, 6 August 2006.

199　**"In the McCarthy movement":** Woodward, quoted in Brown, *Richard Hofstadter*, 115.

200　**"The difference I hope to establish":** Hofstadter, *The Age of Reform*, 323.

200　**"inspiration . . . was much more informed by administration":** Ibid., 325.

200　**"clearly underestimated the degree to which progressive ideology":** Brinkley, *Liberalism and Its Discontents*, 147.

200　in a book whose title, ***The End of Reform:*** Alan Brinkley, *The End of Reform: New Deal Liberalism in Recession and War* (New York: Vintage Books, 1995).

200　**Goodwyn's *Democratic Promise:*** Lawrence Goodwyn, *Democratic Promise: The Populist Moment in America* (Oxford: Oxford University Press, 1976).

200　**"coherent, enlightened, and fundamentally democratic":** Brinkley, *The End of Reform*, 138.

201　**"To describe the origins of Populism in one sentence":** Goodwyn, *Democratic Promise*, xviii.

201　**"as the self-empowering fulfillment of real democracy":** Ivins, " 'Populism' a Label Too Easily Thrown."

201　**"Populism was up-from-the-bottom politics":** Ibid.

201　**"most studies of the last quarter century have depicted American Populism":** McMath, *American Populism*, 210.

201　**"Neither proto-fascists nor proto-New Dealers":** Ibid., 210–11.

202　**More recent scholarship has forcefully challenged:** Charles Postel, *The Populist Vision* (New York: Oxford University Press, 2007), 4, 6, 17, 288.

202　**"incurious, phony populist":** Alec Baldwin, "Sarah Palin: Faux Populist," *Huffington Post*, 9 February 2010.

202　**"a pitch-perfect recital of the populist message":** David Broder, "Sarah

Palin Displays Her Pitch-Perfect Populism," *Washington Post*, 11 February 2010.

203 **in *The Radical Right*, an important collection of essays:** Daniel Bell, ed., *The Radical Right* (New York: Doubleday, 1963).

203 **book published eight years earlier as *The New American Right*:** Daniel Bell, ed., *The New American Right* (New York: Criterion Books, 1955).

203 **"Social groups that are dispossessed invariably seek targets":** Daniel Bell, "The Dispossessed," in Bell, ed., *The Radical Right*, 3.

203 **"discharged many university professors in state universities":** Seymour Martin Lipset, "The Sources of the 'Radical Right," in Bell, ed., *The Radical Right*, 316.

203 **"dismissed teachers who believed in Populist economics":** Ibid.

203 **"so-called experts":** George Wallace, speeches during the 1968 presidential election, quoted in Taylor Branch, "The Politics of Rage: George Wallace, the Origins of New Conservatism, and the Transformation of American Politics," *Washington Monthly*, October 1995.

204 **"He gave every hearer a chance to transmute a latent hostility":** Taylor Branch, *Pillar of Fire: America in the King Years, 1963–1965* (New York: Simon and Schuster, 1998), 340.

205 **"a language that sees ordinary people as a noble assemblage":** Kazin, *The Populist Persuasion*, 1.

205 **"I do not contend that my subjects *were* populists":** Ibid., 3.

205 **"the pietistic impulse issuing from the Protestant Reformation":** Ibid., 11.

205 **"It became a convenient label for left, right, center":** Ibid., 271.

205 **"Activists who blame an immoral, agnostic media":** Ibid., 4.

205 **"major alteration . . . when populism began its journey from left to right":** Ibid.

206 **"The rhetoric once spoken primarily by reformers and radicals":** Ibid.

206 **"gradually and unevenly":** Ibid.

207 **Thomas Frank's *What's the Matter with Kansas?*:** Thomas Frank, *What's the Matter With Kansas? How Conservatives Won the Heart of America* (New York: Metropolitan Books, 2004).

207 **"periodic bouts of leftism":** Ibid., 31.

207 **"every part of the country in the nineteenth century had labor upheavals":** Ibid.

207 **"more men . . . who hate prosperity":** William Allen White, "What's the Matter with Kansas?" *Emporia Gazette*, 15 August 1896.

207 **"Today's Republicans are doing what the Whigs did in the 1840s":** Frank, *What's the Matter with Kansas?*, 196.

207 **"who no longer speak to people on the losing end of a free market system":** Ibid., 245.

207 **"talk constantly abut class":** Ibid.

208   **"intellect and philistinism"**: Richard Hofstadter, *Anti-Intellectualism in American Life* (New York: Vintage Books, 1962), 3.

208   **"national distaste for intellect"**: Ibid., 6.

208   **"a weaker connection with the idea of community"**: Alan Brinkley, "Liberty, Community, and the National Idea," *American Prospect*, 1 November 1996.

209   **"cooperative commonwealth"**: McMath, *American Populism*, 8.

209   **"developed among people who were deeply rooted in the social and economic networks"**: Ibid., 17.

209   **"took place within membership organizations"**: Ibid., 42.

209   **"evolution of a cooperative economic organization"**: Walter Rauschenbusch, *Christianizing the Social Order* (New York: Macmillan, 1914), 367.

210   **"a beloved community"**: Eugene McCarraher, *Christian Critics: Religion and the Impasse in Modern American Social Thought* (Ithaca: Cornell University Press, 2000), 13.

210   **"that the Christian spirit lay not in the manger"**: Ibid.

210   **"contribute in significant ways to the creation"**: Alan Brinkley, "Liberty and Community," in Alan Brinkley, Nelson W. Polsby, and Kathleen M. Sullivan, *The New Federalist Papers: Essays in Defense of the Constitution* (New York: W. W. Norton, 1997), 99.

210   **"From the beginning of his administration, Franklin Roosevelt's rhetoric"**: Ibid.

210   **"It should not surprise us"**: Thomas Frank, "Obama and the Gulf Spill Anger," *Wall Street Journal*, 9 June 2010.

211   **"The people now flocking to the Democratic Party"**: Ibid.

211   **"while it is fun to trash new-style Democrats"**: Ibid.

212   **"We need a vigorous government and a healthy market"**: Brinkley, "Liberty and Community," 101.

CHAPTER IX: THE LONG CONSENSUS
AND ITS ACHIEVEMENTS

214   **"the full dinner pail"**: McKinley presidential campaign slogan, 1900, http://www.whitehouse.gov/about/presidents/williammckinley.

214   **"Burn down your cities and leave our farms"**: William McKinley, "Cross of Gold" speech, Democratic National Convention, Chicago, 8 July 1896.

215   **"After 1900 . . . Populism and Progressivism merge"**: Richard Hofstadter, *The Age of Reform: From Bryan to FDR* (New York: Vintage Books, 1955), 133.

215   **"March without the people and you march into the night"**: Ralph Waldo Emerson, quoted in Michael Kazin, *The Populist Persuasion: An American History* (New York: Basic Books, 1995), 7.

215   **"persistently blunted Bryan's appeal"**: Ibid.

215   **"forged a working coalition between the old Bryan country"**: Ibid.

216 **"Roosevelt borrowed from Bryan, but Bryan came from Nazareth in Galilee":** Ibid.

216 **"ineffectual":** Eldon Eisenach, "Introduction," *The Social and Political Thought of American Progressivism* (Indianapolis, IN: Hackett, 2006), viii.

216 **"symbolized a new national commitment":** Ibid.

216 **"the movement's leading minds founded the modern American university":** Ibid.

217 **Herbert Croly, the progressive thinker:** See Edward Stettner, *Shaping Modern Liberalism: Herbert Croly and Progressive Thought* (Lawrence: University Press of Kansas, 1993).

217 **"to use Hamiltonian administrative nationalism":** Herbert Croly, quoted in Sidney M. Milkis, *Political Parties and Constitutional Government: Remaking American Democracy* (Baltimore: Johns Hopkins University Press, 1999), 66.

218 **"use the whole power of government":** John Milton Cooper, *Woodrow Wilson: A Biography* (New York: Knopf, 2009), 165.

218 **"Have we come to a time":** Michael Sandel, *Democracy's Discontent: America in Search of a Public Philosophy* (Cambridge, MA: Harvard University Press, 1996), 215.

218 **"There is . . . a point of bigness":** Cooper, *Woodrow Wilson*, 167.

218 **"the time when the combined power of high finance":** Ibid.

218 **"A National Government cannot create good times":** William Howard Taft, quoted in Cooper, *Woodrow Wilson*, 167.

219 **"marked an early step toward the ideological transformation":** Cooper, *Woodrow Wilson*, 167.

219 **"agreed despite their differences that economic and political institutions":** Sandel, *Democracy's Discontent*, 221.

219 **"cult of governmentalism":** Chester E. Finn Jr., "Herbert Croly and the Cult of Governmentalism," in Lamar Alexander and Chester E. Finn Jr., *The New Promise of American Life* (Indianapolis, IN: Hudson Institute Inc., 1995), 43.

219 **"preoccupation with strong government, strong leaders and strong nationalism":** Michael McGerr, "Foreword," in Herbert Croly, *The Promise of American Life* (Boston: Northeastern University Press, 1989), xi.

220 **Eisenach notes, while twenty-two states:** Eisenach, "Introduction."

220 **"formed their own municipal corporations to supply transportation":** Ibid., ix.

221 **"If you look at the dates at which they were created":** Robert D. Putnam, "The Decline of Civil Society: How Come? So What?" John L. Marion Lecture, Canadian Centre for Management Development, Ottawa, Ontario, 22 February 1996.

221 **John Louis Recchiuti points to the work of:** John Louis Recchiuti, *Civic Engagement: Social Science and Progressive-Era Reform in New York City* (Philadelphia: University of Pennsylvania Press, 2007).

222 **"Early twentieth-century local, state and national policies":** Theda Skocpol, "Don't Blame Big Government: America's Voluntary Groups Thrive in

a National Network," in E. J. Dionne Jr., ed., *Community Works: The Revival of Civil Society in America* (Washington, DC: Brookings Institution, 1998), 39.

222 **"The GI Bill of 1944 never would have taken the inclusive shape":** Ibid.

223 **"property rights, to the exclusion of human rights":** Theodore Roosevelt, quoted in Sidney M. Milkis, *Theodore Roosevelt, the Progressive Party, and the Transformation of American Democracy* (Lawrence: University Press of Kansas, 2009), 59.

223 **"be submitted for final determination":** Theodore Roosevelt, quoted in Milkis, *Theodore Roosevelt*, 60.

223 **"not a radical rejection of the American tradition'":** Milkis, *Theodore Roosevelt*, 265.

223 **"The most exalted purpose of the insurgency":** Ibid., 71.

224 **"property rights shall not be exalted over human rights":** Ben Lindsey, quoted in William McClay, *The Masterless: Self and Society in Modern America* (Chapel Hill: University of North Carolina Press, 1994).

224 **"fellows":** Herbert Croly, quoted in McClay, *The Masterless*, 160.

225 **"compromised a man as much in his success as in his failure":** McClay, *The Masterless*, 160.

225 **"the achievement of the national purpose":** Herbert Croly, quoted in McClay, *The Masterless*, 160.

225 **"Great Community":** McClay, *The Masterless*, 167–70, 179, 280.

225 **"invaded and partially disintegrated the small communities":** John Dewey, quoted in McClay, *The Masterless*, 167.

225 **"a perception of common interest, a high degree":** McClay, *The Masterless*, 167–68.

227 **"The world must be made safe for democracy":** Woodrow Wilson, "Making the World Safe for Democracy," 2 April 1917, http://historymatters.gmu.edu/d/4943.

227 **"of a steady diet of":** H. L. Mencken, *On Politics: A Carnival of Buncombe* (Baltimore: Johns Hopkins University Press, 2006), 33.

227 **"Tired to death of intellectual charlatanry":** Ibid., 34.

227 **"not heroics but healing":** Warren G. Harding, "Back to Normal" speech, http://www.whitehouse.gov/about/presidents/warrenharding.

227 **"He should have added: not action but alliteration":** Arthur M. Schlesinger Jr., *The Cycles of American History* (New York: Houghton Mifflin, 1999), 32.

228 **"After all, the chief business of the American people":** Calvin Coolidge, "The Press Under a Free Government," 1925, http://www.calvin-coolidge.org/html/the_business_of_america_is_bus.html.

228 **"The chief ideal of the American people is idealism":** Ibid.

228 **"Large and aggressive components":** Arthur S. Link, "What Happened to the Progressive Movement in the 1920s?" *American Historical Review* 64, no. 4 (Chicago: University of Chicago Press, 1959), 850.

228 **"reversals and failures":** Ibid.

228 **"various progressive coalitions controlled Congress":** Ibid.

229 **"He is certainly a wonder":** Franklin D. Roosevelt, http://www.hoover.ar chives.gov/exhibits/Hooverstory/gallery02/index.html.

229 **"the greatest spending Administration":** Franklin D. Roosevelt, Address in Sioux City, Iowa. 1932, http://publicpolicy.pepperdine.edu/faculty-research/new -deal/roosevelt-speeches/fr092932.htm.

229 **"piled bureau on bureau":** Ibid.

229 **"above all, try *something*":** Franklin D. Roosevelt, address at Oglethorpe University, http://newdeal.feri.org/speeches/1932d.htm.

230 **"Franklin D. Roosevelt directed the campaign":** Barton Bernstein, "The New Deal: The Conservative Achievements of Liberal Reform," in Barton Bernstein, ed., *Towards a New Past: Dissenting Essays in American History* (New York: Vintage, 1969), 267.

230 **"anti-monopolists . . . envisioned a frontal assault":** Alan Brinkley, *The End of Reform: New Deal Liberalism in Recession and War* (New York: Alfred A. Knopf, 1995), 5.

230 **"advocates of centralized economic planning":** Ibid., 162.

230 **"the vaguely corporatist concept of business 'associationalism'":** Ibid., 5.

230 **"cartelistic arrangements within major industries":** Ibid., 7.

231 **"When liberals spoke now of government's responsibility":** Ibid.

231 **"controlling or punishing 'plutocrats' and 'economic royalists'":** Ibid.

231 **"providing a healthy environment in which the corporate world":** Ibid.

231 **"In the end . . . it was not as easy as many liberals":** Ibid., 271.

231 **"economic royalists":** Ibid.

231 **"money-changers have fled from their high seats":** Franklin Delano Roosevelt, First Inaugural Address.

233 **"threatened to push him in a direction far more radical":** William Leuchtenburg, *Franklin D. Roosevelt and the New Deal, 1932–1940* (New York: Harper and Row, 1963), 177.

234 **we can, as Harold Meyerson argued:** Harold Meyerson, "The Fallacy of Post-Industrial Prosperity," *Washington Post*, 4 September 2011.

235 **"achieved a more just society by recognizing groups":** Leuchtenburg, *Franklin D. Roosevelt and the New Deal,* 347.

235 **"Governments can err, presidents do make mistakes":** Franklin D. Roosevelt, "Rendezvous with Destiny," speech before the 1936 Democratic National Convention, Philadelphia, http://www.austincc.edu/lpatrick/his2341/fdr36ac ceptancespeech.htm.

235 **"We must lay hold of the fact that economic laws":** Franklin D. Roosevelt, nomination address, 2 July 1932, reprinted in *The Public Papers and Addresses of Franklin D. Roosevelt* (New York: Random House, 1938), 1:647.

235 **"Two more glaring misstatements of the truth could hardly have been packed into so little space":** *Boston Transcript,* quoted in Leuchtenburg, *Franklin D. Roosevelt and the New Deal,* 344 n. 53.

236 **"Hardheaded, 'anti-utopian,' the New Dealers nonetheless":** Leuchtenburg, *Franklin D. Roosevelt and the New Deal,* 345.

236 **"with its model town of Norris"**: Ibid.

236 **"because it represented the 'middle way' of happy accommodation"**: Ibid.

236 **"The sharp contraction in income inequality"**: Carola Frydman and Raven Molloy, "Pay Cuts for the Boss: Executive Compensation in the 1940s," Working Paper 17303, National Bureau of Economic Research, August 2011, http://www .nber.org/papers/w17303.pdf.

236 **"the closest thing to a real social revolution"**: Geoffrey Perret, *Days of Sadness, Years of Triumph: The American People, 1939–1945* (Madison: University of Wisconsin Press, 1985), 1:10.

237 **"barriers to social and economic equality"**: Ibid., 1:11.

237 **"access to higher education became genuinely democratic"**: Ibid.

237 **"was not seen as composed of *us* and *them*"**: Robert Reich, *The Resurgent Liberal: And Other Unfashionable Prophecies* (New York: Crown, 1989), see 278–89 for this and Reich's broader argument about contemporary liberalism.

237 **"The goals of reviving the economy and winning the war"**: Ibid., 333.

241 **"Every man has a right to his own property"**: Franklin D. Roosevelt, Commonwealth Club speech, San Francisco, 1932, http://www.americanrhetoric. com/speeches/fdrcommonwealth.htm.

241 **"The same man who tells you that he does not want to see the government interfere"**: Ibid.

241 **"We know that individual liberty and individual happiness"**: Ibid.

CHAPTER X: THE NEW AMERICAN SYSTEM

245 **"I'll work every day"**: Rick Perry, "Presidential Announcement Remarks," RedState Gathering 2011, Charleston, South Carolina, 13 August 2011, http:// www.rickperry.org/news/text-gov-rick-perry-presidential-announcement -remarks.

245 **"Corporations are people, my friend"**: Mitt Romney, remarks at Iowa State Fair, 11 August 2011, http://www.c-spanvideo.org/program/Romneya.

246 **"Corporations are *not* people" . . . "Due to recent budget cuts, the light"**: Ezra Klein, "The Wonkiest Signs from Occupy Wall Street," Ezra Klein's Wonkblog, *Washington Post*, 17 October 2011.

246 **"Ultimately, inevitably, the route to real change has to run through politics"**: Hendrik Hertzberg, "Occupational Hazards," *New Yorker*, 7 November 2011.

251 **"a time for choosing"**: Ronald Reagan, "A Time for Choosing," 27 October 1964, http://www.reagan.utexas.edu/archives/reference/timechoosing.html.

252 **"Telling Americans to improve democracy by sinking comfortably"**: Robert H. Wiebe, *Self-Rule: A Cultural History of American Democracy* (Chicago: University of Chicago Press, 1996), 264.

254 **"the largest disparity between younger and older voters"**: Pew Social and Demographic Trends, "Millennials: Confident. Connected. Open to Change,"

24 February 2010, http://www.pewsocialtrends.org/2010/02/24/millennials-con
fident-connected-open-to-change.

254 **"after decades of low voter participation by the young":** Ibid.

254 **"Government should do more to solve problems":** Ibid.

255 **"When something is run by government":** Ibid.

255 **"being a good parent":** Ibid.

255 **"when politics goes well, we can know a good in common":** Michael J.
Sandel, *Liberalism and the Limits of Justice* (Cambridge: Cambridge University
Press, 1982), 183.

256 **"Government is the enemy":** Bill Cohen, quoted in E. J. Dionne Jr., "Week in
Politics: Oil Spill, Crist, Immigration," National Public Radio, 30 April 2010.

258 **"When my brother John and I were growing up":** Caroline Kennedy, "A
President Like My Father," *New York Times*, 27 January 2008.

258 **"The mood . . . was strangely blended from ambition and idealism":**
Godfrey Hodgson, *The Gentleman from New York: Daniel Patrick Moynihan: A
Biography* (Boston: Houghton Mifflin, 2000), 73.

259 **world of Bill Bishop's Big Sort:** Bill Bishop, *The Big Sort: Why the Clustering
of Like-Minded America Is Tearing Us Apart* (New York: Mariner Books, 2009).

259 **"their willingness to sacrifice individual interests for the common
good":** Michael Sandel, "Reply to Critics," in Anita L. Allen and Milton C. Re-
gan, eds., *Debating Democracy's Discontent: Essays on American Politics, Law,
and Public Philosophy* (New York: Oxford University Press, 1998), 325.

259 **"those people":** Bishop. *The Big Sort*, 40.

260 **Adele Stan, a thoughtful left-of-center journalist:** Adele Stan, "Dismiss the
Tea Parties at Your Peril—They're a Force to Be Reckoned With," AlterNet,
May 4, 2010, http://www.alternet.org/news/146707/dismiss_the_tea_parties_at_
your_peril_-_they%27re_a_force_to_be_reckoned_with/?page=1. Also, interview with author.

262 **"The end is redemption and reconciliation":** Martin Luther King Jr., originally printed in *Christian Century*, 1957; excerpts available at http://mlk-kpp01
.stanford.edu/kingweb/about_king/encyclopedia/nonviolent.resist.html.

262 **"to speed up that day when all of God's children":** Martin Luther King Jr.,
"I Have a Dream" speech, 28 August 1963.

263 **"Egalitarians of a more radical stripe initially took a dim view":** Jonathan
Rauch, "Not Whether but How: Gay Marriage and the Revival of Burkean Conservatism," *South Texas Law Review*, Winter 2009; also at http://www.jonathan
rauch.com/jrauch_articles/gay-marriage-9-the-conservative-way.

263 **"Note how different these two streams are":** Ibid.

265 **"the very idea of the perfect world in which all good things are realized":** Isaiah Berlin, *The Power of Ideas* (Princeton, NJ: Princeton University
Press, 1998), 23.

Index

A Note on the Author

E. J. Dionne Jr. is a senior fellow at the Brookings Institution, a columnist for the *Washington Post*, and University Professor in the Foundations of Democracy and Culture at Georgetown University. He appears weekly on NPR and regularly on MSNBC and NBC's *Meet the Press*. His twice-weekly op-ed column is now syndicated in 140 newspapers. His writing has been published in the *Atlantic*, the *New Republic*, the *American Prospect*, the *Washington Post Magazine*, the *New York Times Magazine*, *Commonweal*, *New Statesman*, and elsewhere. He is the author, editor, or coeditor of numerous books, including the classic bestseller *Why Americans Hate Politics*, which won the Los Angeles Times Book Prize and was nominated for the National Book Award. His most recent book is *Souled Out*. Dionne lives in Bethesda, Maryland, with his wife, Mary Boyle, and their three children.